NICHE TACTICS

Niche Tactics aligns the relationship between architecture and site with its ecological analogue: the relationship between an organism and its environment.

Bracketed between texts on giraffe morphology, ecological perception, ugliness, and hopeful monsters, architectural case studies investigate historical moments when relationships between architecture and site were productively intertwined, from the anomalous city designs of Francesco de Marchi in the sixteenth century to Le Corbusier's near eradication of context in his *Plan Voisin* in the twentieth century to the more recent contextualist movements. Extensively illustrated with 140 drawings and photographs, *Niche Tactics* considers how attention to site might create a generative language for architecture today.

Caroline O'Donnell is the Edgar A. Tafel Assistant Professor and Director of the Master of Architecture Program at Cornell University in Ithaca, New York, USA. She is the Principal of design firm CODA, winner of the 2013 MoMA-PS1 Young Architects' Program competition for the pavilion at the Museum of Modern Art PS1, New York, and Editor-in-Chief of *The Cornell Journal of Architecture*.

NICHE TACTICS

Generative Relationships Between Architecture and Site

Caroline O'Donnell

NEW YORK AND LONDON

First published 2015
by Routledge
711 Third Avenue, New York, NY 10017

and by Routledge
2 Park Square, Milton Park, Abingdon, Oxon OX14 4RN

Routledge is an imprint of the Taylor & Francis Group, an informa business

Library of Congress Cataloguing in Publication Data
O'Donnell, Caroline.
Niche tactics: generative relationships between architecture and site / Caroline
pages cm
Niche Tactics was originally published under the title: Niche Tactics:
The Giraffe Model in the 101st ACSA Annual Meeting Proceedings (2013):
New Constellations New Ecologies, edited by Ila Berman and Ed Mitchell.
Includes bibliographical references and index.
1. Architecture and biology. 2. Architectural design. I. Ingraham,
Catherine, writer of introduction. II. Title.
NA2543.B56.036 2015
720.9—dc23
2014037941

ISBN: 978-1-138-79311-8 (hbk)
ISBN: 978-1-138-79312-5 (pbk)
ISBN: 978-1-315-73028-8 (ebk)

Acquisition Editor: Wendy Fuller
Editorial Assistant: Grace Harrison
Production Editor: Christina O'Brien

Typeset in Bembo
by Swales and Willis Ltd, Exeter, Devon, UK

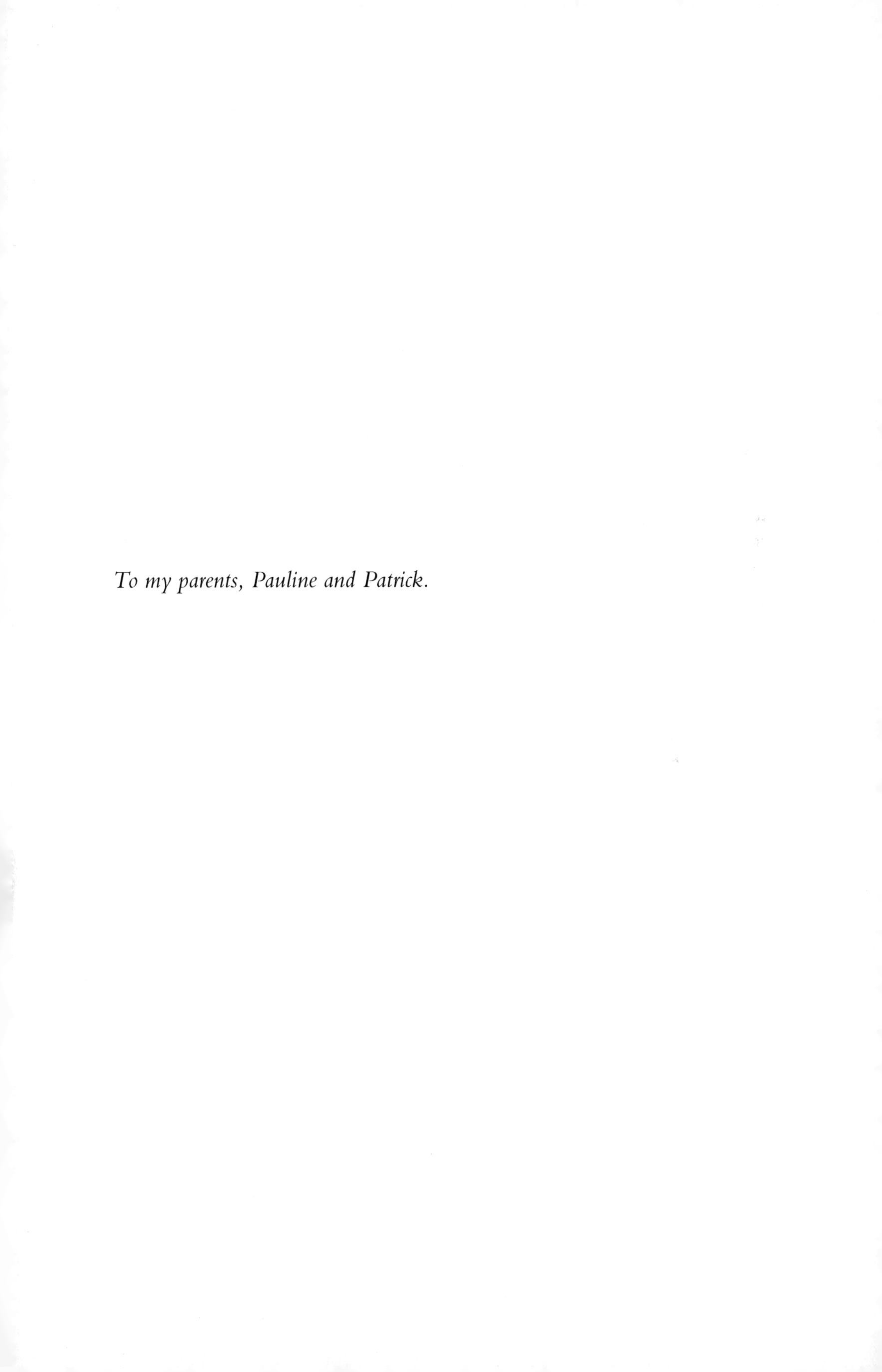

To my parents, Pauline and Patrick.

CONTENTS

FIGURES

FOREWORD

Catherine Ingraham

This book picks up a conversation that has been underway for some time and gives it a new clarity in what some have called (somewhat sardonically at the time) strictly architectural terms. The wayward animality in contemporary architectural work—bio-mimicry, morphogenesis, developmental and evolutionary logics, iterative dynamic systems—is not harnessed here in any pedantic sense but it seems less on the loose, which is a good thing. Niche Tactics argues, significantly, that our recent attempts to compute forces to create patterns and multi-operational surfaces may be missing that element of design that can transform a site into a milieu, and equip form and pattern with tactical talents. The book is not giving us general environmentalist advice. It goads architects to look harder and more carefully at contexts—the *niches* of the book's title—without the sentimentality that accompanies a return to strictly vernacular examples or the confusion produced by that most obtuse of concepts, sustainability.

A designer and professor of Architecture at Cornell University, Caroline O'Donnell provides here an unusual sharpness and persuasiveness around this difficult subject matter. Her analytic drawings, which supplement a lucid text, envision mobile rather than static architectural contexts. She takes us back—as it seems we are destined to go for all of our analytic lives—to those Modernist dictums and Renaissance practitioners, whose sponsors are now semi-reformed and pining for variation and locality. O'Donnell is a close reader of the architects Palladio, Francesco de Marchi, Le Corbusier, and Peter Eisenman, critics Nikolaus Pevsner, Rudolf Wittkower, and Colin Rowe, as well as a range of figures from outside the discipline of architecture. Her studies nimbly move from Renaissance villas and defensive cities, through the Picturesque, Modernism, and Contextualism, to film theory, aesthetics, and the structure of jokes and, all at once, confront current and urgent perplexities in architecture.

From time to time, in architecture's history, we have wandered into foreign territory that is not easily convertible to architectural principles. The analytic treatment of those forays has always required a certain delicacy of translation that I think is present in this book. Great care is taken here to underpin the book's arguments with specific architectural work while resisting didactic or reductive logic. These case studies are expanded and critiqued through specific theoretical frameworks. For example, the book gives us a way to use James Gibson's brilliant discussion of 'affordances' in *Ecological Perception*—a concept that has been on our minds for a long time but has been difficult to incorporate into current architectural discussions. The book also revisits D'Arcy Thompson. The oddness of D'Arcy Thompson's transformational logics—which most of us first encountered in Greg Lynn's very influential application of Thompson's animal morphology theory to the evolution of digital design— resides in what O'Donnell calls an "under-specification of external influences and an over-simplified mapping of development."

The evolutionary biologist Stephen Jay Gould greatly admired D'Arcy Thompson. Gould admits, however, that Thompson's methods were severely hampered by not having the apparatuses we now have—specifically the computer—to model the development of a complex form in three dimensions. Of interest to those who would claim that architectural design can be, in part, formally developmental, Gould believes that physical laws (forces) are not directly the cause of forms per D'Arcy Thompson. Instead, Thompson's diagrammatic descriptions *indirectly* provide "blueprints for optimal shapes." An organism's form, in other words, is not a direct result of physical forces (gravity's effect on the form of elephants, for example) but evidence instead of complex compensatory solutions developed in response to and within environmental forces in order to establish an organism's particular niche, its *fit*. This may include mechanisms of equilibrium that, in fact, avert deformations by forces that the organism might routinely encounter in its environment. Such mechanisms enable an organism to manage oscillations in forces such as weather or food availability. Gould's crucial point is that there is no direct relationship between forces and formal morphology.

If we have found guidance in architecture (particularly in early digital work) from Greg Lynn's early forces-to-forms techniques, we have also suffered from taking those forces as literal lines of force. Lynn himself frequently writes of vicissitudes that are part of complex systems, but architecture has tended toward the dogma of linear registration. Optimization studies (generative components and modularity) often configure wind or solar energy collection (or in a more sociological spirit, circulation or traffic) as force maps to which architectural design, as well as infrastructure and urban organization, can directly respond. The variation in daily shifts in the path of the sun or unpredictable climatic conditions give such force maps a dynamic character that architecture attempts to capture and register in the unfolding of a variegated, yet static, form. Such architectural forms become, thus, a tracking of energy diagrams. This may be exciting but it leaves out of its purview massive swaths of information that deal with landing an energized material object in a particular time and space. It leaves out too the asymmetrical and heavy load *use* imposes on all aspects of architecture and site. *Niche Tactics* enters the discussion at just this point. It urges architecture toward an honesty that is not a banality or a fall into realism but a deep attentiveness to the systemic forces it brings to bear, and serendipitously encounters, through its formation on-site. Architecture both creates and confronts a niche, not only for itself in the midst of human desires and concerns, but also necessarily as part of intricate non-human systems. Consideration of context also informs architecture's aesthetic logic, whatever it may be, which neither rides on top of architecture nor lies entirely within it.

When O'Donnell laments our loss of attention to context in architecture she is not recommending a return to what she calls a "symbolic vernacular" architecture, which is primarily retrospective. She recommends a tactical approach—niche *tactics*—such as that any life system would use to weigh its affordances. Niche tactics are not idle forms of counsel to architects to look beyond the autonomy of architectural languages to a surrounding milieu or context. They are a commentary on pivotal relations between design and computation and an urgent appeal to architects that they not only look more closely at the river that may lie next to their building site but that they, *we*, take account of the "multi-dimensional space of resources." "It is not the defining of the context that allows the giraffe to emerge," she writes, "but the *abstraction* of that context."

The giraffe. Yes, in a minute. But the word *abstraction*—a translation from Gibson—is pivotal. Gibson asks "What is offered to the animal, what is provided and furnished to it by its environment?" What is afforded to a living system refers not merely to external resources but also to the talents and cognitive specificity possessed by every animal, including, of course, human animals. Every living being must interpret its landscape, research and test its potentials on a daily basis (because everything is in flux), and continuously compute a pattern of affordance that enables its survival and, indeed, its creativity. It cannot calculate everything, but it designs a system.

Tactical niche-thinking is, thus, both opportunistic and creative. It potentially brings architectural negotiations between forces and forms into the same indirect relationship that Stephen Jay Gould indicates: tactical processes, in effect, create a system of fit. This is neither an automatic processing that, in its mimicry of evolutionary logics, attempts to produce complex form, nor is it a series of pattern book templates or design theories. Flourishing is life's tendency, given enough affordances, not a luxury. But flourishing does not mean optimization. D'Arcy Thompson's shapes and nets are general analogies for how form adaptively changes but they miss almost all the components of a complex adaptive system, many of which are now emerging from the fog of our theories of nature.

Humans, of course, have a particular arsenal of talents that come into play all the time, in the midst of technical powers. We process the context of each moment of our existence constantly and also have mechanisms that give us a chance to rest from that processing—homeostasis, regulation of body temperature, sleep, dreams. Our powers of abstraction necessarily include humor, irony, technologies such as writing and imaging, and that great morass of mental activity we call thought and sensation. It is always odd when we decide—as we often have in architecture—to arbitrarily rule out certain cognitive talents in order to formally control a specific process or theory. Our almost three-hundred year privileging of vision and its technocratic domain is a good example of this. Architecture is at our disposal, so to speak. Buildings and infrastructures themselves are not living systems. As Giorgio Agamben and others have articulated, non-living systems are adept at creating living subjects for themselves and architecture is no exception. In every other respect, architects are able to tactically abstract physical and metaphysical dimensions in the interest of designing systems that endure. That architecture has to do with keeping life alive to itself is obvious. That architecture's vast array of ingenuity is never incidental to its performance is also obvious. That architecture exists in the midst of evolutionary processes and is embedded in systems of all kinds, yet has choices and creative range about how to deploy itself there is, in fact, what has constituted, and continues to constitute, architecture's deep historical significance. So, this book asks with great clarity, why has architecture been so myopic and simple-minded about its engagement with environments?

A list—unless in the hands of Luis Borges—is never the most effective way to enliven a topic, but I want to list, all the same, a few of the tactical maneuvers this book offers to us:

- Niche-thinking encourages a shift in focus from enclosure to system.
- Analytic drawings reintroduce movement vectors into Palladian villas and call attention to Pier Vittorio Aureli's and Peter Eisenman's exposure of the barchesse, or barn, that Rudolf Wittkower and Colin Rowe excised in favor of symmetrical geometries. Going further, O'Donnell calls the barn "a gasket or docking mechanism" for connecting a villa to its site.
- Reinsertion of the breath of *poché* into Wittkower's diagrams.
- Rethinking context as a field of asymmetrical and sometimes invisible forces that may cause architecture to twist, shift, and bend as if dancing with an "invisible partner."
- Discovering opportunities for suppleness: Francesco de Marchi's "site-deformed cities" suggest that cities have "buckled under the pressure of site."
- Opening the cold-case: re-investigation of the "neglected fragmentary urban remnants" in Le Corbusier's *Plan Voisin*.
- Admission of joke structures and "hopeful monstrosities" into the architectural realm.
- Weaving together Pevsner's functionalist-picturesque with Gibson's concept of 'affordance' to produce an ecological picturesque.
- Investigations of the filmmaker Lev Kuleshov's experiments in montage that affected viewers' perceptions of figure/ground and foreground/background.
- And a final hint at the translation of these maneuvers into a design oeuvre (in the coda) that suggests that this book is not merely analytic, but has output.

Oh yes, and the giraffe. I have perhaps given the impression that the book is interested in animals. It is, but not as such. O'Donnell uses the giraffe, donkey, and duck as ways of 'drawing' architecture out. The giraffe—beloved by Lamarckian and Darwinian theorists alike for its demonstration of diametrically opposed relations between morphology and external contexts (trees, specifically)—inaugurates the discussion. The giraffe is morphologically peculiar, without question: exceptionally long neck, huge arteries, and heart to sustain a sophisticated blood system that has to be pumped great distances to energize the head yet not explode the relatively delicate veins and arteries that feed its thin long legs. It is an engineering experiment that improbably succeeds—as do so many patently awkward animal organizations that seem massively inefficient. Two esoteric benefits are achieved by the giraffe's elongations and organs: the first is a food source for which it does not need to compete (leaves and branches that no other ground animal is tall enough to reach) and the second is speed. There is, also, grace, which I think has to be part of the giraffe's abstracting of its niche but which we refuse, for some reason, to describe as an aesthetic talent.

Context becomes the more finely tuned niche, which couples architecture inextricably, and precisely, with both internal and external forces. This is not the autopoietic system as it has been repurposed for architecture by Patrik Schumacher (for me, a nearly scandalous distortion) but, more pointedly, the autopoietic system defined in 1972 by the Chilean biologists Maturana and Varela. The key character of autopoiesis is that every living system is organizationally closed in order to bind and give structure to its existence, yet this same system has to be energetically open in order to gather resources for survival. Both of these dispositions are absolutely necessary. When Jacob von Uexküll argued that species do not share the same worlds, he argued for the radical closure of each animal's world. When he observes moments of contact between living systems—such as predator and prey, bee and flower—he describes these acts as episodic isolated probes. In this view, there is no environment, no *outside* of any kind. Maturana and Varela, however, describe just the opposite: a world defined by living beings that are inextricably intertwined. Contact between different animal species, as well as an organism's interaction with its environment, is not a singular probe. It is, instead, a necessary engagement that forms the organizational independence and energetic interdependence of organism and environment. Living beings exist inside immense environments—too complex for any living system to fully manage. However, every animal, humans included, routinely and strategically accesses this environment to capture specific kinds of energy and, as Niklas Luhmann would have it for social systems, knowledge. Subtract an apex species from a landscape and the landscape will collapse. Kill the wolves in Yellowstone National Park and whole swaths of animals, niches, and systems of cognition will be deeply altered.

In more succinct terms, then, Professor O'Donnell's book provides very sharp insights into what it might mean to *draw*, as an architect or urban designer, in order to *draw out*, in an ecological sense, the 'missing perspectives' of diverse and complex contexts in past, contemporary, and future architectural work.

July 28, 2014

ACKNOWLEDGMENTS

This book began as a series of articles in 2008. In order to arrive at the point where these sometimes unlikely issues were colliding productively, it was necessary to have had a diverse and not immediately obviously connected trajectory through the Manchester School of Architecture in the UK (with a specialization in bioclimatics), and at Princeton School of Architecture in the US. For this dueling pair of inputs, I wish to thank on the east side of the pond, Greg Keeffe and Geoff McKennan, and on the west side, Peter Eisenman, Sarah Whiting, Stan Allen, Spyros Papapetros, Manuel de Landa, Robert E. Somol, Jesse Reiser, Ed Eigen, Michael Young, Jane Harrison, and finally Greg Lynn who, unbeknownst to him, was with me on both sides.

This collection has been motivated and influenced by friends and colleagues whose input, advice, encouragement, and generosity have been essential: Cynthia Davidson, Alicia Imperiale, James Lowder, Sabine Müller, Andreas Quednau, Val Warke, Jeremy Foster, David Salomon, Mark Morris, Richard Harrison, Catherine Ingraham, Matthew Lutz, Mathew Aitchison, Lydia Kallipoliti, Stuart Cohen, Peter Stec, Neema Kudva, Ila Berman, Pedro Gadanho, Ryan Paxton, Helene Furján, Sanford Kwinter, Preston Scott Cohen, Mohsen Mostafavi, Pietro Todeschini, and the Todeschini Family.

The work has been tested, in different formats, in several studios and seminars at Cornell University, Department of Architecture. Thanks to all of my colleagues, who have been exceptionally inspiring in these explorations, and in particular to Jerry Wells, Val Warke, and Arthur Ovaska, who made presentations in these seminars, but also to Andrea Simitch, Lily Chi, Mary Woods, Werner Goehner, Francois Roche, Dagmar Richter, and especially to department Chair Mark Cruvellier, and Dean Kent Kleinman, for their unwavering support and encouragement. Thanks to all of the students in the culmination seminar "Contexts: Niche Thinking and the Possibility of Ugliness," for discussing these ideas: Christopher Battaglia, Carly Dean, Gokhan Kodalak, Tiffany Jin, Erin Pellegrino, James Slade,

Owen Smith, Lily-Love Toppar, Daniel Torres, and Xueting Wei, and also students in the previous seminars: "Unideal: Deviations from the Architecture of the Ideal," "Perceptual Genius: Experiencing Architecture from the Eye to the Mind," and "Mutations: Architecture, Genetics and the Niche." Thanks also to the Irwin S. Chanin School of Architecture of the Cooper Union, New York, especially to Anthony Vidler, Elizabeth O'Donnell, Guido Zuliani, Ricardo Scofidio, and Pablo Lorenzo-Eiroa, and to the EnvironMENTAL group at TU Delft, Netherlands.

This work is written from the perspective of a designer seeking both to ground and to project the ideas put forth here in the realm of design. In that respect, my design collaborators have been as important as my text collaborators: thanks, in particular, to Troy Schaum, Ajay Manthripragada, Mike Green, Erana Samarasundera, Aoibheann Ní Mhearáin, COMMA, and SMAQ, and to the designers and researchers at CODA: Suzanne Lettieri, Michael Jefferson, Steven Clipp, Juan Carlos Artolozaga, Rachel Tan, Joseph Kennedy, Jessica Levine, Jerry Lai, Noah Ives, Lucas Greco, Yeung Shin, Daniel Salomon, Nathan C. Friedman, John Lai, Courtney Jiyun Song, Sarah Haubner, Leslie Mignin, Jessica Tranquada, Richard Nelson Chow, Joon Choe, Mike Babcock, and all of the PS1 team.

This project as a whole—both text and design—has, at various points, been supported by: Cornell Department of Architecture and College of Architecture, Art and Planning, Cornell PCCW, Cornell Council for the Arts, Akademie Schloss Solitude, Fonds BKVB (Netherlands), the Arts Council of Ireland, Princeton University, Elise Jaffe and Jeffrey Brown, and MoMA/PS1.

Thanks to Edith Fikes, through whose fingers this text has been combed at many stages of completion. Her patience, perseverance, and continued good spirits have been unmatchable.

And thanks, finally, to John Zissovici, who should appear in many of the paragraphs above, but as usual belongs in a paragraph of his own.

Credits

Text editing and research: Edith Fikes.
Images: all CODA images by Caroline O'Donnell, Suzanne Lettieri, and John Lai.

INTRODUCTION

Bubbles Burst

The Architectural Soap-Bubble

Architecture's unlikely yet persistent reluctance to engage fundamentally with issues of context can most notably be traced to Le Corbusier's renowned comparison of architecture and the soap-bubble. "This bubble," he famously postulated, "is perfect and harmonious if the breath has been evenly distributed and regulated from the inside."[1] This primacy of the interior was, despite their many differences, shared by modern architects, among whom, as contextualist Thomas Schumacher has noted, "few . . . would have allowed that the outside surface ought to determine the interior distribution."[2]

Reiterated in language more appropriate for the 1990s, Rem Koolhaas's provocation to "fuck context" reinvigorated this tendency to favor programmatic, and thus interior-dominated, concerns. Koolhaas's study of architecture's relationship to its urban environment in his oft-quoted essay on *Bigness* is in many ways a call to understand the building as an isolated object, uninterested in and unfettered by external conditions.[3] Koolhaas argues for an architecture that "through its independence from context . . . does not take its inspiration from givens too often squeezed for the last drop of meaning" but that is instead "its own raison d'être."[4]

More recently, this situation has been defined as "absolute architecture," by Pier Vittorio Aureli, who notes that "the very condition of architectural form is to separate and be separated."[5] Aureli masterfully charts the struggle between the separated form and its other, yet the root of his definition lingers: why is this separation a given, and why, consequently, has the relation between architecture and context been so antagonistic?

The bubble, in fact, has a short lifespan. Even when floating in space, it is subject to several external deformative forces: gravity pulls the water molecules to the bottom of the orb, causing unevenness in the membrane; changes in air pressure

FIGURE 0.1 Bubble before bursting.

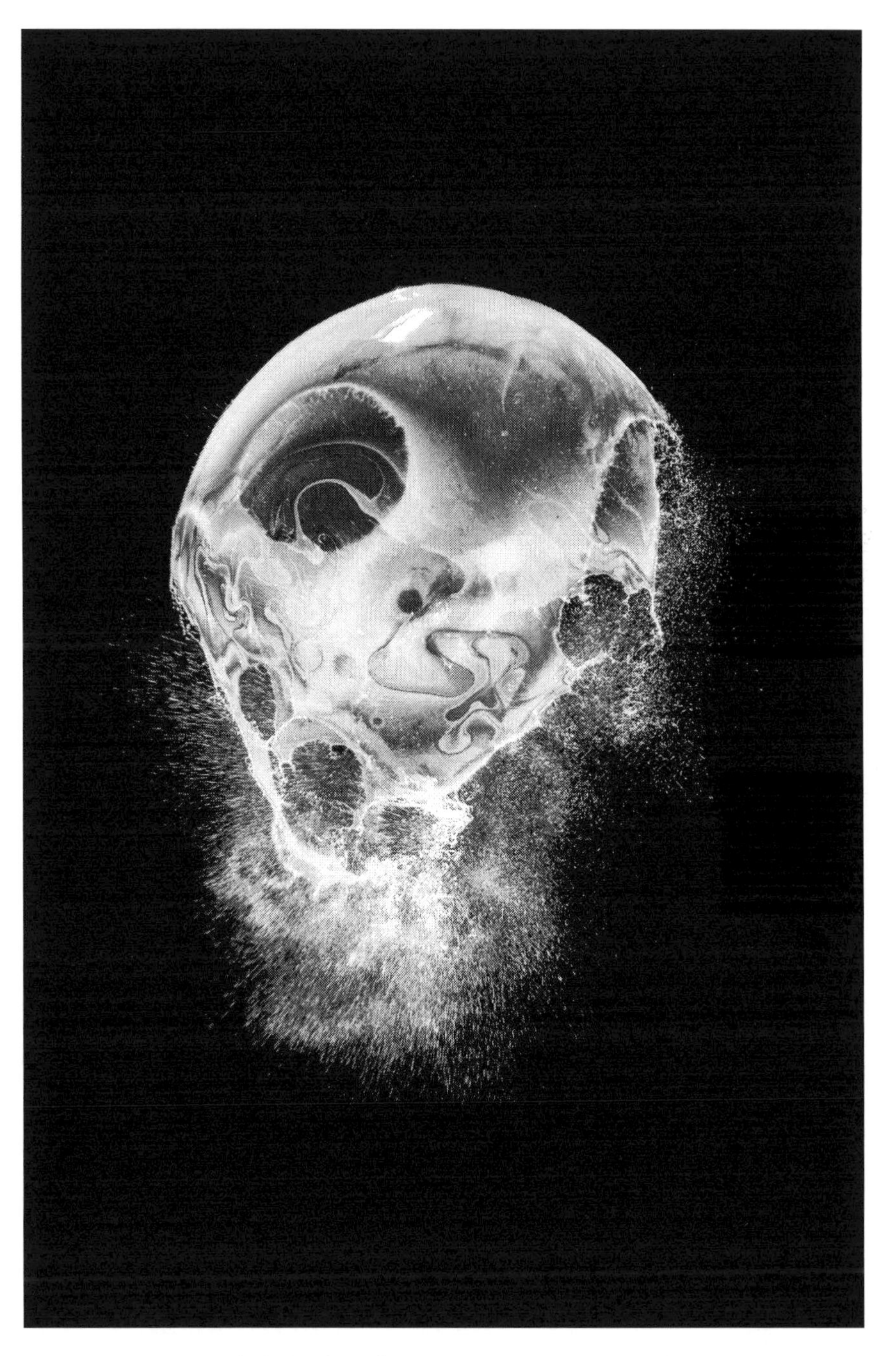

FIGURE 0.2 Bursting bubble. © William Horton 2013. Used with permission.

cause surface deformation. Eventually, the bubble comes into contact with a surface or object and bursts. For the bubble, an encounter with and deformation by the context is inevitable.

The Ecological Bubble

In the same decade as Le Corbusier's original bubble was born, Estonian biologist Jakob von Uexküll proposed a different kind of bubble. Standing in a flower-strewn meadow, Von Uexküll imagined blowing a soap-bubble around each creature, representing the creature's world and its own specific perceptions of that world:

> When we ourselves then step into one of these bubbles, the familiar meadow is transformed. Many of its colorful features disappear, others no longer belong together but appear in new relationships. A new world comes into being. Through the bubble we see the world of the burrowing worm, of the butterfly, or of the field mouse; the world as it appears to the animals themselves, not as it appears to us.[6]

Von Uexküll named this phenomenal- or self-world '*umwelt*.' The organism, having abstracted its particular version of the world, is "so wrapped up in its own *umwelt* that no other worlds are accessible to it . . . as though each one were floating in its own particular 'bubble' of reality."[7]

Von Uexküll's illustrator, Georg Kriszat, attempted to represent the *umwelts* of various animals: it was clearly a challenge to depict the bubble encompassing and drawing in (in both senses of the word) the select and salient elements of the organism's environment. The bee's world, for example, was shown as an abstraction or distillation of the entire (human) environment, but inevitably fell short of expressing the sensorially loaded and memory-rich abstract world of the bee.

This bubble-making gives meaning to reality: a different reality for each animal. Von Uexküll described, for example, the very particular bubble of a tick, which has a limited number of triggers and responses:

> Light affects it and it climbs on to the end of a branch. The smell of a mammal affects it and it drops down on to it. The hairs get in its way and it looks for a hairless place to burrow under the skin and drink the warm blood. Blind and deaf, the tick has only three affects in the vast forest, and for the rest of the time may sleep for years awaiting the encounter. What power, nevertheless![8]

No elements exist in the tick's *umwelt* other than the three triggers and their responses: light-climbing, smell-dropping, and skin-burrowing. The drawing that the tick would make of the world—those elements that would be *drawn* into his bubble—would include only these three components. This representation of the

FIGURE 0.3 Jacob von Uexküll, "Surroundings (top) and environment (bottom) of the bee." From Jakob von Uexküll, *A Foray into the Worlds of Animals and Humans*, trans. Joseph D. O'Neill (Minneapolis, MN: University of Minnesota Press, 2010), 85. Originally published in Professor J. Baron Uexküll, G. Kriszat, Streifzüge durch die Umwelten von Tieren und Menschen Ein Bilderbuch unsichtbarer Welten, "Form und Bewegung als Merkmale," V. 21, 1934, Fig. 23, p. 46, © Julius Springer, Berlin, 1934. With kind permission of Springer Science+Business Media.

world, then, is linked to action-possibilities and form of the organism. In turn, the form of the organism points backward to the actions and abstractions of the environment.

Von Uexküll's bubble, considered as a model for architecture, could not be more opposed to its Corbusian cousin. While Le Corbusier's bubble represents an architecture formed from internal forces, Von Uexküll's bubble points to an architectural organism[9] which 'perceives' and thus responds to a select set of external forces. Moreover, Le Corbusier's bubble is the object of architecture itself, floating in a void, whereas Von Uexküll's bubble reaches out, wraps around, and draws in many excerpts of its environment.[10]

The Uexküllian bubble is conceived through the eyes of the organism 'in' (and not isolated from) the earth. This significant difference between these two points of view is illustrated by anthropologist Tim Ingold in his essay "Earth, Sky, Wind and Weather."[11] Ingold argues that there is no abstract, planar surface on which to dwell. Instead, the rain softens the ground, the winds erode the land, the forests extend to the sky, so that:

> to inhabit the land is not, then, to be stranded on a closed surface but to be immersed in the incessant movements of wind and weather, in a zone wherein substances and medium are brought together in the construction of beings that, by way of their activity, participate in stitching the textures of the land.[12]

Ingold's diagrams show the opposite conditions of living 'on' (Left) and 'in' (Right). In the first, the human is a neutral generic stick figure. In the second, the 'in,' the human has acquired a few attributes. First, he has an orientation. He has turned his back to the wind and is facing the gentle lee zone. Second, the figure now has a stance, a gait, with which he is poised on the ground as if ready to act. Third, the figure has acquired hair, perhaps a material necessity of being 'in.' Finally, nothing about Diagram B is fixed but rather appears in a general state of interrelated flux.

Take the representation of the environment away in Diagram A, and nothing is lacking. Do the same in Diagram B, and the figure continues to suggest something around him. His gait, orientation and material *imply* something about his context.

If we imagine, as architects may be wont to do, that the human is surrounded by an enclosure, in Diagram A, Right, that enclosure might be a generic house. It addresses the sky and the earth but, like its enclosed figure, assumes the default symmetricality on the vertical axis. Consider now a house 'in' the land. Presumably, it must also change its gait, orientation, and materiality. Extrapolated from the diagram into a real environment that includes many complexities besides earth, sky, and wind, one imagines the architecture responding accordingly complexly.

That is to say, whereas the Corbusian-become-Koolhaasian bubble model for architecture is analogous to living *on* the earth, the Uexküllian bubble model aligns better with the idea of living *in* the earth, a scenario in which the architectural organism is considered as part of a complex and idiosyncratic network.

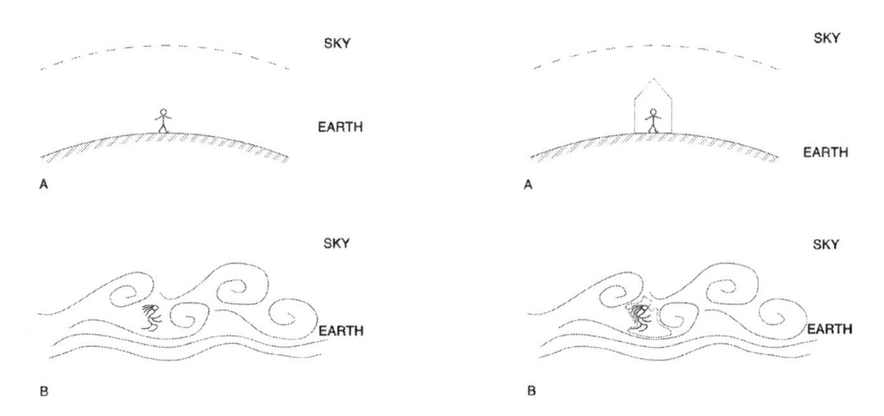

FIGURE 0.4 (Left) After Tim Ingold in "Earth, sky, wind, and weather." (Right) With enclosure added. CODA, 2012.

The architectural consequences of such an approach—which we will call 'niche-thinking' (and the concept of the niche will be more fully developed in Chapter 1, "Niche Tactics")—could be profound. But despite various attempts to shift the discipline toward the ecological model, similar generic prototypes persist and proliferate today, irrespective of climate, culture, or material geography. Ironically, Rem Koolhaas, in his announcement of "Fundamentals," the theme for the 2014 Venice Architectural Biennial, laments this sacrifice of "national identity to modernity" (a sacrifice that he himself propagated), and calls for an acknowledgment of the "process of the erasure of national characteristics in favor of the almost universal adoption of a single modern language in a single repertoire of typologies."[13] The exhibitions, he proposes, will demonstrate the evolution toward the global, but at the same time celebrate, "the survival of unique national features and mentalities that continue to exist and flourish even as international collaboration and exchange intensify."[14]

This global problem can only have worsened since Paul Ricoeur wrote, in 1961, that everywhere in the world one finds, "the same bad movie, the same slot machines, the same plastic or aluminum atrocities, the same twisting of language by propaganda."[15] Koolhaas, it seems, has come full-circle, realizing at last that, unlike movies and slot machines, architecture has a site. Site is, in fact, alongside inhabitation, one of architecture's defining characteristics. Movies and slot machines, plastic and aluminum products, paintings, poems, or music: these can be considered in isolation. Architecture cannot. However, although architecture usually *has* a site, it is not always in generative dialogue *with* it. In Ingold's terms, it may be *on*, without being *in*.

Instances of architecture's productive engagement with its surroundings—that is, of architecture being *in*—date back to the commonly accepted origins of Western architecture.[16] In "On Climate as Determining the Style of the House," Vitruvius opens an early discussion of context by comparing climatic variation in the human body to architectural variation. The segment begins with the common-sense statement that:

> as the position of the heaven with regard to a given tract on the earth leads naturally to different characteristics, owing to the inclination of the circle of the zodiac and the course of the sun, it is obvious that designs for houses ought similarly to conform to the nature of the country and to the diversities of climate.[17]

Vitruvius notes that the effects of climate are "not only discernible in nature, but they are also observable in the limbs and bodies of entire races."[18] He proceeds to draw an analogy between buildings and body size, complexion, hair color, and vocal pitch at different latitudes.

However, the hierarchies present in Vitruvius's treatise are revealed when, in the chapter that follows, he writes that "symmetry and order are *primary*, and only *after* these considerations have been made, should one consider the nature of the site (as well as use and beauty)."[19] This is an important moment to pause, and acknowledge the coup won by symmetry and order over responsiveness at this moment (and, consequently, perhaps, over ugliness.) Vitruvius's hierarchy would prove difficult to challenge. Even today, the dominance of order and symmetry remains pervasive in architecture and has been a trap that has routinely befallen architects. It is still precisely this issue (and the preconceived notions of form with which it is associated) that limits architecture's ability to respond adequately to its environment.

Renaissance translations of these ideas, found in the many architectural treatises that proliferated around 1,500 years after Vitruvius, tend to be much more pragmatic. Alberti, for instance, in his first book of *The Art of Building in Ten Books*, devotes parts three through ten to careful consideration of the details—both in nature and in human cultural life—that constitute the site, which he refers to more precisely as *locality* and *area*.[20] In so doing, Alberti advises the architect to make both calculations and observations before determining the building's design and orientation. He suggests that elements of the existing context can and perhaps should determine early decisions in the process of architectural production. This predetermined object, however, is a far cry from Vitruvius's unexplored allusion to site-motivated variation in morphology, materiality, and temperament, but understandably so, since such an exploration had been made impossible by the predominance of formal rules over morphological responsiveness.

Beginning again then from this well-grounded but secondary emphasis in Vitruvius, this collection of essays examines moments of being not *on* but *in*, in a variety of ways. The opposition between the two bubble models—Le Corbusier's isolated bubble and Von Uexküll's selectively encompassing bubble—sets up an oscillation back and forth between the pole of contextual engagement and its various inverses. This sinusoidal line through time follows the trajectory of contextual thinking and production through all of these realms, even those seemingly opposed to it.

Having set out the ecological argument in Chapter 1, "Niche Tactics," in Chapters 2 and 3 we revisit two case studies in Renaissance Italy: "The Thirteenth Villa" investigates Palladio's much-analyzed 'brood' of villas and searches for evidence of context-motivated variation, while "The Deformations of Francesco de Marchi" charts the revolutionary work of the Renaissance military architect, whose site-deformed cities opposed the mainstream of pure geometric urban design in the hypothetical realm of the treatise. Chapter 4 takes us to eighteenth-century England, where contextual thinking begins in earnest through the Picturesque movement: "An Ecological Approach to the Picturesque," in discussing the upswing of the role of site in design, the movement's postwar interpretation as 'Townscape,' and its alignment with functionalism, returns us to functionalist thinking in ecology and potential new modes of operating today.

In the early twentieth century, as the pendulum swung away from contextualism once again, fragments of resistance are discovered at the heart of the Modern movement. Chapter 5's case study, "The Donkey's Way," investigates the neglected urban remnants in Le Corbusier's *Plan Voisin* and extrapolates the significance of their presence to produce an entirely new set of locally affected towers within the plan.

As a consequence of the declared failures of Modernism, the conflict between the architectural bubble and the external world became the subject of much study in the 1960s, and it was at one pole of this debate that Colin Rowe and his students initiated the 'Contextualist' movement.[21] Chapter 6, "All Dressed Up," examines the successes and failures of these various contextual movements and Chapter 7's case study, "Santa Maria Deformata," questions the existence of ideal form following Colin Rowe and Fred Koetter's comparison of two churches in *Collage City*, identifying and interpolating the already deformed conditions of their so-called pure form. Together these chapters come closest to a manifesto for alternative paths for contextualism that aims to sidestep the pitfalls of the original movements.

At around the same time that contextualism was born, the eco-architecture movement (brought to us most forcefully through John McHale's *The Ecological Context* (1970) and Ian McHarg's *Design with Nature* (1969)) formed the core of what we might today consider to be 'sustainability.' Zooming out to see the earth from space showed the world as a fragile sphere (a bubble, we might say) and provoked the arresting realization of our "responsibility for the viable maintenance of the planet as life-space."[22] McHale likens the relationship between humans and planet Earth to that of a medic and a sick patient: a desperate call for an architecture of remediation.

The importance of these issues cannot be overstated. It seems, however, that the reality and urgency of these various crises have distracted us from alternate or parallel paths for ecological thinking: that is, the thinking of architecture as an ecological system and legibility of site through form.[23] While contextualism at times began to do that, it headed eventually down a dead-end path toward fitting-in and the architecture of neighborly mimicry.

In order to find these alternatives, this collection too zooms out—outside the discipline of architecture—to ecology, to film theory, and to linguistic and joke theory: disciplines in which the role of context has been particularly significant. By escaping the bounds of the discipline of architecture, the role of context in other disciplines becomes a means of re-approaching this most architectural of problems with new tools. Chapter 1, "Niche Tactics," as we know, develops the analogy between evolutionary and architectural generation and, in particular, the role of the niche that lies at the core of that relationship; Chapter 8, "Kuleshov Effects," investigates filmmaker Lev Kuleshov's experiments into the role of background in the perception of the object and its applicability for architecture; and Chapter 9, "Duck Jokes," investigates the role of context in joke theory and its possible alignment with architecture's own potential for the transformation of expectation.

Following these various probes outside the discipline, the consequences of such 'niche-thinking' are considered: if those forces to which the (architectural) organism is responding are asymmetrical, the resultant form, in all likelihood, will be equally disordered. Due to the commonly accepted notions of beauty being tied to order, proportion, and symmetry, the inevitable formal conclusion of this type of production is the ugly. Chapter 10, "Fugly," presents Karl Rosenkranz's nineteenth-century notion of ugliness, which defines it not only in our commonly accepted terms, but additionally in its relationship to the unfamiliar and the expected. Finally, Chapter 11, "Hopeful Monsters," returns the thinking about ugliness to evolution and the productive role of the monstrosity in the production of 'successful' form in nature.

The nodes of the oscillation that are presented here, far from claiming to be comprehensive, are intended to connect a series of points that chart the fluctuations in contextual-thinking in architecture with another series of trajectories from outside the field.[24] By connecting these various contextual dots, the aim is to open up new ways of thinking and engaging context that can be productive and generative in design today.

While a coda is usually considered to be a concluding remark, the CODA at the end of this book refers as well to a series of design experiments that test the ideas presented here. As such, it is less an end than the beginning of a new approach that will play itself out through a design practice: not just the practice presented there but, hopefully, through many others as well.

Such new approaches are necessary because the contextualists' own bubble burst when it became apparent that their architecture was incapable of escaping from a reverence to, and continuation of, existing conditions. Deformation seemed to act only between known ready-made types and, even then, appeared to take the form of well-behaved adjustments to blend in with the existing. Rem Koolhaas's expletive was perhaps a necessary slap in the face to that moribund trajectory.

However, it does not follow that the engagement and response to contextual forces must arrive at a banal architecture of retrospective copies. Von Uexküll's bubble is useful here because it goes further than the contextualists' proposition of deformation as a response to the visible world. It proposes instead that the *world* is first pulled inside the bubble, and, moreover, that the meaning of '*world*' is interpreted differently by each organism, due to the nature of the interactions between it and the environment. The organism, then, evolves in a relationship with its extracted world, formed and materialized by the forces produced by that world. This is why Von Uexküll wrote: "The question as to meaning must therefore have priority in all living beings."[25]

In this way, architectural context can be considered a field of meaningful forces; sometimes asymmetrical, sometimes invisible. The architecture that is a consequence of its context can be rethought; not as fitting in, but as a forceful offensive reaction that is capable of communicating that reaction through its form and materiality. As such, it may be an architecture that twists, shifts, and bends in ways that imply its invisible partner, whether in fight or in dance.

Notes

1 Le Corbusier, *Toward a New Architecture*, trans. John Goodman (Los Angeles: Getty Publications, 2007), 216.
2 Thomas L. Schumacher, "The Outside is the Result of an Inside: Some Sources of One of Modernism's Most Persistent Doctrines," *Journal of Architectural Education*, 56, 1 (2002), 22–33.
3 Rem Koolhaas, "Bigness or the Problem of Large," in *S,M,L,XL* (New York: The Monacelli Press, 1995), 502.
4 Ibid., 502–515.
5 Pier Vittorio Aureli, *The Possibility of an Absolute Architecture* (Cambridge, MA: MIT Press, 2011), 201, ix.
6 Jakob von Uexküll, "A Stroll Through the Worlds of Animals and Men: A Picture Book of Invisible Worlds," in *Instinctive Behavior: The Development of a Modern Concept*, ed. and trans. Claire H. Schiller (New York: International Universities Press, 1957), 5.
7 Tim Ingold, "Point, Line and Counterpoint," in *Being Alive, Essays on Movement, Knowledge and Description* (New York: Routledge, 2011), 80. In reference to J. von Uexküll, "A Stroll Through the Worlds of Animals and Men: A Picture Book of Invisible Worlds," *Semiotica*, 89, 4 (1992), 319–391.
8 Von Uexküll, "A Stroll Through the Worlds of Animals and Men," in *Instinctive Behavior*, 5.
9 One pertinent example is to be found in Le Corbusier's *Toward a New Architecture*, in which he considers the architect a "creator of organisms." Le Corbusier, *Toward a New Architecture* (1927), trans. Frederick Etchells (New York: Holt, Rinehart and Winston, 1986), 103.
10 This description aligns to some extent with the biological definition of the 'niche'—a concept that will be elaborated in Chapter 1, "Niche Tactics."
11 Tim Ingold, *Being Alive: Essays on Movement, Knowledge and Description* (New York: Routledge, 2011).
12 Ibid., 121.
13 "Rem Koolhaas Revisits Fundamentals for the 2014 Venice Architecture Biennale," *Design Boom*, January 25, 2013, www.designboom.com/architecture/rem-koolhaas-revisits-fundamentals-for-the-2014-venice-architecture-biennale/ (accessed April 17, 2013).
14 Ibid.
15 Paul Ricoeur, "Universal Civilization and National Cultures," in *History and Truth*, trans. Chas. A. Kelbley (Evanston, IL: Northwestern University Press, 1965), 276–277.

This piece was quoted at the beginning of Kenneth Frampton, "Towards a Critical Regionalism: Six Points for an Architecture of Resistance," in *Anti-Aesthetic, Essays on Postmodern Culture* (Seattle, WA: Bay Press, 1983), 16.

16 This collection limits itself (mainly) to Western architecture and assigns Vitruvius as the first true architect. Of course, many instances of the productive engagement between site and architecture are to be found in non-Western traditions, as well as pre-Vitruvian Western vernacular architecture, and both deserve more attention.

17 Vitruvius, *The Ten Books on Architecture*, trans. Morris Hicky Morgan (New York: Dover, 1960), 170.

18 Ibid.

19 Ibid., 174.

20 Leon Battista Alberti, *On the Art of Building in Ten Books*, trans. Joseph Rykwert, Neil Leach, and Robert Tavernor (Cambridge, MA: MIT Press, 1988), 6.

21 Rowe was not alone in his engagement with context. Simultaneously, Ernesto Rogers, Also Rossi, and Vittorio Gregotti were publishing prolifically on similar subjects in Casabella, Christian Norberg-Schulz wrote on *Genius Loci*, Kevin Lynch wrote on the *Image of the City*, and Robert Venturi wrote *Complexity and Contradiction*.

22 John McHale, *The Ecological Context* (New York: George Braziller, 1970).

23 Such thinking may result in sustainable architecture without that being its sole purpose.

24 And there are, of course, many other oscillations and sub-wobbles in this story that are not touched upon here.

25 Jakob von Uexküll, *A Foray into the Worlds of Animals and Humans*, trans. Joseph D. O'Neill (Minneapolis, MN: University of Minnesota Press, 2010), 151.

1

NICHE TACTICS

Darwin's theory of unmotivated variation and the subsequent 'editing' process that drives evolution have been mirrored by a contemporary trend toward the production of variation in architecture. As scripts have become capable of generating multifarious options, evolutionary terminology has crept into the language of architecture: words such as *species*, *iteration*, *generation*, *variation*, *mutation*, and *autopoiesis* have by now become commonplace.[1] While this interdisciplinary borrowing has enriched our ability to produce and accept the unexpected, and to think processually about architectural generation, developments have at times tended to neglect the contextual logics that underlie these evolutionary transformations.[2]

For the identification of a fundamental nexus between evolutionary theory and architecture, the discipline of architecture owes much to D'Arcy Thompson.[3] Thompson's diagrams, depicting species through continuous and simple geometric transformations, render the biological development of physical forms graphically legible.[4] The grid, which represents the forces of deformation across species, suggests an underlying ordering system in the natural world. 'Force,' as understood by Thompson is: "the appropriate term for our conception of the causes by which these forms and changes of form are brought about."[5] However, while many environmental factors (gravity, energy, motion, and so on) are mentioned, and Thompson notes that transformations may depend on various phenomena "from simple imbibition of water to the complicated results of the chemistry of nutrition,"[6] environmental forces are not specifically mapped in the transformations.

Further, in nature, the transformation of parts is not necessarily proportional to the whole.[7] Thompson details the transformation of the part, for example, by relating the cannon bone of the ox, sheep, and giraffe (with the ratio $x'' = x/3$) and by demonstrating the smooth continuity of this proportion through a series of bones in the legs of those animals.

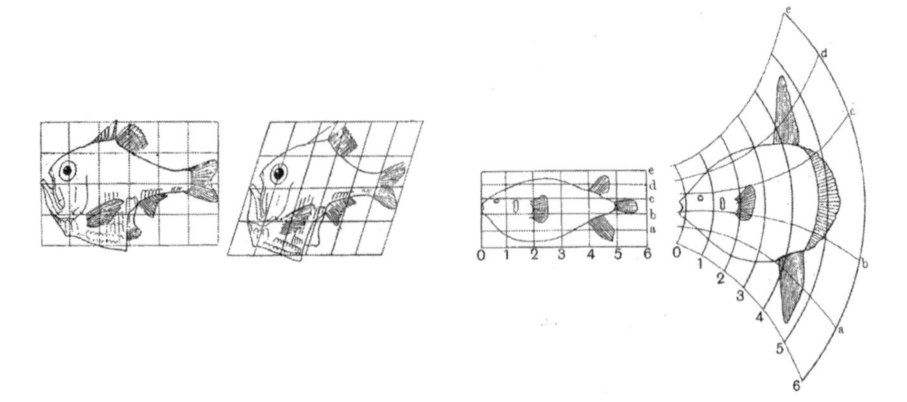

FIGURE 1.1 Thompson, "Evolution of body form." The transformation of Cartesian coordinates from (left) (A) the body plan of the fish *Argyropelecus olfersi* to (B) the body plan of the fish *Sternoptyx diaphana* (Figs 517 and 518, p. 1062) and (right) from (A) the body plan of the fish *Diodon* to (B) the closely related fish *Orthagoricus* (Figs 525 and 526, p. 1064). D'Arcy Wentworth Thompson, edited by John Tyler Bonner, *On Growth and Form*. © 1961 Cambridge University Press. Reprinted with the permission of Cambridge University Press.

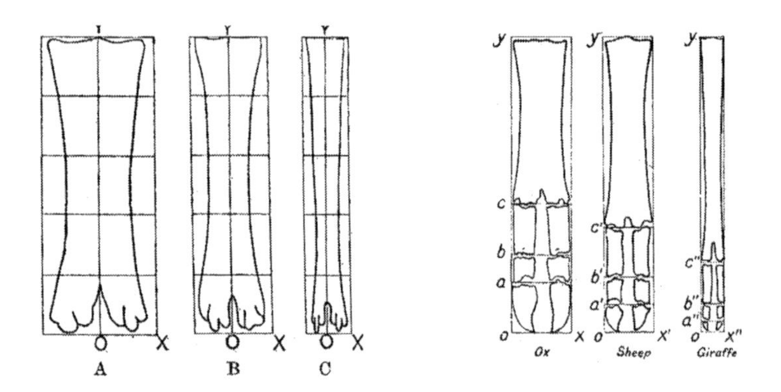

FIGURE 1.2 Thompson, "Comparison of the cannon bone and foot in a coordinate system for several ungulates." D'Arcy Wentworth Thompson, *On Growth and Form*, ed. John Tyler Bonner (Fig. 493, p. 1039 and Fig. 506, p. 1052). © 1961 Cambridge University Press. Reprinted with the permission of Cambridge University Press.

However, he does not continue to diagram the parts *within* the whole; say, for example, the leg-bones of the giraffe inside its vast and differentiated body. Had this been attempted, a series of bulges would have appeared within the smoothness of the grid.

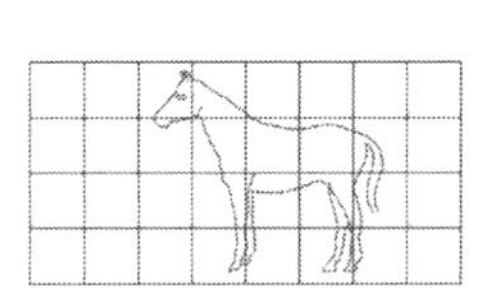

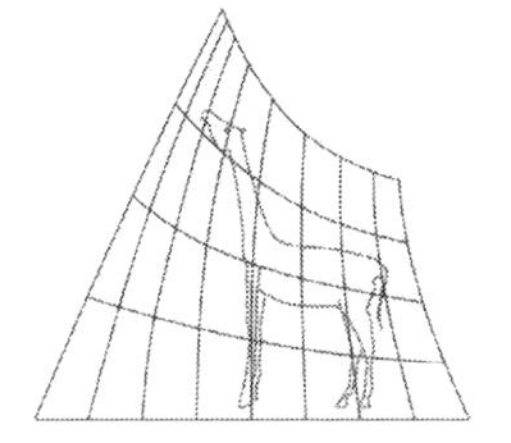

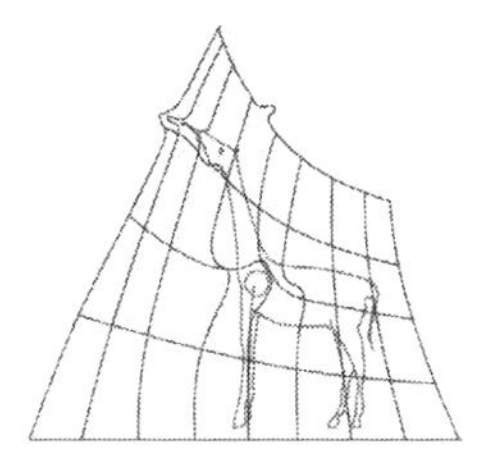

FIGURE 1.3 Horse–giraffe diagram, after Thompson. CODA, 2012.

The giraffe's heart, for example, is much larger than is normal for its body size—a consequence of pumping blood to its lofty head (the giraffe's heart is 2.3 percent of its body mass, compared to 0.5 percent in other mammals).[8] Also related to differentiated variation across parts within a singular body, the giraffe's neck contains several valves that prevent a rush of blood to the head when lowered for drinking, and its lower legs include a thick layer of tight skin—the "anti-gravity suit"[9]—because the blood vessels in the legs sustain constant and immense pressure. This example alone illustrates a circulatory and mechanical response to a morphological condition, which in turn re-affects the material and formal components, all of which significantly complexify Thompson's simplified diagrams.

An alternative diagram looks at the giraffe instead as a system that includes not only the mechanical and material aspects of the form, but the relevant aspects of the environment too. The giraffe, thus, does not end at its skin, but draws in the essential world around it. Furthermore, what it encompasses affects those related aspects of its body, shifting form, material, and system into equilibrium with each other.

Species

Before species were understood as transformative in this way, new discoveries had been explained as combinations of known types. The genus name of the Giraffe *Camelopardalis*[10] reflects this attitude: considered, as it was, to be a combination of the camel (formally) and the leopard (materially). The error was a consequence of typological thinking, in which fixed types, though immutable, were combinable. Today's understanding of evolution is precisely the opposite: incompatible species have boundaries that change over time (or are different over space). This conceptual shift—from combination to conversion—has percolated beyond evolutionary theory and into our cultural thinking in many fields. In the 1990s, Greg Lynn—one of the original proponents of evolutionary thinking in contemporary architecture[11]—studied and addressed the issue in a series of texts

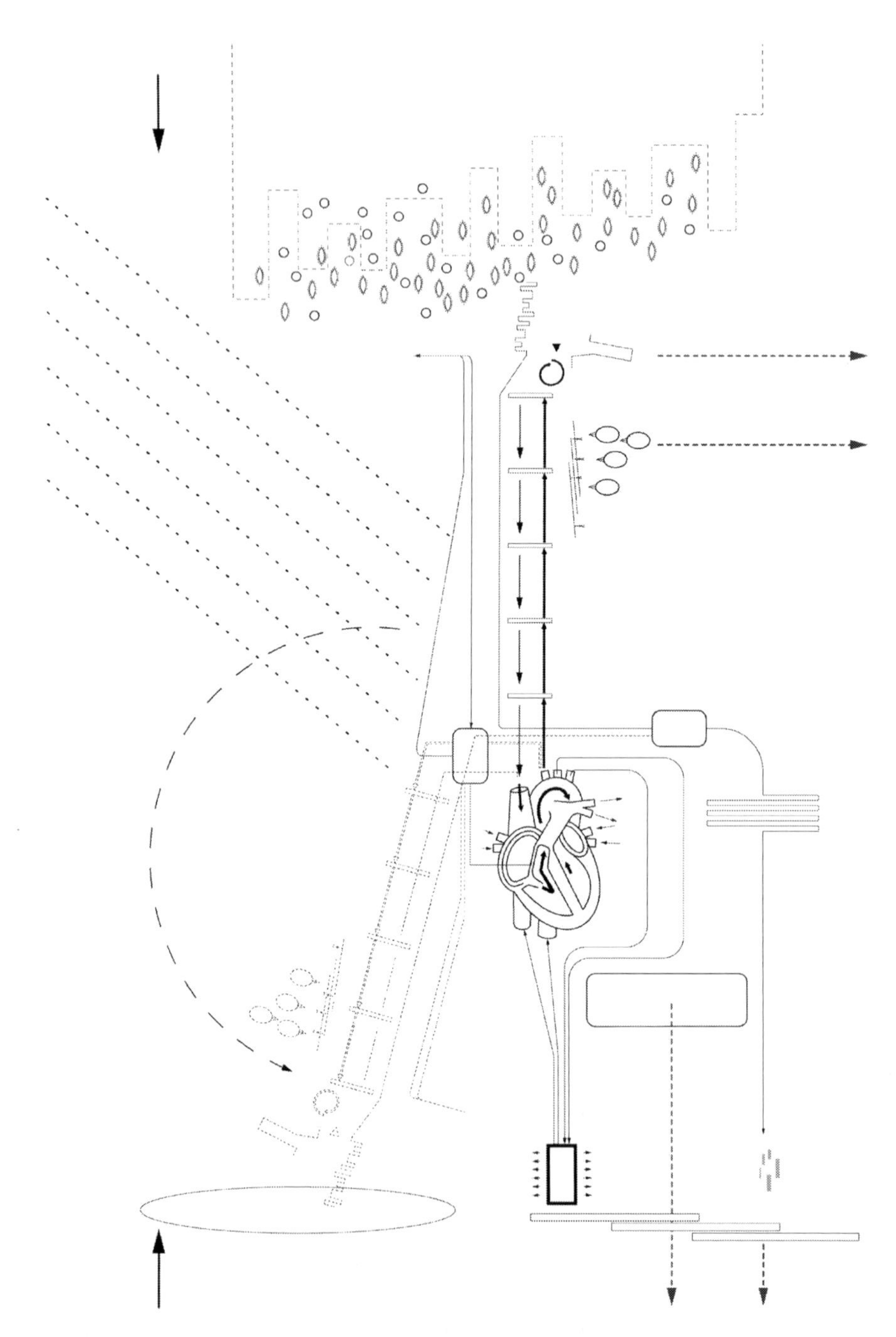

FIGURE 1.4 Giraffe diagram. CODA, 2012.

collected in *Folds, Bodies & Blobs*. Following Thompson's lead, Lynn writes that "the type or spatial organism is no longer seen as a static whole separate from external forces, but rather as a sensibility continuously transforming through its internalization of outside events."[12] Lynn's texts are often paired with design experiments, in which the provocations developed in the text are tested. The projects attack ideas of whole and perfect form, and transform existing or platonic forms into fragmented, striated, or multiplied geometries, motivated by a variety of factors, including program, structure, form, and culture.[13] In *Stranded Sears Tower*, contextual features (the river, the city's gridded structure, and various transportation lines) are considered to be transformative forces. In the *Cardiff Bay Opera House Competition*, site alignments are made with existing buildings and infrastructure.[14] Lynn's break-out of formalism through evolutionary thinking was a radical change from the typological thinking that preceded it, and is the foundation upon which we will build.[15]

To some extent, Thompson's *force* can be aligned with Darwin's *fitness*: that is, the relationship between the animal and its environment. Random mutations in the organism that have a positive effect in the context of the organism allow that organism to gain advantage and thus continue its lineage along with that particular mutation, while mutations that have a negative effect contribute to the demise of the organism and the consequent eradication of that mutation. In Darwin's words:

> Variations, however slight and from whatever cause proceeding, if they be in any degree profitable to the individuals of a species, in their infinitely complex relations to other organic beings and to their physical conditions of life, will tend to the preservation of such individuals, and will generally be inherited by the offspring.[16]

This phenomenon is often illustrated through thirteen species of finch identified in the Galápagos Islands, each having evolved in isolation—according to the theory of 'adaptive radiation'[17]—in relation to specific local conditions, from one original ground-dwelling, seed-eating finch.[18]

Some of the ground finches have developed large stout beaks for eating large seeds, while the tree finches have developed beaks that are better adapted to eating insects or nectar, or for wood-pecking. Further, these beak morphologies have been linked with foot and claw morphology[19] (for clasping a branch versus walking on the ground), as well as overall size and song.[20] The bird diagram implies all of these conditions—seeds, insects, nectar, wood, branches, ground, mates, other body parts—by depicting variation that cannot exist independently of them. Mapped in a Thompsonian manner, these birds may represent twelve steps in a smooth transition, without contextual information.[21] Alternatively, we might envision a counterpart to the bird diagram that shows the environmental forces to which the birds have fit.

FIGURE 1.5 Darwin, Galapagos finches. Based on a drawing in Biological Sciences Curriculum Study, *Biological Science: Molecules to Man*, Houghton Mifflin, 1963. CODA, 2012.

Such environmental forces are not always visible, however. On a global scale, Carl Bergmann described (in 1847) a relationship between body size and geographic location in closely related kinds of birds and mammals. He found, for instance, that as latitude increases toward the poles, the same is true for body size. Bergmann's explanation of this phenomenon was based on heat conservation: the lower surface/volume ratio in larger animals being advantageous for conserving heat in colder climates.[22] Despite more recent claims that the changing morphology is related to other factors (food supply or predator population, for example), the thermoregulatory basis of Bergmann's argument has been supported by studies showing changing body size in a fixed location during climate change.[23]

Following Bergmann's rule, Joel A. Allen (in 1877) proposed a corresponding relationship between the location and the size of an animal's appendages: in the example shown, the ears of the desert fox (left) appear to have been enlarged, in comparison to the mid-European fox, while ears of the arctic fox (right) appear to have been reduced.[24]

Of course, beyond morphology, skin color and other skin components also affect thermoregulation. However, skin color is often associated with camouflage, and in fact has the opposite response than would be expected from a thermoregulatory response: colder climates, where we might expect darker, more absorptive skin, tend to work in favor of light-colored skin, which conceals the animal from view, and, conversely, the thick vegetation in the equatorial zones creates shadows, in which darker-skinned animals are better concealed.[25] In this case, the condition of hiding from predators (or prey) supersedes thermoregulation.

FIGURE 1.6 Allen's rule: variation in the relative sizes of foxes' ears (from left, *Fennecus zerda* (hot desert habitat), *Vulpes vulpes* (temperate habitat), and *Alopex lagopus*) (cold tundra habitat). From "Single Species Patterns" in *Biogeography*, 2nd ed., by Mark V. Lomolino, Brett R. Riddle, and James H. Brown, Sinauer Assoc., 1998–1999, p. 490.

This complex symbiotic relationship—between the many qualities of the environment and the many needs of the organism—is fundamental to the work of perceptual psychologist J.J. Gibson, who writes:

> it is often neglected that the words animal and environment make an inseparable pair. Each term implies the other. No animal could exist without an environment surrounding it. Equally, although not so obvious, an environment implies an animal (or at least an organism) to be surrounded.[26]

As the environment is described, the animal that inhabits it can be defined, and vice versa.[27] If it is hot and dry, if there is stalky, yellowish grass underfoot, if Acacia trees are dotted around, giraffes may emerge; or, conversely, if the animal is tall, long-necked, with dappled skin, savannah emerges.[28] This relationship is what produces the ecological *niche*, and it is precisely this relationship that has been lost in the translation from evolution to architecture.

Coined by the naturalist Joseph Grinnell in 1917,[29] a *niche* was initially understood to mean the collection of components of an organism's habitat that influence its survival and reproduction. Zoologist G. Evelyn Hutchinson[30] later elaborated upon the meaning of the term. He specified that the multi-dimensional space of resources (e.g., light, nutrients, structure, etc.) within a habitat could be occupied by multiple species and that the niche was a subset of that habitat containing particular resources imperative to one particular species: whereas different species can occupy the same habitat, they cannot occupy the same niche.[31] In Gibson's words: "Let us observe that in one sense, the surroundings of a single animal are the same as the surroundings of all animals, but that in another sense, the surroundings of a single animal are different from those of any other animal."[32]

This clarification is imperative to the understanding of the term *niche* for the architect. Just as the act of defining an environment is not enough to define the resources required for a species to survive, the oft-misused strategy of 'site analysis' is not enough for the generation of architecture.[33] While the standard site analysis might be capable of describing a habitat for several species, it is too generic as a process to abstract in the way that would be necessary to create the diversity of species that exist in a single environment.

The standard site analysis will, ecologically speaking, produce a generic animal, to exist on one site (versus the diversity of animals to be found in the same site in nature).[34] Though nearly impossible to accomplish, the thorough, all-encompassing site analysis would lead to a nondescript hybrid of all species inhabiting one environment, like the greyish-brown blob of paint resulting from the mixing of many colors. This all-mapping, all-responding organism would lead, quickly, to its own extinction because every constraint cannot be mapped and subsequently responded to. A series of potentially random aspects would be collected and subsequently lead to the production of a weak hybrid that recalls the mixing of species, much like the giraffe's mistaken identity as a combination of the leopard and the camel: a *Girabra*, an *Elefaffe*, a *Zion*. This chimeric combination of species is the consequence of an imprecise and overlapping 'abstraction' of information from the environment. Instead it is the *selective and subjective abstraction* of components of a habitat that forms the conditions for a specific response.

The map of the niche, as a hypothetical *abstraction* made by the giraffe, for example, is a map particular to the specific species, containing treetops, some watering holes, and some speedier predators (man and the lion are the giraffe's only real threats). Other species in the same habitat might respond to other factors: the zebra's map may be dominated by the lower branches (on which to dine), the elephant may focus on the tree trunks (on which to scratch), and the lion may map the long grass (from which to pounce). It is not the defining of the context that allows the giraffe to emerge but the *abstraction* of that context.

The seemingly self-evident relationship of the giraffe's formal attributes with its environment has resulted in its use as an example in many evolutionary discussions. Jean Baptiste Lamarck used it to support 'Soft Inheritance,' a theory in which features acquired throughout the lifespan of the animal were inherited by its offspring: in this

FIGURE 1.7 Girabra, Elefaffe, and Zion. CODA, 2012.

case, the giraffe's habit of stretching the neck and fore-legs. Darwin's subsequent theory proposed instead that these transformations were *unmotivated*: that is, the variations were not *striving* to reach the tree-tops, rather, that:

> those individuals which had some one part or several parts of their bodies rather more elongated than usual, would have survived under typical circumstances. These will have intercrossed and left offspring that either inherit the same bodily peculiarities or a tendency to vary again in the same manner; whilst the individuals less favored in the same respects will have been the most likely to perish. By this process long-continued, an ordinary hoofed quadruped might be converted into a giraffe.[35]

Many subsequent theorists have proposed more complex alternatives: that the giraffe's neck is secondary to the elongation of its legs, which served to outrun its predators;[36] that its increased surface area is primarily a function of cooling;[37] or that the use of the neck and head for fighting in order to gain social dominance is a primary concern.[38] Regardless of the specific hierarchy of these features, each theory points to some hypothetical *abstraction* of the environment made by the organism in the process of perception.

Even simply considering the treetops as having been primary in the giraffe's particular abstraction, the relationship is much more reciprocal and complex than it would at first appear. It unravels into a web of interrelationships with arrows in both directions. For example, studies have shown that the thorniness of the East African Acacia tree—the Giraffe's preferred food—is induced by herbivorous activity.[39] In return, the lips, tongue, and inside of the mouth of the giraffe are covered in papillae and its skin is thick, to protect against these very thorns. Further, the aggressive ants that inhabit the Acacia appear to act symbiotically with the tree in its defense: the ants inhabit the shoot tips of the upper branches—the Giraffe's preferred plant part—and are more likely to inhabit trees with more foliage.[40] This is only one strand of a complex web of reciprocal relationships that exists for all species of plants and animals. Following this, it becomes rather easy to imagine the many more relationships between the giraffe and other species—and, potentially, the further evolution of the giraffe. A change in any of these values—ants, thorns, tongue, skin, ticks, birds, lions, grass, gazelle, deer, and so on—each of which is a consequence of other factors such as climate, predators, hunting, etc. can affect the others. The constant adjustment and negotiation is what nudges evolution forward, niches and species, constantly diversifying.

A fundamental part of the process of *abstraction* is described by Gibson as the *affordance* of an object: "what it *offers* the animal, what it *provides* or *furnishes*, either for good or ill."[41] Affordances exist as 'action possibilities' latent in the environment, existing independently of the animal's ability to recognize them, but always in relation to and dependent upon the animal's capabilities.[42]

Alternatively, Jakob von Uexküll's notion of *Umwelt* suggests that the meaning is not intrinsic to the thing but *bestowed* upon it by the animal, or "*acquired* by virtue of having been drawn into that creature's activity."[43] Thus, rather than the animal fitting to its environment, the animal fits its 'perceived' environment to itself and gives it meaning through use. The meaning is based on a need and therefore implies an action: it tells the animal how to act in its world. Since no animal (including the human one) is capable of observing from a position of neutrality, the very act of perception, in which the meaning of use is direct and primary, inevitably implies an action.[44]

Returning to the niche then, the process by which an animal *abstracts* its environment can be considered to reside partially in the environment and partially in the animal. Ecological abstraction involves an extraction but also a projection of some kind of meaning in order to isolate the specific and useful elements from the white noise of generic perceptual world. The *niche* can be considered to be a concise collection of *affordance–umwelt* arrows, back and forth, between animal and environment, each propelling the other forward.

A simplified version of this relationship has been fundamental to many vernacular architectures—for instance, the color and minimal fenestration of Mexican adobe construction as a negative response to solar incidence, the double-jigged entrance in the Scottish stone hut as a response to the treeless windy hillside, the steeply pitched roofs of the Malaysian stilt-dwelling as a response to heavy rains and uncertain ground conditions, or the domed form and interior step of the igloo for minimal heat loss and pooling of cooler air below the sleeping surface, and so on. For a long time, even the high discipline of architecture maintained the faint traces of the vernacular responsiveness, embedded, as it was, in the strict laws of architectural orders. Marc-Antoine (Abbé) Laugier's Primitive Hut (1755), of course, was a reminder of the origins of architecture and a call, amid the high ornamentation of the Baroque, to return to essentials, to reconnect the elements of architecture with their responsive origins in nature, to remember "man in his first origin, without any help, without other guide, than the natural instinct of his wants."[45] In his famous etching, the architecture seems bound to its environment.

Despite similar calls for essentialism, Modernism's preference for internationalism over any 'natural instinct' led to an architecture absolutely contrary to the architecture of the niche. Whatever its intentions, it became a standardized and globalized style that smoothed out all special diversity and responsiveness, and it is from this idea of the generic, and all of its misinterpretations that proliferate today, that we are still attempting to recover.

So why all of this wandering around in the savannah, when the vernacular could be our model? An iterative process by definition, using local materials and traditional technologies handed down through the generations, such a model would seem appropriate, and less removed from the discipline at hand.

Yet, look more closely: even Laugier's image has things the wrong way around. The image shows nature manipulated into the preconceived form of architecture's most primary object: the hut. The image exists before the context and inevitably dictates the response.[46]

FIGURE 1.8 Laugier, frontispiece to second edition of *Essai sur l'architecture*, 1753.

Anthropologist James Deetz has explained this phenomenon using the notion of the "mental template," an ideal prototype, which, he suggests, exists in the mind of the vernacular maker as a preconceived notion of how things *ought* to be made.[47] Such a desire for appropriate form is, as has been described, absent in evolution, and it is precisely the lack of appropriateness that allows the niche-thinking model to stealthily evade preconceptions of the expected.

Though not without immense value, the vernacular model is further undermined by its increasingly retrospective associations. With the advance of globalization, and the increasing loss of original local architectures, "the vernacular itself becomes a lost world—and with it, its field of study becomes the exclusive domain of historians."[48] As local responses to context have become historicized, they have been further internalized into the culture and symbolism of the place, bound to their own self-image, trapped in a loop of continuity without forward-moving, progressive, evolutionary change.

Limited to representing the image of their type, like Thompson's transformations, iterated vernaculars often miss the internal and systematic 'bulges' that occur as a result of parts reacting to disparate but related elements. Niche-thinking encourages a shift in focus from enclosure to system, where form and skin are merely a part of a complex web of connections within both the animal and the environment. In short, while the vernacular as a model of adaptation may have begun with a responsive impulse, its reactions, with each generation, can become dulled by its own self-image.

This dominance of this preconceived image persists today, especially in so-called sustainable architecture in which a sustainable solution is found for something that looks like architecture. Niche-thinking proposes instead an ecological way of thinking (in the case of the primitive hut, about the trees, their branches, their bark, their roots, their ground, their nutrients, their rain, their solar energy, their birds' nests, their birds, etc.) in order to produce a form of enclosure that is a responsive component of that system. Niche-thinking opens up physical form to the complexity and contingencies of contexts, in which the environment is not singular, but consists of different potential *umwelten*.

Going one step further, niche-thinking might be considered to be tactical, based, as it is, according to Michel de Certeau's definition, on actions produced out of moment-to-moment reactions to localized constraints, "always on the watch for opportunities that must be seized 'on the wing' . . . constantly *manipulat[ing]* events in order to turn them into 'opportunities.'"[49] Similarly, Darwin describes natural selection as:

> daily and hourly *scrutinizing*, throughout the world, the slightest variations; rejecting those that are bad, preserving and adding up all that are good; silently and insensibly working, whenever and wherever opportunity offers, at the improvement of each organic being in relation to its organic and inorganic conditions of life.[50]

That is to say: evolution does not have any overview; it has no goal; it cannot plan. The term *plan* here becomes tantalizingly ambiguous: a tactical practice cannot plan in either sense of the term, whether foreseeing in time, or drawing orthographically in space, and thus seems incongruous with the world of design. A tactical practice, De Certeau elaborates:

> does not . . . have the options of planning general strategy and viewing the adversary as a whole within a distinct, visible, and objectifiable space. It operates in isolated actions, blow by blow. It takes advantages of "opportunities" and depends on them.[51]

Tactical practices, nonetheless, are familiar, everyday activities: De Certeau describes, for example, the experience of grocery shopping in which the shopper, "confronts heterogeneous and mobile data—what she has in the refrigerator, the tastes, appetites and moods of her guests, the best buys and their possible combinations with what she already has on hand at home, etc."[52] Traditional design, via the plan, on the other hand, implies forethought: a shopping list with little or no possibility for on-site deviation. In the context of grocery shopping, such strategic acts seem ludicrous. More sensible, in our everyday example, is a plan with suppleness: the possibility of change in the plan as information and opportunities become available.

Such unmotivated reaction to the local, as evidenced by the giraffe, can produce surprising and monstrous effects. Using the model described here, what we might now more properly call 'Niche Tactics,' initiates a suppleness in the design process, a reactiveness to the need- or desire-based abstractions of the complex context, without the shackles of fixed types embedded within local culture. Niche Tactics proposes a more nuanced response to site: a response not only to the visible, the whole, and the objective, but also to the hidden, the systematic, and the idiosyncratic. Each final design, like each organism, is the result not only of a series of iterations or tests, but one judged and edited by the dialogue that is produced with its niche. Furthermore, in addition to its presence inevitably affecting changes and continuities in future versions of its type, it may continue to evolve itself.

Today, the natural processes of evolution are circumvented by artificial means: life support systems keep bodies—and thus lineages—alive, independent of the organism's fitness to its environment. Likewise in architecture, additive artificial systems—air-conditioning, for example—allow habitation to venture into and survive in environments without any fitness in the architecture's inherent formal-mechanical-material systems. Thus, any potential response is superseded by the possibility of additive solutions. While the discipline has already started to acknowledge the negative consequences that such architectural life-support systems have for the environment, what is perhaps less acknowledged is the effect that the life-support systems (as well as some so-called sustainable responses) have had on the legibility of this relationship between the architectural organism and its niche.

In a *Niche-Tactical* design practice, as the morphology and the system co-evolve, some awkward stretches, contortions, bulges, or splays may result in relation to opportunities and their counterparts in the environment. As the form strives to collect water, light, space; to mediate temperature, visibility, and solar gain; to dispose of waste; to defend itself; to attract, to display, to hide; and to do this in perhaps more extreme ways due to existing surrounding competition, new morphologies and systems emerge. These new forms may not fit into our expectations of known types but are a complex transformation of body and parts that is a specific response to the environment, an abstraction that allows the rereading of the notion of environment in relation to its new species.

Notes

"Niche Tactics" was originally published under the title "Niche Tactics: The Giraffe Model" in the 101st ACSA Annual Meeting Proceedings (2013): *New Constellations New Ecologies*, edited by Ila Berman and Ed Mitchell.

1 This thinking is described as having shifted from a focus on form to one "focused on the process of formation, to dynamic constitutive systems and ecologies, to techniques, building blocks, modules, evolution and diversity." Detlef Mertins, "Variability Variety and Evolution in Early 20th Century Bioconstructivisms," in *Research and Design: The Architecture of Variation* (New York: Thames and Hudson, 2009), 55.

2 Several digital practices today, however, are leading the way in engaging dynamic, biological, responsive systems, including, to name a few, Jenny Sabin Studio/Sabin Design Lab at Cornell AAP, Kokkugia, Smart Geometry Group, Philip Beesley, Ecologic Studio, MinimaForms, and Epi-phyte Lab. Such practices are drawing into the whiteness of the computer's background dynamic systems and forces to which their outputs must respond, as well as drawing in scientific models for architectural production.

3 Today, Thompson's simple transformations are no longer viewed as representative of how biological change occurs. His diagrams are useful mostly as convenient visual diagrams of morphological change.

4 The occurrence of Thompson's work in architectural publications is innumerable. See, for example, Philip Beesley and Sarah Bonnemaison's *On Growth and Form: Organic Architecture and Beyond* (Toronto: Riverside Architectural Press, 2008), which includes essays relating Thompson's work with architecture, as well as a bibliography.

5 D'Arcy Thompson, *On Growth and Form*, ed. John Tyler (Cambridge: Cambridge University Press, 1961; orig. 1917), 11.

6 Ibid., 10.

7 The study of proportions in biology is referred to as allometry. For more, see Michael J. Reiss, *The Allometry of Growth and Reproduction* (Cambridge: Cambridge University Press, 1989).

8 T.J. Pedley, B.S. Brook, and R.S. Seymour, "Blood Pressure and Flow Rate in the Giraffe Jugular Vein," *Philosophical Transactions: Biological Sciences*, 351, 1342 (1996), 855.

9 A.R. Hargens, R.W. Millard, K. Petterson, and K. Johansen, "Gravitational Haemodynamics and Oedema Prevention in the Giraffe," *Nature*, 329 (1987), 59–60.

10 The giraffe was one of the many species first formally described by Carl Linnaeus in 1758. He gave it the binomial name *Cervus camelopardalis* in the tenth edition of his *Systema Naturae*. Morten Thrane Brünnich classified the genus Giraffa in 1772.

11 See also Martin Kemp, "Doing What Comes Naturally: Morphogenesis and the Limits of the Genetic Code," *Art Journal*, 55, 1 (*Contemporary Art and the Genetic Code*) (Spring, 1996), 27–32.

12 Greg Lynn, "Multiplicitous and Inorganic Bodies," in *Folds, Bodies and Blobs* (Brussels: La Lettre Volée, 1998), 39.
13 Ibid., 47.
14 Greg Lynn, "The Renewed Novelty of Symmetry," in *Folds, Bodies and Blobs*, 76.
15 While form and its responsiveness are radically reconsidered, the rethinking of context itself is not the focus of Lynn's trajectory. Lynn writes that contexts, "lack specific organization and the information that they provide tends to be general," and that context "is meaningless in and of itself [if] it is unorganized, and 'organized context' requires an agent of differentiation" (Greg Lynn, "The Renewed Novelty of Symmetry," *Assemblage*, 26, April 1995, 14). Perhaps this inevitable generic-ness of context is what leads Lynn away from this path in the end.
16 Charles Darwin, *On the Origin of Species*, 6th ed. (New York: Digireads Publishing, 2010), 48.
17 Adaptive radiation is defined as a process in which organisms diversify rapidly into a multitude of new forms, particularly when a change in the environment makes new resources available, creates new challenges, and opens environmental niches (Dolph Schluter, *The Ecology of Adaptive Radiation* (Oxford: Oxford University Press, 2000), 10–11).
18 Another theory called 'character displacement' proposes that two lineages will become different as a result of selection against competition for the same resources. This will lead to niche displacement.
19 Grant and Weiner 1999, from Joseph M. Craine, *Resource Strategies of Wild Plants* (New York: Princeton University Press, 2009), 6.
20 Jeffrey Podos, "Correlated Evolution of Morphology and Vocal Signal Structure in Darwin's Finches," *Nature*, 409, 11 (2001), 185–188.
21 The term contextual here refers to the surroundings of the animal. In evolutionary biology, the understanding of finch evolution depends critically on the phylogeny (history of splitting events that gave rise to current diversity) and thus in a way the 'historical context' of the organism itself becomes relevant.
22 Following many studies supporting this correlation, the phenomenon became known as Bergmann's rule. Additional studies have attributed the correlation to other factors, such as food requirements, predator populations, etc. For more information, see Mark V. Lomolino, Brett R. Riddle, and James H. Brown, "Single Species Patterns," in *Biogeography*, 2nd ed. (Sunderland, MA: Sinauer Associates, 2006), 490.
23 Elizabeth A. Hadley, "Evolutionary and Ecological Response of Pocket Gophers (*Thomomys talpoides*) to Late-Holocene Climatic Change," *Biological Journal of the Linnean Society*, 60 (1997), 277–296; and M.F. Smith and J.L. Patton, "Subspecies of Pocket Gophers: Causal Bases for Geographic Differentiation in *Thomomys bottae*," *Systematic Zoology*, 37 (1988), 163–178.
24 While Bergmann's explanation was based on increased heat-loss in small bodies (having a low volume : surface ratio), more recent studies have proposed lack of predators, lack of food, or other factors for the phenomenon.
25 Gloger's rule (1833) states that species of birds and mammals in warmer climates are more darkly colored than in colder/drier regions.
26 James J. Gibson, *The Ecological Approach to Visual Perception* (Hillsdale, NJ: Lawrence Erlbaum Assoc., 1986), 8.
27 Although, as Ingold notes in "Point, Line and Counterpoint," in *Being Alive, Essays on Movement, Knowledge and Description* (New York: Routledge, 2011), Gibson is ambivalent on the equality of this relationship.
28 This example is a paraphrasing of the example used in the Synergistics and Synaesthetics units of the Manchester School of Architecture's Bioclimatic School by Professors Greg Keeffe and Geoff McKennan.

29 J. Grinnell, "The Niche-Relationships of the California Thrasher," *The Auk*, 34, 4 (1917), 427–433.

30 George Evelyn Hutchinson (1903–1991) was a British ecologist and limnologist. Following Grinnell, Charles Elton defined the ecological niche as the organism's "place in the biotic environment, *its relations to food and enemies"* (Charles Sutherland Elton, *Animal Ecology* (University of Chicago Press, 2001), 64). Hutchinson subsequently redefined it as the "highly abstract multi-dimensional hyperspace in which the organism's needs and properties were defined as dimensions" (L.B. Slobodkin, "An Appreciation: George Evelyn Hutchinson," *Journal of Animal Ecology*, 62, 2 (1993), 391).

31 A fundamental difference between the Grinnellian and Hutchinsonian niche is the idea that one is seen as a property of the environment (Grinnell), whereas the other is a property of the organism (Hutchinson).

32 James J. Gibson, *The Ecological Approach to Visual Perception*, 7.

33 For an elaboration on site analysis, see "Why Site Matters," the introduction to *Site Matters: Design Concepts, Histories, and Strategies*, ed. Carol J. Burns and Andrea Kahn (New York: Routledge, 2005).

34 There is considerable debate in evolutionary biology about the nature of transitions between generalists and specialists. Specialists have high performance over a limited range of conditions and generalists have a limited performance over a broader range of conditions. For more, see George W. Gilchrist, "Specialists and Generalists in Changing Environments. I. Fitness Landscapes of Thermal Sensitivity," *The American Naturalist*, 146, 2 (August, 1995), 252–270.

35 Darwin, *On the Origin of Species*, 6th ed., 177.

36 Chapman Pincher, "Evolution of the Giraffe," *Nature*, 164 (1949), 29–30.

37 A. Brownlee, "Evolution of the Giraffe," *Nature*, 200 (1983), 1022.

38 Robert Simmons and Lue Scheepers, "Winning by a Neck: Sexual Selection in the Evolution of the Giraffe," *The American Naturalist*, 148 (1996), 771–786.

39 Antoni V. Milewski, Truman P. Young, and Derek Madden, "Thorns as Induced Defenses," *Oecologia*, 86, 1 (1991), 70–75.

40 In addition, species of Acacia without the ants tended to have longer thorns (Derek Madden and Truman P. Young, "Symbiotic Ants as an Alternative Defense against Giraffe Herbivory in Spinescent *Acacia drepanolobium*," *Oecologia*, 91 (1992), 235–238).

41 Gibson, *The Ecological Approach to Visual Perception*, 7. Italics in original.

42 See Chapter 5, "An Ecological Approach to the Picturesque," for more on affordance.

43 Ingold, "Point, Line and Counterpoint," 79. Makes reference to J. von Uexküll, *The Theory of Meaning*, trans. B. Stone and H. Weiner from *Bedeutungslehre*, ed. T. von Uexküll, *Semiotica*, 41, 1 (1982), 25–82.

44 For more on the difference between Affordance and Umwelt, see Ingold, "Point, Line and Counterpoint," 79–80.

45 Marc-Antoine (Abbé) Laugier, *An Essay on Architecture* (London, 1755), 9, www.archive.org/stream/essayonarchitect00laugrich#page/15/mode/1up.

46 James Lowder has likened this problem to Slavoj Zizek's criticism of Caffeine-Free Diet Coke, a product deprived of all of its malignant properties, which Zizek refers to as drinking "nothing in the guise of something . . . merely an envelope of a void" (Slavoj Zizek, *The Fragile Absolute* (New York: Verso, 2009), 22–23). Lowder argues: The same psychological forces that shape an object like Caffeine-Free Diet Coke are also present in architecture. For example, the desire for a sustainable or eco-friendly building that has a zero-carbon footprint while maintaining the historical and stable image of architecture

is, in effect, the desire to produce architecture in the semblance of architecture while removing from it all of its impurities, much in the same way Caffeine-Free Diet Coke operates. In the manifestation of this desire, we eventually end up with a "surface form deprived of content," and prevent the possibilities for a new, or at least different, origin of architecture (in James Lowder, "Skin Problems," in the Proceedings of the 103rd ACSA Annual Meeting: *The Expanding Periphery and the Migrating Center*, edited by Lola Shepperd and David Ruy, ACSA, 2015).

47 James Deetz, *Invitation to Archaeology* (New York: Doubleday, 1940), 46.

48 Marcel Vellinga, "The Inventiveness of Tradition: Vernacular Architecture and the Future," *Perspectives in Vernacular Architecture*, 13, 2 (2006/2007), 115–128.

49 Michel de Certeau, *The Practice of Everyday Life* (Berkeley: University of California Press, 1984), xix.

50 Darwin, *On the Origin of Species*, 6th ed., 65.

51 De Certeau, *The Practice of Everyday Life*, 37.

52 Ibid., xix.

2

THE THIRTEENTH VILLA

In his 1949 diagram, *Schematized Drawing of 11 of Palladio's Villas*, Rudolf Wittkower redraws eleven self-similar Palladian villas[1] and ponders: "What was in Palladio's mind when he experimented over and over again with the same elements?"[2] In answer, Wittkower proposes what he calls a "geometric formula" or "pattern" that he imagines to have been absolutely set in Palladio's mind as he designed the villas of Veneto over the course of his career.

In the almost seventy years since the posing of question of "*What was in Palladio's mind?*"—the issue has been probed ad nauseam. Its inclusion here, however, is essential, not only to establish the lineage along which architecture became separated from its context, but also, by joining the dots of questions asked about Palladio's motives, to dig beyond the formalist crust that has formed over Palladio's work, and to find, instead, evidence of responsive and evolutionary thinking in what has been upheld as a formalist model and an ideal-oriented practice.

Wittkower's *twelfth villa*, the first graphic translation of Palladio's adherence to universal rules, is described as a "rectangle divided by two longitudinal and four transverse lines."[3] It is a template, a static representational device, meant to explain the consistencies and similarities across the eleven selected villas. Wittkower's disregard for the deviation from the rule, for the contingent, or the erroneous, is characteristic of his renowned reading of Palladio. Despite some tantalizing wanderings, Wittkower's focus consistently returns to the fixed geometric ideal. For example, of the villas selected, he writes:

> While in looking at these facades one cannot escape the impression that an inexhaustible wealth of ideas lies behind them, it must yet be kept in mind that they are all generated from the same fundamental principle. Palladio's buildings have been considered as variations on a basic geometric theme, different realizations, as it were, of the platonic idea of the Villa.[4]

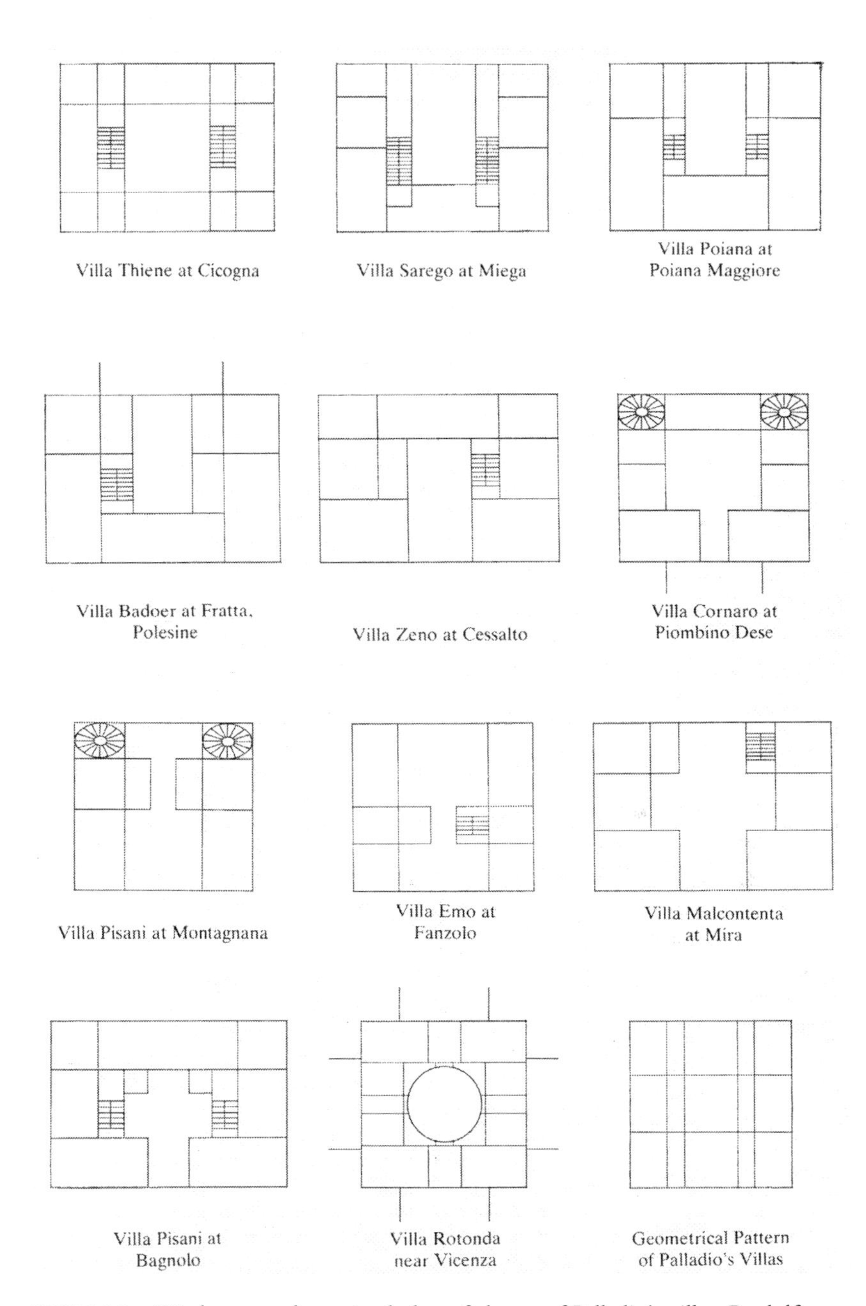

FIGURE 2.1 Wittkower, schematized plan of eleven of Palladio's villas. Rudolf Wittkower, *Architectural Principles in the Age of Humanism*, © Academy Editions, London, 1988. Courtesy of John Wiley & Sons, London.

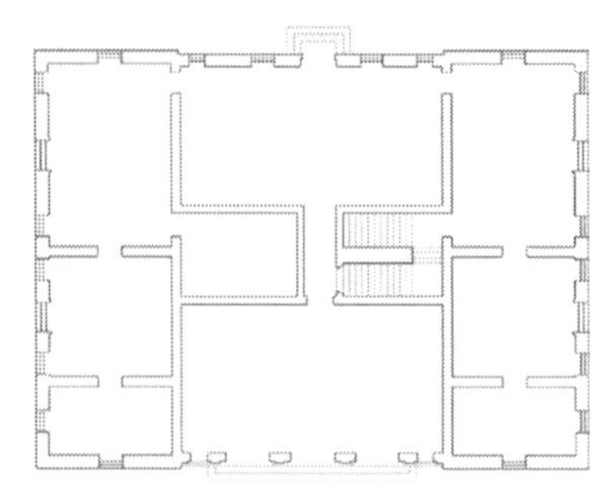

FIGURE 2.2 Palladio, *Villa Trissino*, Cricoli. Redrawn after Scamozzi (1778) by CODA, 2014.

According to Wittkower, the original pattern for the villa is to be found at *Villa Trissino* at Cricoli (1530–1538), a project that Palladio worked on as a young sculptor. "Everything later undertaken by Palladio," Wittkower writes, "is a development of this archetype."[5] From here, the typological thinking inevitably fixates upon similarities in the architectural object rather than the deviations and their motives.

Wittkower's study of the Palladian villa was furthered almost immediately by Colin Rowe with his *Mathematics of the Ideal Villa*, which labels Wittkower's twelfth villa as the "ideal," and demonstrates its universality through time, from the Renaissance to Modernism.[6] In this well-known and influential analysis of Le Corbusier's *Villa Stein* and Palladio's *Villa Malcontenta*, the underlying structure is championed as a mathematical truism, indifferent to style.

A new response to Wittkower's question of what was in Palladio's mind was pioneered in 1978 by G. Stiny and W.J. Mitchell, with their publication of *The Palladian Grammar.*[7] Stiny and Mitchell recognized the villa variations as a potential example of *Shape Grammars*. Consistent with its name, their system fits into a linguistic grammatical frame derived from Noam Chomsky's work on the topic.[8] Where Chomsky proposes that language involves a type of 'rule-governed creativity,' in order to put words together correctly to produce sentences, Stiny and Mitchell translate the theory and apply it to shapes and patterns that accrue form incrementally (examples include Chinese lattice and ice-ray designs). In the same way that words obey grammatical rules as sentences unfold, so do shapes obey a finite number of form-giving rules to produce an infinite number of designs. Stiny explains:

> [Phrase structure grammars] define languages of expressions comprised of linear strings of symbols, and [shape grammars] define languages of designs comprised of plane or solid shapes. Both use replacement rules to change objects of certain kind-strings or shapes into new objects of the same kind.[9]

Palladio's *Quattro Libri* "sets out rules of classical architectural usage in much the same way as a traditional grammar sets out rules of Latin usage,"[10] and Stiny asks the inevitable follow-up question to Wittkower: "Can these rules be formalized in a shape grammar to define a language of designs in the Palladian style?"[11] However, where Wittkower sets up a template, Stiny deploys a set of instructions or guidelines. He proposes a series of basic operations that must occur in order to generate a villa: 1. grid definition, 2. exterior wall definition, 3. room layout, 4. interior wall realignment, 5. principal entrances, 6. exterior ornamentation, 7. windows and doors, and 8. termination (combined into six steps in the diagram.)[12]

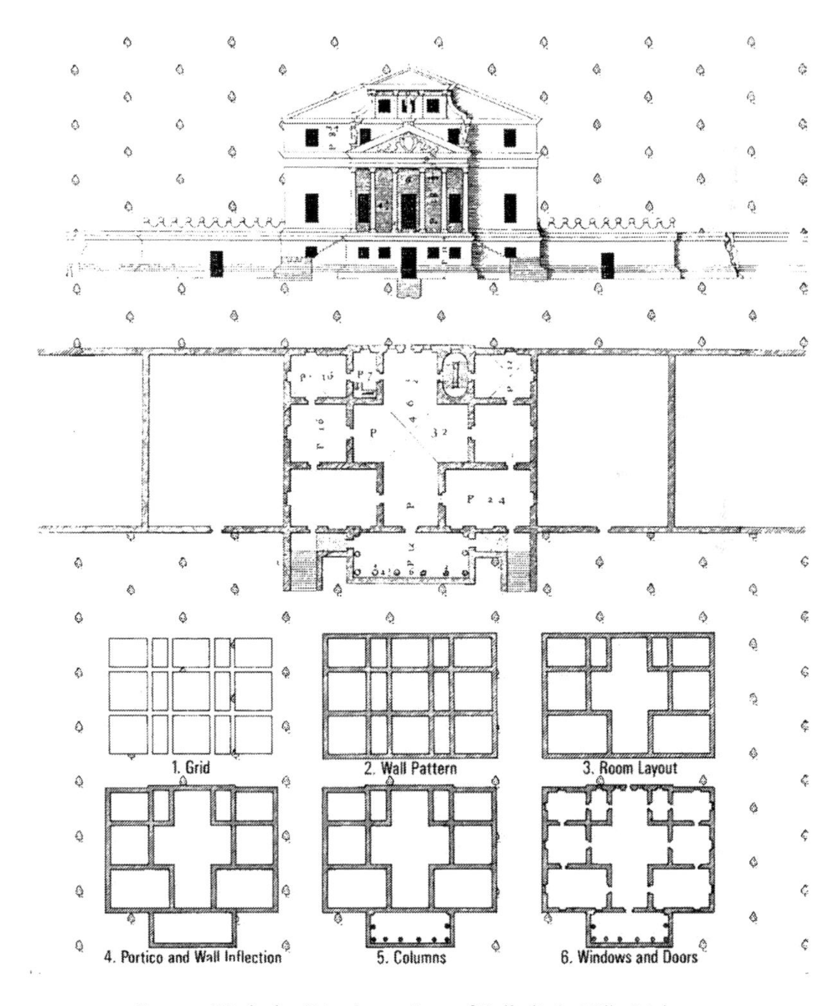

FIGURE 2.3 George Nicholas Stiny's version of Palladio's *Villa Malcontenta* generated by parametric shape grammar. George Nicholas Stiny, "Computing with Form and Meaning in Architecture," *Journal of Architectural Education* (1984–), 39, 1 (Autumn, 1985), 10. Reprinted by permission of Taylor & Francis (www.tandfonline.com).

Some of these guidelines are taken directly from explicit instructions given by Palladio in his *Quattro libri*. For example, Palladio stipulates that: "The rooms ought to be distributed on each side of the entry and hall: and it is to be observed, that those on the right correspond to those on the left, that so the *fabrik* may be the same in one place as the other."[13] Other operations are deduced from an analysis of the plans and drawings themselves—for example, the predominance of the 5 × 3 grid (as in Wittkower's twelfth villa), or the necessity of a wide central bay along the y-axis.[14]

Stiny and Mitchell "clarify the underlying commonality of structure and appearance," to generate rules of style by characterizing likeness.[15] Like Wittkower, their emphasis is on the given villa's consistency and obedience to rules. Differences and deviations are again negated. While the authors acknowledge that their study is incomplete, their suggestions for further study go only as far as to suggest a possible grammar for façade generation and more detailed treatment of proportion.

In 1985, George Hersey and Richard Freedman, who developed computational rules in order to produce all "Possible Palladian Villas," took up their suggestions.[16] Whereas their predecessors' first operation was to set out a grid, their program, *Planmaker*, began by randomly selecting the dimensions of a starting perimeter rectangle and subsequently operated by 'splitting' the repeated subdivision of the original rectangle until certain conditions of configuration, number, and proportions were generated. The splitting rules are based on Palladio's rules and, as an extension of Stiny and Mitchell's work, the frequency with which he used (and broke) them.

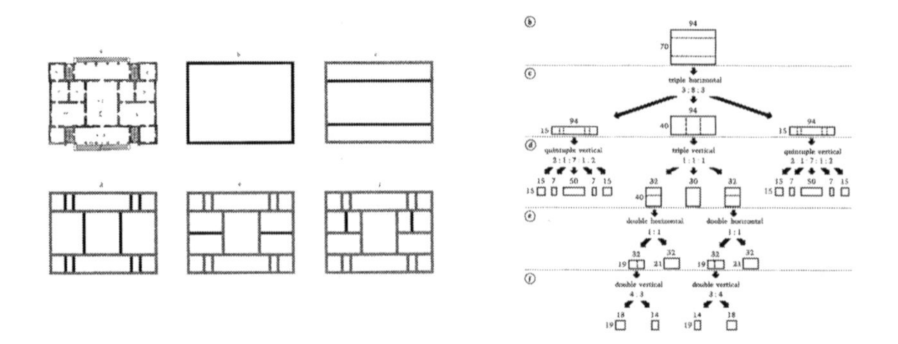

FIGURE 2.4 George L. Hersey and Richard Freedman, "Split tree for the *Villa Valmarana*, Lisiera da Balzano Vicentino, from the *Quattro Libri*, and the corresponding split description." George L. Hersey and Richard Freedman, *Possible Palladian Villas: (Plus a Few Instructively Impossible Ones)*, diagrams, pp. 42–43, © 1992 Massachusetts Institute of Technology. Reprinted by permission of The MIT Press.

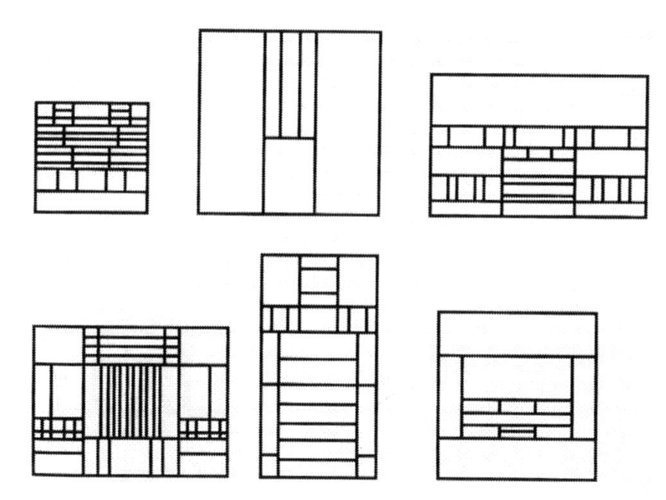

FIGURE 2.5 George L. Hersey and Richard Freedman, "Foibles." George L. Hersey and Richard Freedman, *Possible Palladian Villas: (Plus a Few Instructively Impossible Ones)*, diagrams, p. 52, © 1992 Massachusetts Institute of Technology. Reprinted by permission of The MIT Press.

After several iterations, Hersey and Freedman discovered that, while the rules *can* generate new Palladian plans, they can also generate some decidedly un-Palladian plans. A crucial schism occurs in the study at the moment where the computer, following the rules, begins to generate villa plans that are, according to the authors, "ridiculous" (for example, mal-proportioned plans or plans with too many rooms). Hersey and Freedman step in to edit. Most of these "foibles," say the authors, "could and should eventually be programmed out of existence."[17] Stiny, along with another colleague, James Gips, had already noted that, given the potential infinite number of possibilities, such an editing operation must occur. They wrote that, "a mechanism, a selection rule, is required to determine which of the shapes in the language defined by the shape grammar is used. The selection rule acts as a halting criterion for the shape generation process."[18]

While the deduction of Palladian rules is relatively straightforward, the question of editing is more obscure. As mentioned, Hersey and Freedman program their variations using a formula that relates to the frequency with which Palladio applied the rules. In place of any other information, this approach is used because, according to Hersey and Freedman, "we may never be able to do better . . . because there is little likelihood that we will ever know all of the conditions that lead Palladio to select or break his rules."[19]

Wittkower was no less in the dark. His only reference to the logics of the variations was part of his original question: "Once he had found the basic geometric pattern for the problem 'villa,' he adapted it as clearly and as simply as possible to the special requirements of each commission."[20] But what were these special requirements?

While it may have been overlooked in the search for rules undertaken by the above collection of scholars, Palladio's *Quattro Libri* does provide clear reasons for deviation. Palladio cites two principles: the client and the site. Palladio writes that "more or fewer rooms could be included than I have designed, depending on the site and the needs and convenience of those who would be living there."[21] Indeed, it is these two criteria that contribute to *naming* the villa. Each title is presented as client plus site, as in "Villa Zeno at Cessalto," for example.

While Palladio gripes that the architect is "frequently obliged to accommodate himself to the wishes of those who are paying rather than attending to what he should,"[22] his conceptual belief in the reflection of the client in the architecture is clear. He stipulates that one must "pay particular attention to those who want to build, not so much for what they can afford, as for the type (*qualità*) of building that would suit them."[23] Following Vitruvius, he believes that men in public office should have the most ornate houses, while smaller and less expensive buildings are appropriate for men of lower status.[24] However, while Palladio is clear that villas must be differentiated by rank, he also purposefully omits the rank in his work, stating that: "I have taken no notice of the status or rank of the gentlemen who are mentioned, though of course they are all extremely distinguished."[25] Client variations aside, then, what evidence exists for site-motivated variation?

Lineage

It is not surprising that our scholars neglect the influence of the natural environment. Wittkower begins his analysis by stripping the villa to its marrow (bones removed with poché) and looks instead at the formal object. Stiny et al. begin with the grid, and Hersey with the enclosure, after which both studies proceed inward. In all cases, external conditions are negated at the first step and never re-enter their processes as possible motivators. The hypothesis that the villa variations are a consequence of site forces is incongruous with a lineage of thought that, since Wittkower, has used Palladio's villas as a foundation for an architecture of formal order and rules.

Countless critiques of Palladio's villas have been written, many concerned with the rule and with part-to-whole relationships, and some more than others search for site motivations in Palladio's variations. James S. Ackerman muses that the cause for the more independent blocks at villas *Cornaro*, *Pisani* at Montagnana, and *Malcontenta*, for example, could be that the center of agricultural activity was distant from the villa or that the swampy ground conditions did not allow for a

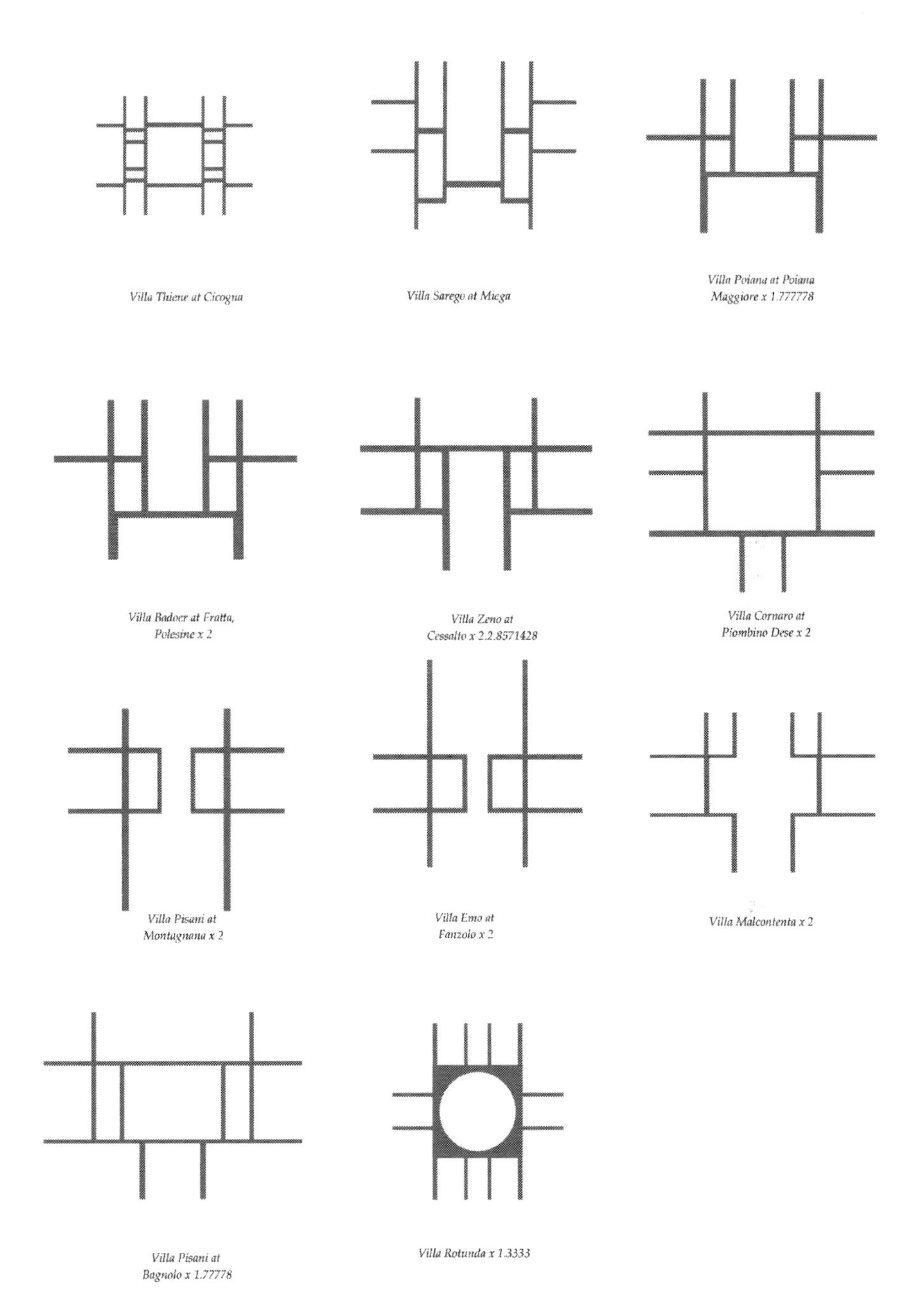

FIGURE 2.6 Wittkower's missing poché (interior). CODA, 2005.

Note: multiplication factors indicate the scale distortion performed by Wittkower, taking *Villa Thiene* as × 1.

basement, thus kitchens and service spaces were located at ground level and pushed other spaces upwards.[26] Ackerman also describes *Villa Sarego* at Santa Sofia (not on Wittkower's list), a wall-less façade with "the vigour of an Egyptian temple," whose isolation geographically from the others prompts him to ask "whether geography influenced distinctions in type."[27]

Denis Cosgrove's description of *Villa Godi* (also not on Wittkower's list) is a case in point regarding the struggle and eventual dominance of architectural form over landscape or site. Cosgrove presents the two forces as equal, writing that *Villa Godi*'s "specific site and orientation maximize the possibility of well-composed views out over the surrounding countryside," and also that "the building itself recomposes the landscape in which it stands."[28] A closer look at *Villa Godi*, however, reveals that these three statements are not equal: a strong hierarchy exists between them. First, is the architectural form, second is the orientation to views (a rotation but hardly a 'recomposition' of the form, which has been shaped to reference a traditional type) and third is the landscape, which, adherent to less strict rules perhaps, is malleable enough to be recomposed. As in the Vitruvian model, site considerations are relegated to at best a secondary concern.

More recent critics/designers have sought to break open this adherence to rule and form. Greg Lynn, for instance, framed Wittkower's selection of villas not as a type but rather as a "brood;" a "species."[29] Opposed to Wittkower's fixed set of formal exemplars, Lynn insists upon the consideration of their less predictable contextual affiliations and resultant transformations. And so, while he understands the reduction of familial forms to general principles, Lynn laments that "the prejudice toward fixed orders is achieved at the cost of repressing local differences of program, structure, form, and culture."[30] Hersey and Freedman's computations are, for Lynn, no better than those set out by Wittkower, Stiny, Rowe, and others. Lynn sees them merely as an "extension of a previously delineated and closed set of potential forms whose characteristics can be stated in advance through an ideal mathematics."[31]

In response to Wittkower's brood then, Lynn poses a question of his own. He asks: "Might there be another way to respect particularities and differences without 'returning our inquiry' to universal types?" His own inquiry, one characterized by "more pliant systems of description," is generative and inductive rather than reductive. His study is a departure from the "single organizational idea," and favors "a system of local affiliations outside itself."[32]

This system is open and exploratory rather than constrained by the notion of an established formal family or type.[33] Lynn's found affiliations allow for modification and variation to occur in architecture via a building's relation to its context rather than its obligation to geometry. Likewise, the correspondence of part-to-whole relationships in buildings is inclusive of relationships of part-to-site.

Pier Vittorio Aureli has, more recently, advanced this end of the debate on forces in situ by taking a stance *against* the possibility of an absolute architecture. For Aureli, an architecture separate from its environment, specifically the space of the city and its political and logistical accoutrements, is itself an illusion propagated by architects and theorists who seek principles exclusive to autonomous form at the expense of richer consideration of the specifics of the site. For instance, Aureli asserts that Colin Rowe "deliberately extrapolates the villas of Palladio and Le Corbusier from their geographical and political context;" and "reinforces Wittkower's radical denial of Palladio's site-specificity, apparent in the removal of the *barchesse* (barns) in his schematic drawings of the villas."[34] In his own analysis, Aureli reinserts the barchesse and underscores their importance to understanding the villas as a geopolitical project that tied it to its time. In this view, the villa is no longer seen as a set of rules or a pattern, but rather as "one element within a larger, latent project."[35] *Villa Emo*, for example, is framed by its barchesse. Palladio, the designer of both, has considered the object as well the object's frame. The volume of the villa, as well as having its own formal logic, is also "inflected so as to react to its specific site condition."[36] Thus, Palladio's villas were not simply objects enclosed within a reconstructed context, but were specific objects that frame and redefine the existing landscape as an economic, cultural, and political counter to the city.

Peter Eisenman as well addresses the issue of the barchesse and their exclusion in his exhibition, *Palladio Virtuel*, at Yale University (2012). Doing so wholly shifts the frame for study away from mathematical idealism and toward one characterized by observing "disarticulation, disjunction, or disaggregation" in the villas and their sites. Eisenman includes the barchesse in his study of Palladio's villas to demonstrate that, "their syntactic rules . . . are different, making each villa a unique example of Palladio's work, rather than one in a series of variations on an ideal."[37]

Through their non-object-focused and typology-averse analyses, the above critics provide a sizeable point of entry for broader consideration of the debate on autonomy, form, and site in the Palladian villa. However, while the barchesse have indeed been neglected and are important considerations moving forward, they represent only one component among many to be found at the site of Palladio's villas. The questions of how and why the objects and frames relate differently at different sites remain open. Furthermore, the more forceful inclusion of context in recent analyses begs a larger question, which will be the subject of the investigation to follow: *Might the villa variations be considered to be a consequence of external forces, particularly the forces of the site?*

An overlay of Wittkower's twelfth villa on to each specific villa reveals the individual transformations embodied by the eleven transformations. Each villa, then, appears as a buzzing, fluctuating vibration between two states. The vectorization and animation of the villas suggests that they are headed somewhere; that they are on the move—but what are their motives?

Site

Among the numerous drawings in Palladio's *Quattro Libri*, no site drawings are included. All references to site are textual, and Palladio includes a chapter on site

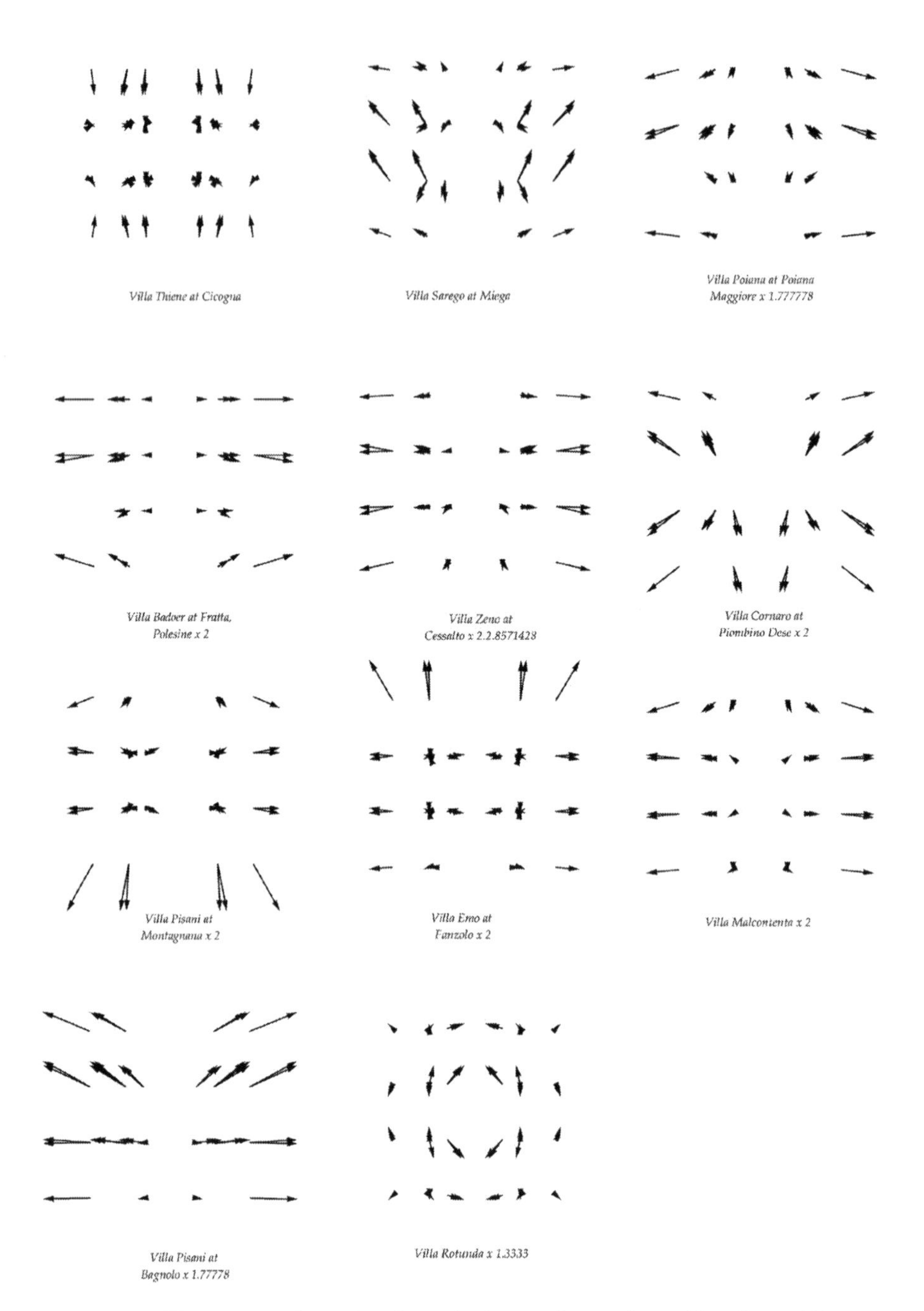

FIGURE 2.7 Vectors: transformation from the 'pattern' to each specific villa. CODA, 2005.

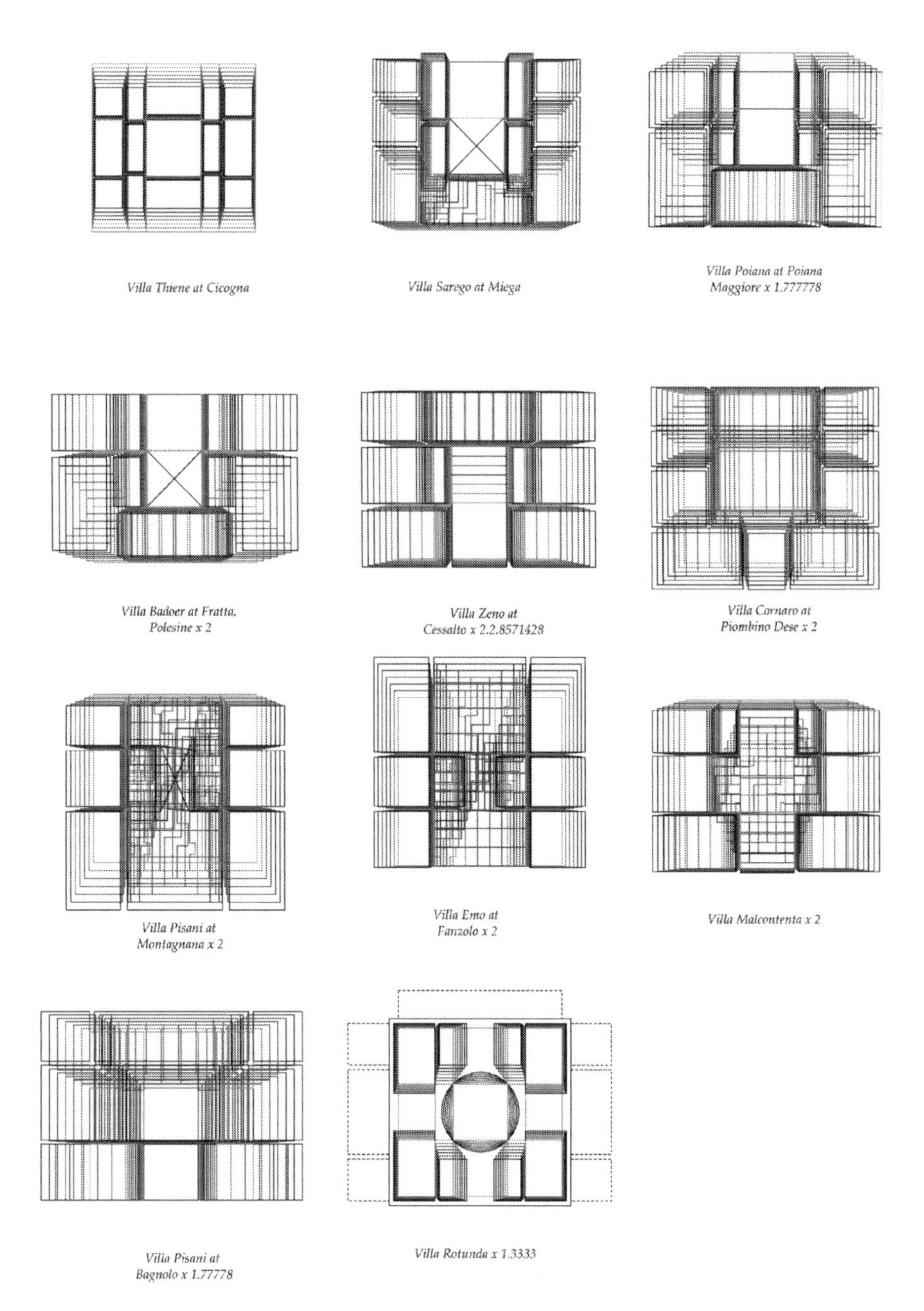

FIGURE 2.8 Blend: transformation from the 'pattern' to each specific villa. CODA, 2005.

choice as well as site planning. It is here that he addresses issues of light, water, heat, wind, and other contextual constraints. While conceding, as Alberti does, that urban contexts force the architect to "abide by the constraints of the site,"[38] Palladio does not make the same definitive statement about the ex-urban villa. However, he does note the importance of the relationship between orientation, use, season, and size of specific rooms. In many cases, he is concerned with the pragmatics of the farm's production: the proper storage of foodstuffs, for example, or the disposal of animal excrement at an appropriate distance from the house. However, he also writes, again reiterating Alberti,[39] that it would also be beneficial to the inhabitant himself:

> if the Summer rooms were large and spacious and oriented to the north, and those for Winter to the south and were small rather than otherwise, because in Summer we seek the shade and breezes and in Winter, the sun, and smaller rooms get warmer more readily than large ones. But those we would want to use in the Spring and Autumn will be oriented to the east and look out over gardens and greenery.[40]

Furthermore, when describing *Villa Capra*, Palladio writes a passage that could leave no doubt as to his passion for the landscape surrounding the villa:

> The site is one of the most pleasing and delightful that one could find because it is on top of a small hill which is easy to ascend; on one side it is bathed by the Bacchiglione, a navigable river, and on the other is surrounded by other pleasant hills which resemble a vast theater and are completely cultivated and abound with wonderful fruit and excellent vines. So because it enjoys the most beautiful vistas on every side, some of which are restricted, others more extensive, and yet others which end at the horizon, loggias have been built on all four sides.[41]

Conversely, less spectacular site conditions receive a more terse description: *Villa Badoer*, for example, is "at a place called the Frata, on a fairly raised site bathed by a branch of the Adige where some time ago there used to be a castle."[42]

Despite these clues, Palladio does not confirm textually that the villa variations are a consequence of site forces. To investigate this hypothesis further, the villas themselves must be analyzed.

In order to uncover the logics of variation, let us first examine the transformation from the Palladian drawing to the Wittkowerian, in order to understand what has been omitted. Palladio's drawings, crowded into the Wittkowerian layout, include many more components than their twentieth-century counterparts. The re-inclusion of *barchesse* contributes to some of the villas' (*Villa Emo*, for example) legibility as a continuum of barchesse-villa-barchesse rather than as an object building wholly

In one of the covered out-buildings at the side of the courtyard there are cellars and granaries, in the other, stables and spaces for farm use. The two loggias projecting like arms were built to connect the owner's house with the farm building; in this building there are two courtyards, one for threshing grain, the other for less important servants.

Villa Thiene at Cicogna

Next to this building is the courtyard for farm use, with all the places appropriate to that function.

Villa Sarego at Miega

On one side are the courtyard and other places essential for farm life, on the other a garden which mirrors that courtyard, and in the area at the back, the orchard and a fishpond. Such is the extent to which this gentleman ...has done everything he could to produce all those beautiful and practical things to make his house attractive, pleasing delightful and convenient.

Villa Poiana at Poiana Maggiore

[On] ground level, there are the rooms of the estate manager, the accountant, the stables and the other essential offices for the estate.

Villa Badoer at Fratta, Polesine

This building has gardens, a courtyard, a dovecot, and everything essential for a farm.

Villa Zeno at Cessalto

On one side there is the kitchen, and the rooms for the housewives, and on the other the rooms for the servants.

Villa Cornaro at Piombino Dese

There are two streets down the sides of this building where there are two doors, above which are passages which lead to the kitchen and rooms for the servants.

Villa Pisani at Montagnana

The cellars, granaries and other farm buildings are on either side of the owner's house and at the ends there are dovecots that are useful for the owner and add beauty to the place; **one can move under cover throughout it, which is one of the principal features required in a house on an estate**...Behind this building is a square garden...through the middle of which runs a stream that makes the site very pretty and delightful.

Villa Emo at Fanzolo

Villa Malcontenta

Villa Pisani at Bagnolo

The loggias which follow a circumference make an immensely pleaseing sight; nearer the ground level there are haylofts, cellars, stables, granaries, the rooms of the accountant, and other rooms for farm use.

Villa Rotunda

FIGURE 2.9 Palladio's site descriptions. CODA, 2005.

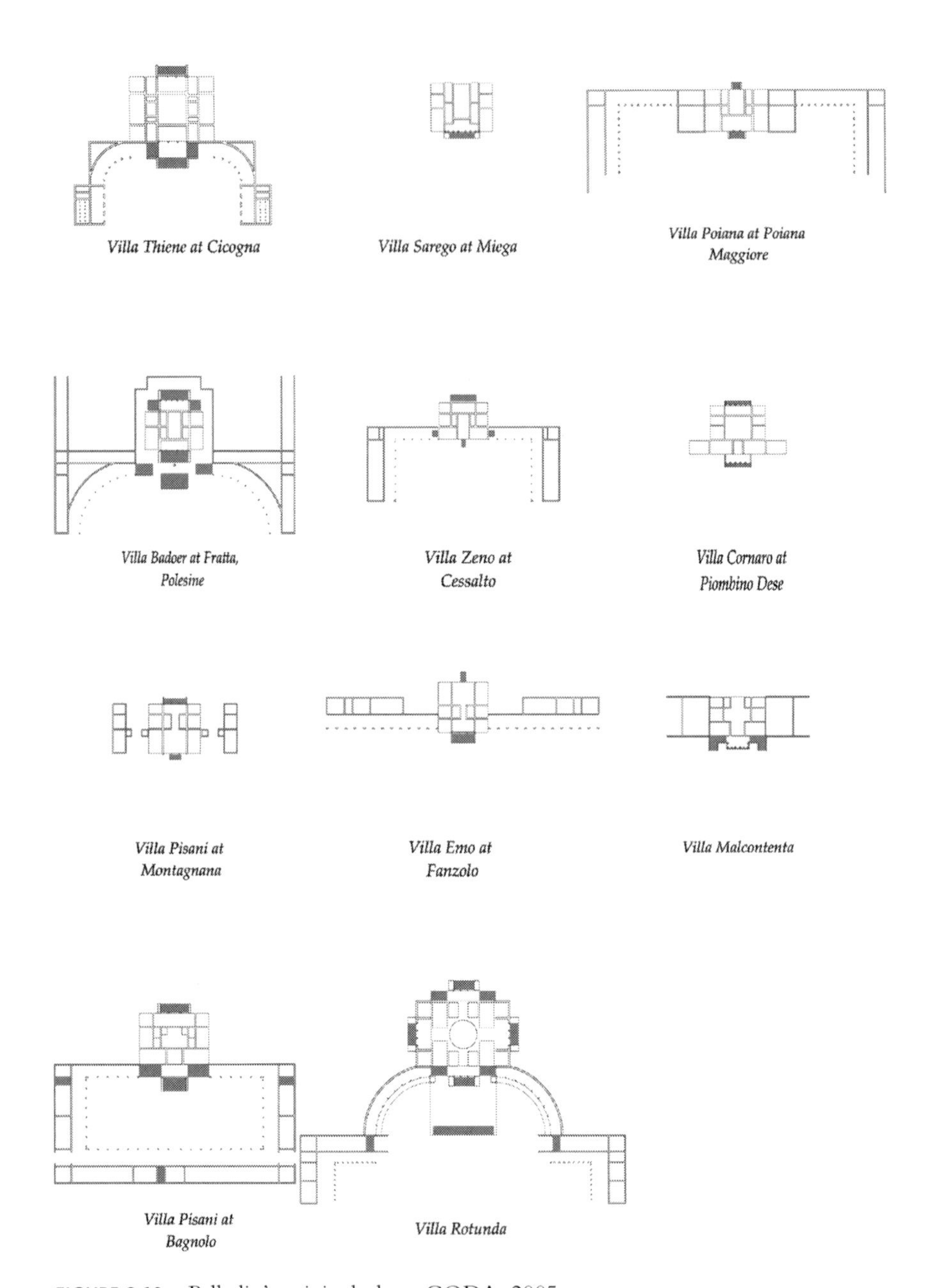

FIGURE 2.10 Palladio's original plans. CODA, 2005.

detached from its outbuildings (such as *Cornaro*). Wittkower, however, would have us believe that each villa is equally detached.

The barchesse, in fact, act as both a buffer and a connective tissue between site and object. *Villa Capra*, albeit built as a freestanding volume, was drawn with its front clearly differentiated through its attachment to curved and rectilinear barchesse. When Rowe describes it as "the most ideal,"[43] he has clearly edited this lopsided component out of his mental image. In fact, only the 'urban' *Cornaro* and *Sarego* are originally represented as freestanding objects. Even then, *Cornaro* has its small wings clipped by Wittkower. The third of the 'urban' group, *Pisani* at Montagnana, has barchesse that have become compressed to become flanks. In all other cases, the barchesse are linear extensions (*Foscari*, *Emo*, *Poiana*), semi-circular partial enclosures (*Capra*, *Badoer*, *Thiene*) or full rectilinear courtyards (*Zeno*, *Pisani* at Bagnolo). These secondary components, which were neglected in the studies by Wittkower and many of those who followed, act as a frame that supports the position of the house object within the context. This frame is almost always positioned between the main entry to the site and the main entry to the villa. In this way, the barchesse act as a significant gasket or docking mechanism through which the site connects directly to the villa and vice versa.

In addition to removing the poché, eliminating the barchesse, and rescaling the villas so that their sizes are more comparable, Wittkower's stripped-down, single line-weight diagrams give the sense that each 'object' is all-sided and even. On the contrary, the sides of each villa differ greatly. Palladio's villas are organized around a single axis of symmetry to produce relative front, back, and side conditions. The approach façade most clearly represents the values of the client and causes the dominant symbolism and ornamentation to gravitate to the 'face' side of the villa. While

FIGURE 2.11 Palladio, *Villa Badoer*, front and rear façades. CODA, 2012.

the main façade is distinguished by a portico—perhaps the 'mouth'—in antis or prostyle, the secondary façade contains either a portico in antis, an impacted portico, or none at all. Compare, for example, *Villa Badoer*'s front and back façades. The rear façade addresses the agricultural fields, and is appropriately austere and functional. On the contrary, the front façade addresses the town of Fratta Polesine, and both its road and canal connections to Venice. This façade is the representative façade, the display of the wealth and success of the villa's client.

Given the importance of the facing direction of each side, the fact that Wittkower orients the villa diagrams orthogonally on the page for comparison becomes problematic. This is a standard device for architectural plan drawing at the building scale, and is naturally employed by Palladio in his plan drawings of these villas in his *Quattro Libri*. Yet doing so feigns regularity across both the various villas and their sites. When the villa diagrams are arranged according to their true orientation at the site they appear more disjointed and the visual emphasis is placed on their apparent responsiveness to external factors.

While it is conceivable that the orientations relate to the sun, as most loggias face north and thus provide shaded outdoor space, it is more likely that these orientations are a response to dominant infrastructural trajectories of road and waterways. When viewed at a larger scale,[44] the logics of the alignments become clear.

It is perhaps not surprising that the zoomed-out view shows alignment with water- and roadways, but closer inspection suggests more complex relationships. The villas are noticeably stretched as a function of proximity to navigable water. *Badoer* and *Malcontenta*, two villas directly adjacent to the waterway, have the highest ratio of longitudinal extension. Conversely, the two villas most distant from water, *Rotonda* and *Emo*, remain closest to square in form. In fact, when the façade-length proportion is mapped against the villa's distance to water, there is a positive correlation in general.

Corresponding asymmetries between the object, its façades, and its site deserve attention as well. *Villa Badoer*, as has been shown, exhibits one of the most extreme differences between front and back façades. The front portico in antis is the center point of an arcing colonnade that lines the barchesse, while the rear is austere, functional, and devoid of any symbolism or ornamentation. In *Badoer*'s surroundings, the road and water access are both to the front or approach side of the villa, which leaves the rear to address only the fields beyond.

Conversely, *Villa Capra* (*Rotonda*) is clearly the most unique of all the villas in its (as built) all-sidedness. *Rotonda*'s context is also very different from that of the other sites. While most sites are flat as a consequence of their proximity to water, *Rotonda* sits atop a hillside and is perhaps the most removed from its context. *Villa Rotonda*, it would seem, is the most stable, ideal, and symmetrical form, as a consequence of its environment. As James Ackerman simply puts it: "The site urged a central plan."[45]

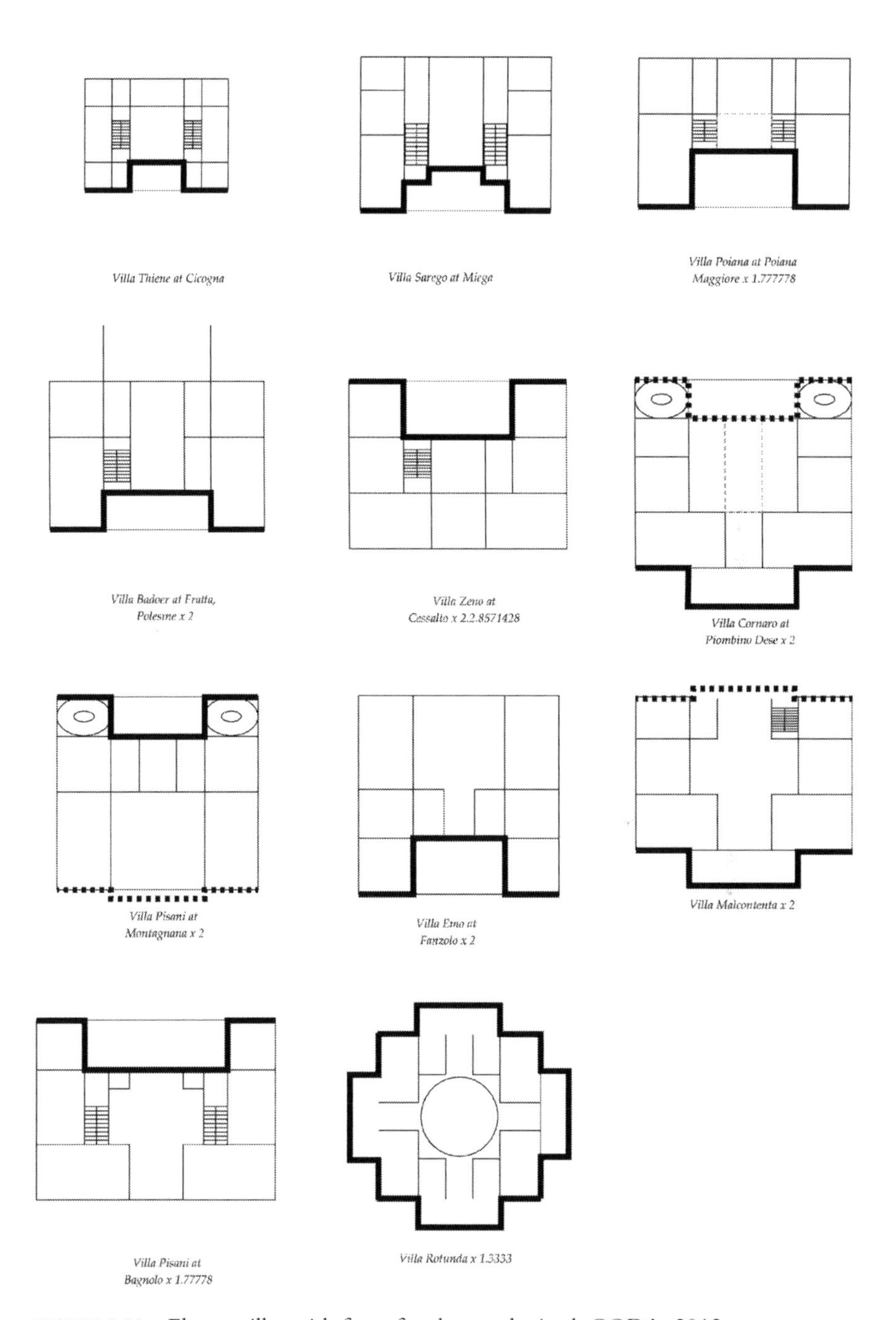

FIGURE 2.12 Eleven villas with front façades emphasized. CODA, 2012.

Note: continuous line denotes 'front'. Dashed line denotes 'back'.

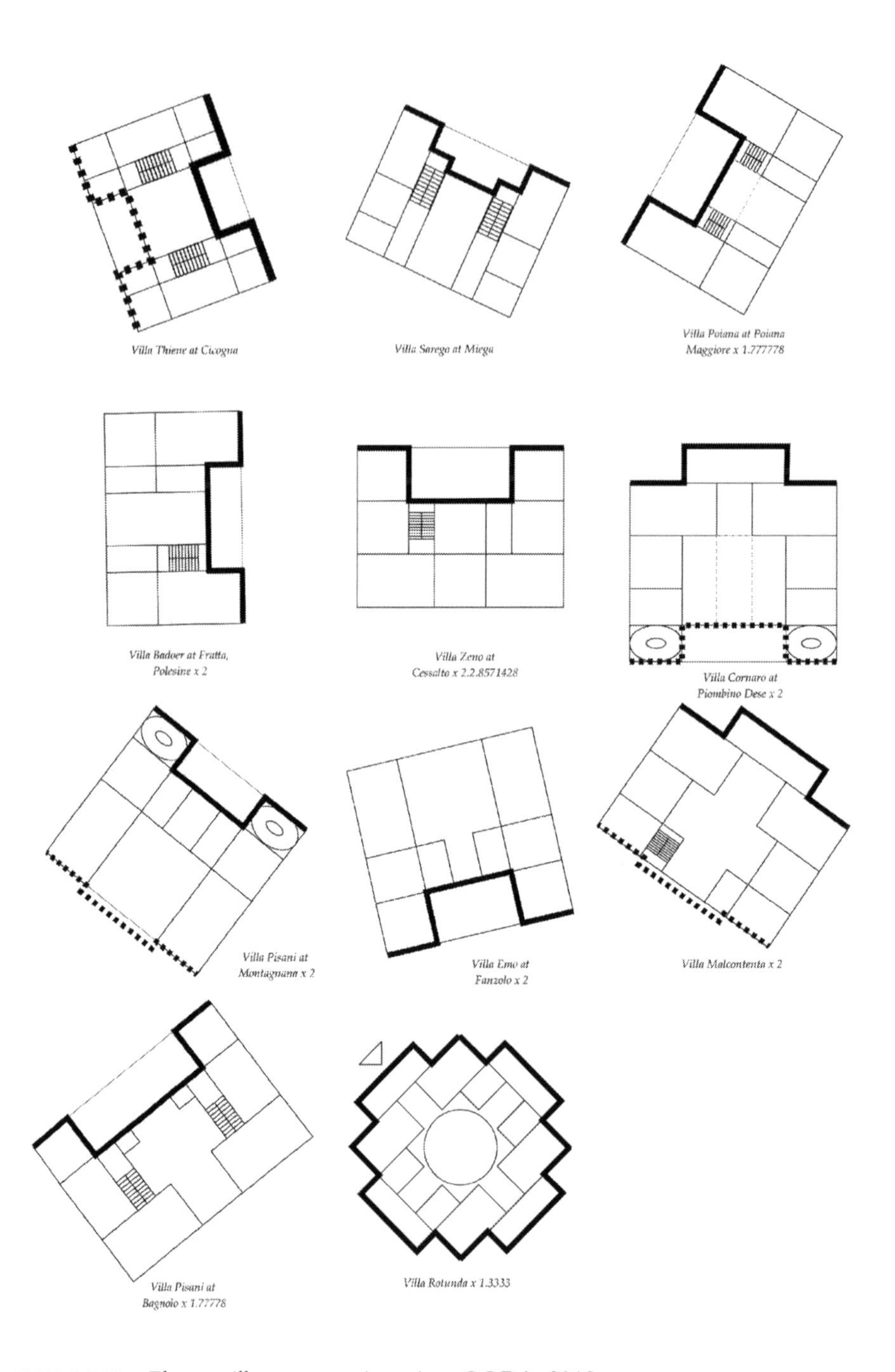

FIGURE 2.13 Eleven villas at true orientation. CODA, 2012.

FIGURE 2.14 Eleven villas' sites. CODA, 2012.

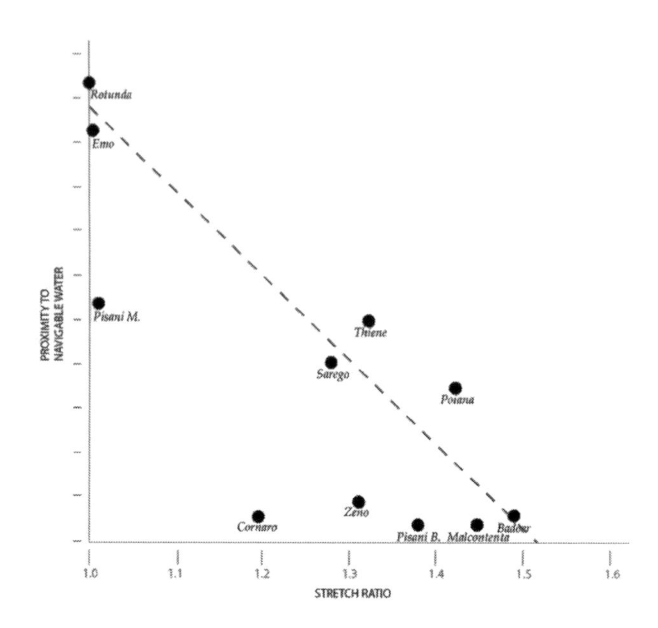

FIGURE 2.15 Eleven villas with length:depth ratio plotted against proximity to navigable water. CODA, 2012.

Only *Villa Cornaro* has two real porticos, in prostyle to the north and in antis to the south. It follows that, at *Cornaro*, it is difficult to assign 'front' to either side because the villa is situated in a truly double-sided condition. The villa faces both the town of Piombino Dese to the north and the water connection to Venice to the south.

The proximity of a given villa to urban contexts is yet another determinate of form. The portico itself reflects unique site conditions as the number of levels in the portico corresponds to the distance from the villa to the urban street. Three of Palladio's villas have double-story porticos: *Villa Pisani* in Montagnana, *Villa Cornaro*, and *Villa Sarego*—the only three villas situated in an urban or semi-urban context.

Parts

Now that these villas have been read not as static, lumpish objects but as elastic, spinning, and buzzing systems, perhaps we can take a further step: by breaking the geometric enclosure line and allowing the parts (which are much more present in Palladio's original drawings) to follow the guidelines of transformation independently. While the above analysis maintains the unity of the whole as reinforced by Wittkower and his followers, the recent investigations that include the barchesse zoom out to include fragments in the site. Similarly, looking inward, the interior parts, too, can be liberated from each other by the reinsertion of poché, a detail, as we have seen, startlingly lacking in Wittkower's diagram. Through this

FIGURE 2.16 Palladio, *Villa Cornaro*, front and rear façades. CODA, 2012.

reinsertion, the villa's component pieces gain an independence that suggests the application of transformation vectors to the part as well as the whole. The eleven sets of vectors shown describe the eleven transformations experienced independently by each part in Wittkower's transformations.

While Figure 2.17 is purely a mapping of Wittkower's transformations seen from the perspective of the part, if a bias is added, for example if we insert a river (we might also consider the sun's trajectory, the wind, and other less physical or visible site phenomena) into the site, we may generate rules for a particular kind of movement. In the next figure, the potential of the parts to stretch in response to the river is investigated.

If the villas can be seen not as a fixed expression of ancient principles but rather as form that is driven by motivations, attractions, repulsions, and the other many reactions that result from merely existing on a site, then this opens—perhaps—new ways of thinking about architectural production.

In proposing a reactiveness embedded within Palladio's logic, then, this analysis argues for a potential latent reactiveness in the architecture that follows. It is both a call for the inclusion of the context into the frame of the architect and a challenge for architects to react assertively to the forces incident upon their precious objects.

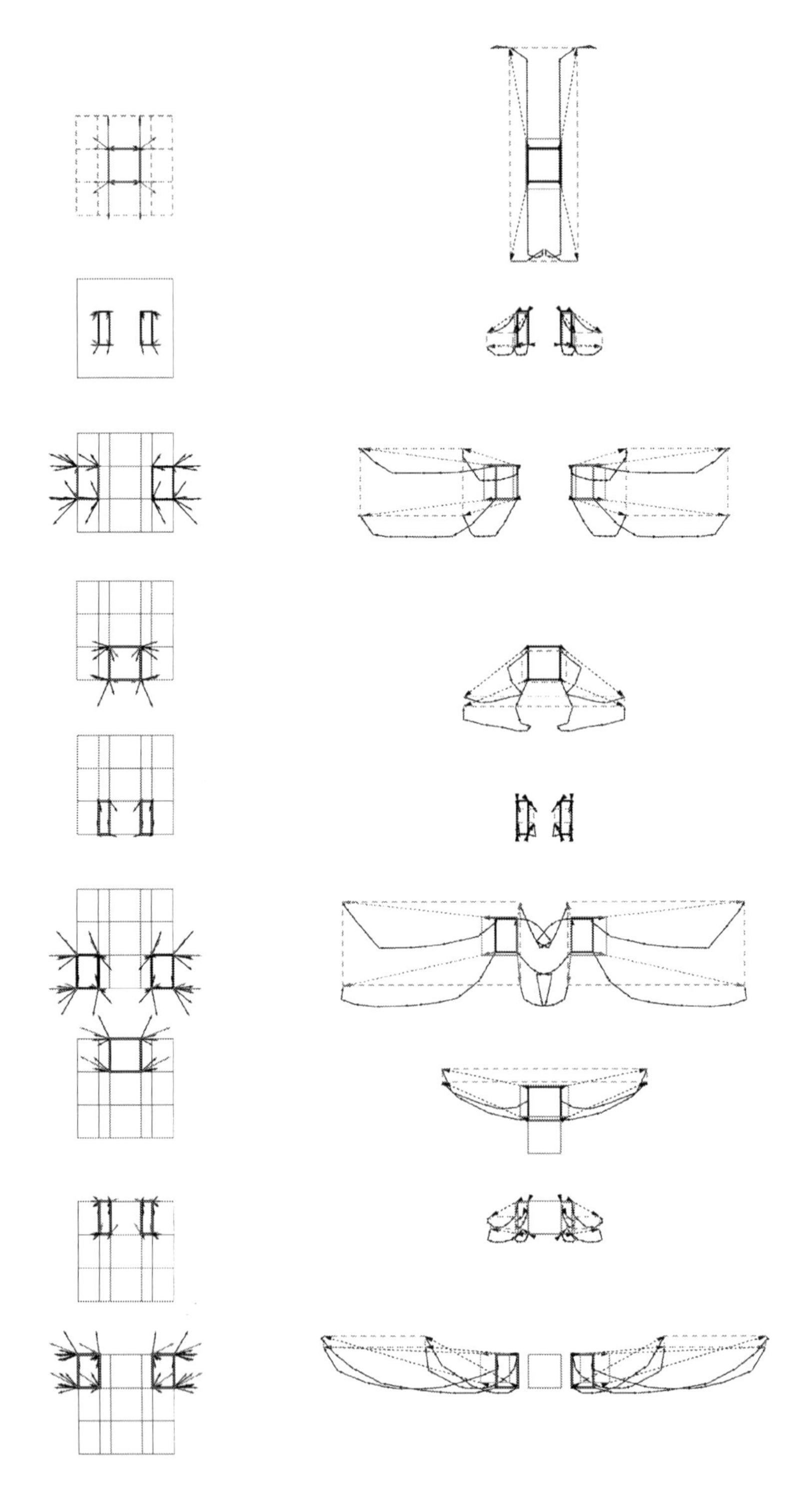

FIGURE 2.17 Movement vectors of the parts of the twelfth villa. CODA, 2005.

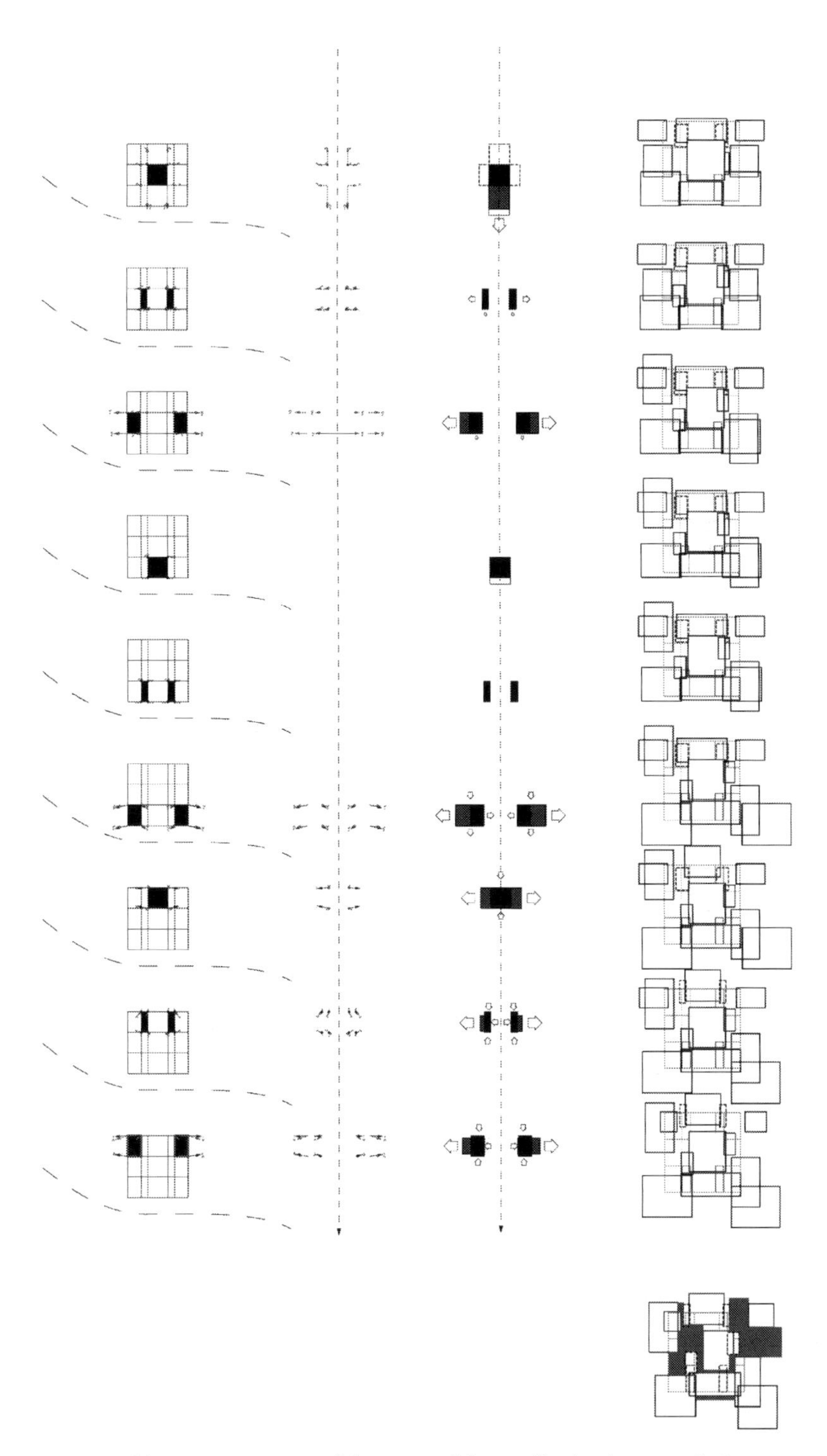

FIGURE 2.18 Movement vectors of the parts of three villas in close proximity to water. CODA, 2005.

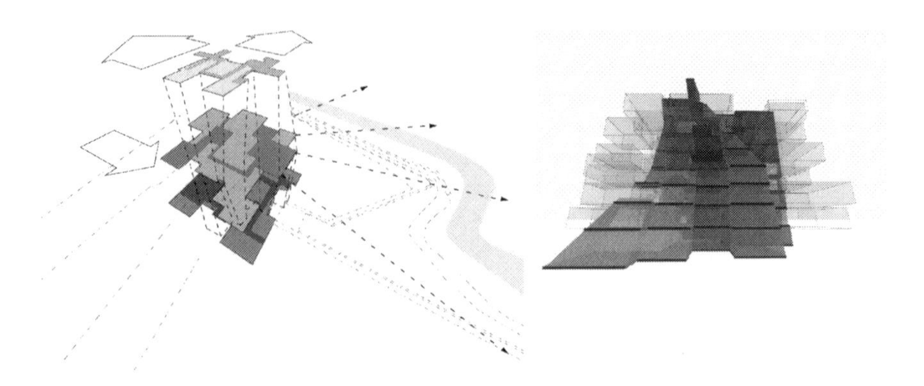

FIGURE 2.19 Diagram: One possible thirteenth villa. CODA, 2005.

Notes

1 A version of this diagram had appeared in 1944 in Wittkower's essay, "Principles of Palladio's Architecture," *Journal of the Warburg and Courtauld Institutes*, 7 (1944), but contained only ten villas, and the pattern, excluding *Villa Capra* (*Rotonda*).
2 Rudolf Wittkower, *Architectural Principles in the Age of Humanism* (New York; London: W.W. Norton, 1971), 111.
3 Ibid.
4 Ibid., 112.
5 Wittkower, "Principles of Palladio's Architecture," 67.
6 Colin Rowe, *The Mathematics of the Ideal Villa, and Other Essays* (Cambridge, MA: MIT Press, 1976).
7 George N. Stiny and W.J. Mitchell, "The Palladian grammar," *Environment and Planning B: Planning and Design*, 5, 1 (1978), 5–18.
8 See, for example, George N. Stiny, "Introduction to Shape and Shape Grammars," *Environment and Planning B: Planning and Design*, 7 (1980), 343–351. Of further interest, in the context of this collection, may be the overlap between Chomsky and Von Uexküll in Prisca Augustyn, "Uexküll, Peirce, and Other Affinities Between Biosemiotics and Biolinguistics," *Biosemiotics*, 9 (2009), 1–17.
9 George N. Stiny, "Computing with Form and Meaning in Architecture," *Journal of Architectural Education*, 39, 1 (1985), 9.
10 Stiny and Mitchell, "The Palladian Grammar."
11 Stiny, "Computing with Form and Meaning in Architecture," 8.
12 Stiny and Mitchell, "The Palladian Grammar." Note that, for their sample, Stiny and Mitchell take the 40+ villas that appear in *Quattro Libri*, as opposed to Wittkower's sample of 11.
13 Andrea Palladio, *Quattro Libri*, trans. Isaac Ware (London: Dover, 1965). Dover reprint edition.
14 All plans are generated with respect to a north–south axis of this coordinate system.
15 Stiny and Mitchell, "The Palladian Grammar," 17.
16 George L. Hersey and Richard Freedman, *Possible Palladian Villas: (Plus a Few Instructively Impossible Ones)* (Cambridge, MA: MIT Press, 1992). *All Possible Palladian Villas* was the original title of the book, until it was pointed out that, despite the thousands of variations, the options that had been produced did not represent a comprehensive set.
17 Ibid., 125.

18 George N. Stiny and James Gips, *Algorithmic Aesthetics: Computer Models for Criticism and Design in the Arts* (Berkeley, CA: University of California Press, 1978), 131.
19 Thomas Seebohm, **"**Response to the Review by Terry Knight of *Possible Palladian Villas* (Cambridge, MA: MIT Press, 1992)," *Journal of Architectural Education*, 49, 1 (1995), 59.
20 Wittkower, "Principles of Palladio's Architecture," 111.
21 Andrea Palladio, "Book II," *The Four Books on Architecture*, trans. Robert Tavernor and Richard Schofield (Cambridge, MA: MIT Press, 1997), 24.
22 Ibid., 3.
23 Ibid.
24 Vitruvio, *I dieci libri dell'architettura tradotti e commentate da Daniele Barbaro*, ed. M. Tafuri and M. Morresi (Milan, 1567), 1.2.5–7, 6.5.1–3.
25 Palladio, "Book II," *The Four Books on Architecture*, 4.
26 James S. Ackerman, *Palladio*, ed. John Fleming and Hugh Honour (Harmondsworth: Penguin Books, 1966), 55.
27 Ibid., 56.
28 Denis Cosgrove, *The Palladian Landscape: Geographical Change and Its Cultural Representations In Sixteenth-Century Italy* (University Park: Pennsylvania State University Press, 1993), 11.
29 Greg Lynn, "Multiplicitous and Inorganic Bodies," in *Folds, Bodies and Blobs* (Brussels: La Lettre Volée, 1998), 34.
30 Ibid., 47.
31 Greg Lynn, "New Variations in the Rowe Complex," in *Folds, Bodies and Blobs*, 212.
32 Lynn, "Multiplicitous and Inorganic Bodies," 56.
33 Ibid., 43.
34 Pier Vittorio Aureli, *The Possibility of an Absolute Architecture* (Cambridge, MA: MIT Press, 2011), 48.
35 Ibid., 49.
36 Ibid., 66.
37 Peter Eisenman, *Palladio Virtuel Exhibition Catalog*, Yale School of Architecture Gallery, August 20–October 27, 2012.
38 Palladio, "Book II," *The Four Books on Architecture*, 4.
39 Leon Battista Alberti, "(5.17 and 9.2)," in *On the Art of Building in Ten Books*, trans. Joseph Rykwert, Neil Leach, and Robert Tavernor (Cambridge, MA: MIT Press, 1988), 145–147, 23.
40 Palladio, "Book II," *The Four Books on Architecture*, 4.
41 Ibid., 18.
42 Ibid., 48.
43 Colin Rowe, "Mathematics of the Ideal Villa," in *Mathematics of the Ideal Villa and Other Essays* (Cambridge, MA: MIT Press, 1982), 2.
44 These are contemporary plans of the villas' sites. Although it is acknowledged that the situations will have changed somewhat, it is also assumed that the very presence of the villa will have maintained a certain amount of stasis, especially concerning the positions of roads and waterways.
45 Ackerman, *Palladio*, 170.

3

THE DEFORMATIONS OF FRANCESCO DE MARCHI

Nowhere has the role of the ideal been more relentlessly investigated than in urban history. Among the various platonic shapes proposed, the circular, or radial, city emerged as perhaps the most perfect form. The circular form allowed a range of meanings to be communicated: to the Platonist, the circle meant ideality; to the humanist, nature; to the astronomer, the universe; and to the military engineer, security. When Plato advocated round cities, his arguments were both pragmatic and abstract. "The temples are to be placed all around the agora," he wrote, "and the whole city built on the heights in a circle, for the sake of defense and for the sake of purity."[1] From its inception, then, the city form has been known to not merely be *doing*, but very much *meaning* something through its form.

Vitruvius propagated Plato's advice when he wrote that "towns should be laid out not as an exact square, nor with salient angles, but in circular form," but his motives are edited to the purely defensive: "to give a view of the enemy from many points."[2] While purity may have been eliminated in this translation of Plato, the relationship between geometry, nature, and architecture was often central for Vitruvius. In his *Ten Books on Architecture*, he frequently aligned architecture and nature—and in particular the natural as expressed through the form of the human figure—writing, for example, that, "in the human body there is a kind of symmetrical harmony between the forearm, foot, finger, and other small parts; and so it is with perfect buildings."[3] The circular city satisfied all practical demands and at the same time represented more: the city's aspirations, its purity, its spirituality, its morals, and its connection to nature and the universe.

In the Italian Renaissance, the circular city saw a resurgence. At first, Leon Battista Alberti effectively skewed the platonic reading away from pragmatism and toward its implications for natural harmony: "It is obvious from all that is fashioned, produced, or created under her influence, that nature delights primarily in the circle," he wrote. "Need I mention the earth, the stars, the animals, their

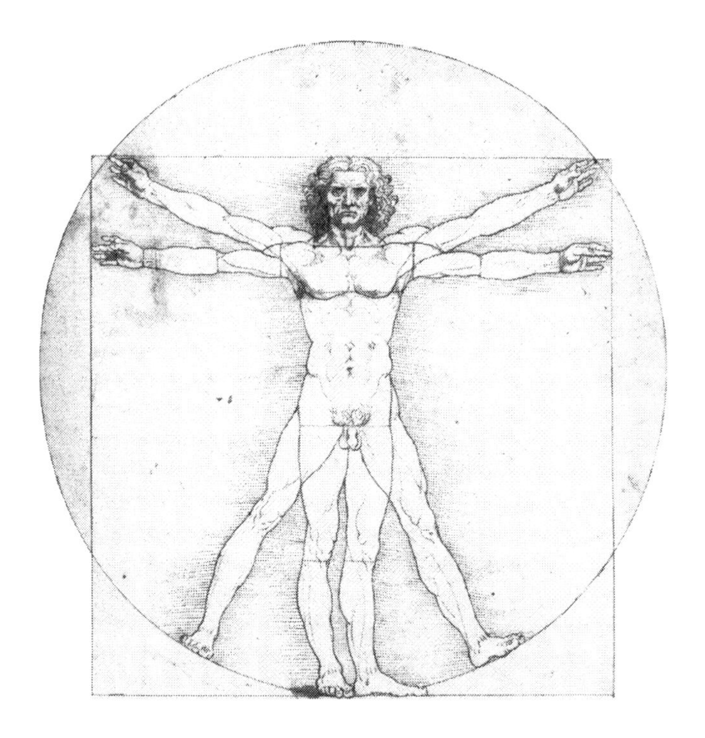

FIGURE 3.1 *Vitruvian Man*, Leonardo da Vinci, *c.*1490.

nests, and so on, all of which she has made circular?"[4] While his preponderance for delight and beauty was evident, Alberti was not averse to bolstering his case by making use of the more pragmatic argument. He believed, as well as consideration being given to the "delight of the mind," that each work "owes a part to necessity and a part to commodity."[5]

Alberti, however prolific as an architect, did not design cities. But among many an animated textual reference to the circular city, we find the earliest *graphic* example in this lineage of architectural treatises is Filarete's rudimentary drawing of *Sforzinda* (1465).[6] The basic diagram is an eight-pointed star, formed out of two squares, bounded by a circle. Although there are references to Vitruvius,[7] the mathematical order of the drawing, combined with the fact that the graphic itself had appeared previously in astrological texts representing both the disposition of the elements and the image of the world,[8] suggests that Filarete's motivations were, like his predecessors, as much symbolic as practical.

The development of the diagram shows a radial network to connect bastions and gates, a ring of public spaces, a canal, and an orthogonally organized central piazza with public buildings.

Following these diagrams, many architects, including Leonardo da Vinci and Francesco di Giorgio Martini, experimented with shape variations, including squares, triangles, circles, and rhomboids, in search of a geometry that could best

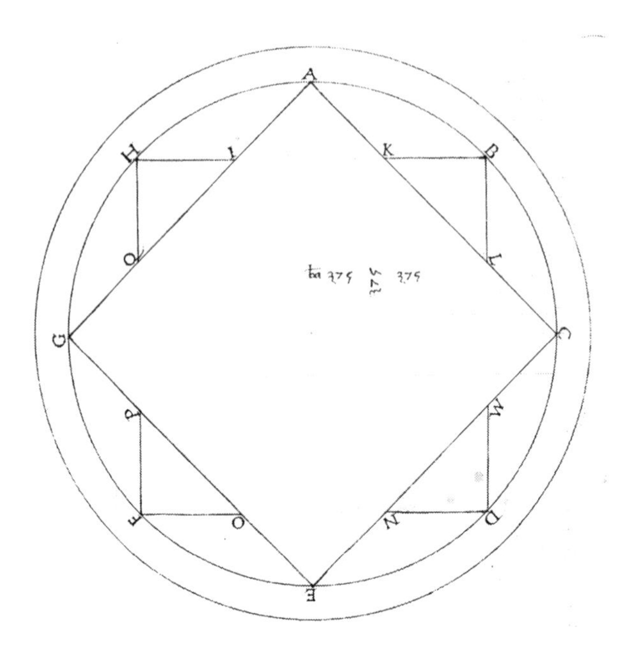

FIGURE 3.2 Filarete, first diagram of the Ideal City of Sforzinda. Filarete's *Treatise on Architecture, Volume 2: The Facsimile* (Yale University Press, 1965), Book II, folio 14r (L).

enclose a city. Whether appearing in their checkerboard or radial versions, the circular city, based unfailingly on the principles of symmetry and proportion, dominated, satisfying, as Filarete's diagram had, "all the longings of the Renaissance for an all-round harmony."[9]

In the mid-sixteenth century, an observable shift in focus occurred in the design of cities as a consequence of improved military technology. The *uomo universale* was supplanted by the military engineer as sophisticated and specialized mathematical skills were required for not only geometric but purely pragmatic schemes for urban development that supported military strategy.[10]

Historian Horst de la Croix goes as far as to claim that "the military architect was an exceedingly practical man and his appreciation of the circle was based exclusively on its functional advantages, untinged by any philosophical cogitation on its symbolic qualities."[11] Yet, inevitably, belief in the significance of the circle remained ubiquitous, and clues from the period exist to illustrate that these concerns *did* seep into military design. Even staunchly pragmatic designers had lapses in their soldierly approach. Giacomo Lanteri, for example, who had been criticized for an overemphasis on the militarization of the city, described the circle, in his 1557 treatise, as "the perfect figure because it reflects the shape and nature of the universe."[12]

It was necessary that the circle be geometrically perfect and consistent around its perimeter. Any irregularities or deformations marked a weakness and a potential

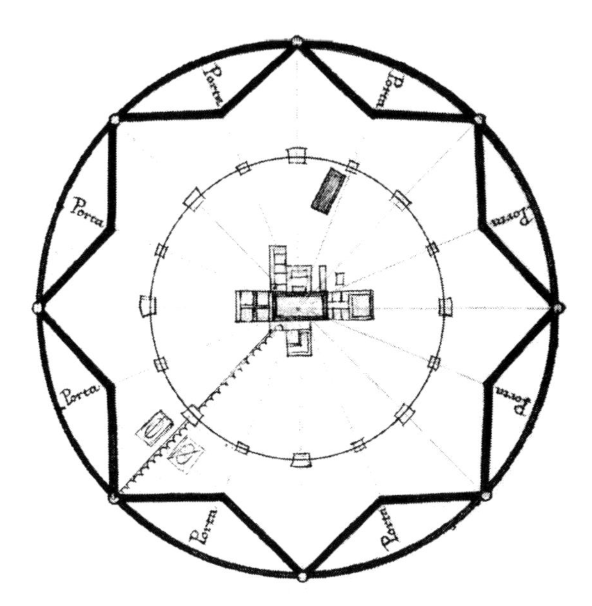

FIGURE 3.3 Filarete, second diagram of the Ideal City of Sforzinda. Filarete's *Treatise on Architecture, Volume 2: The Facsimile* (Yale University Press, 1965), Book II, folio 43r (R).

breach point. Naturally, any inconsistencies in the circle were shunned by military architects on these grounds and, as a result, irregular plans made few appearances in military treatises. Beyond the pragmatics, a certain disdain for irregular form underlying the pragmatic argument might be assumed, since the deformed circle inevitably referenced the imperfect body and a discordant relationship with the universe. The realm of the treatise remained a perfect world in which principles were demonstrated, and so only idealizations were presented in graphic form. Geometries deformed by the site and other contingencies were, on paper at least, considered to be bad examples.[13]

In Filarete's treatise, the Sforzinda diagrams were accompanied by a third illustration—an image of that same Sforzinda, now hovering over a varied landscape. Although Filarete described the site, which he said had been selected after much investigation, the diagram remained unchanged when inserted into its context: it hovered above the flattest part of the site, adjacent to (but unaffected by) a river.

Almost all treatises of this period contained chapters concerning the criteria for the selection of a site for these ideal cities. The argument was polarized between the flat site and the hilly site, each having its own advantages and disadvantages.[14] However, overall, the benefits of the flat site were slightly more persuasive: attacking forces would always be in full sight of defenders, horizontal fire was considered more effective, and the fortress could be supplied and relieved more easily in the case of a siege. More importantly, any disadvantages of the flat site could

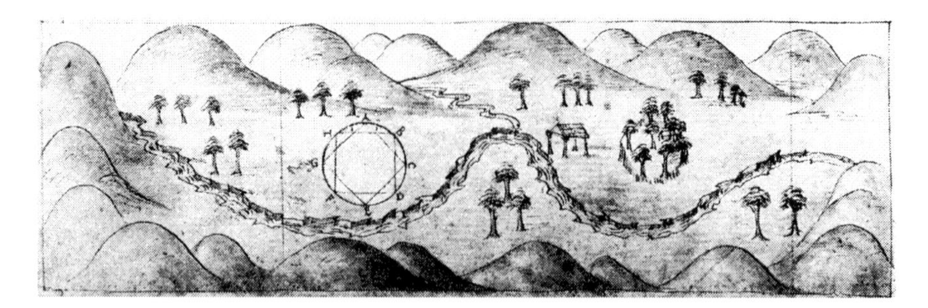

FIGURE 3.4 Filarete, Landscape of Sforzinda. *Filarete's Treatise on Architecture, Volume 2: The Facsimile* (Yale University Press, 1965), Book II, folio 12r.

be offset by the inherently greater strength of the geometric symmetry. Again, this logic implied that asymmetry meant weakness and heightened the potential for vulnerability.

Albeit lengthy and multifarious, the discussion about siting downplayed any response to the inevitable contingencies of the site. While there *are* references to the inevitable deformation of the ideal plan in its *implementation*—for example, Girolamo Cataneo (Lanteri's mathematics teacher and a staunch geometric planner) noted that his geometric designs were intended to be modified by and adjusted to the local conditions of the terrain—the deformations were rarely demonstrated graphically in the hypothetical realm of the treatise.

Enter Francesco de Marchi

More concerned then with principles than reality, the treatise itself was merely the means of communication of urban and architectural *ideals*. It allowed the architect to communicate the way in which a work—from the scale of the column to the scale of the city—*should* be made manifest under ideal conditions. Underscoring this rift that was widening between the world of the ideal and the real, Renaissance mathematician Niccolò Tartaglia, in his preface to the Latin translation of Euclid's *Elements*, stressed that geometry dealt with figures *in the mind* rather than those imperfect forms that we see in nature with the physical eye.[15] In this context of ideals, rules, and *shoulds*, Francesco de Marchi stands alone in his treatment of *what ifs*.

Born in Bologna in 1504, De Marchi practiced as a military engineer in Tuscany and the Low Countries. De Marchi was one of many consultants invited by Pope Paul III to a series of conferences in Rome, beginning in 1534, tasked with the design of a second ring of defenses for the city. Aside from assisting in the construction of the Bastione Sangallo, De Marchi was surrounded by the great military architects who converged on these conferences, and undoubtedly motivated him to begin work on his treatise at this time. Strongly influenced by Alberti, De Marchi was a proponent of the radial plan. Yet, while he acknowledged architecture's less pragmatic attributes, praising, for example, the dignity of architecture and recognizing the importance of Vitruvius, he positioned himself as a soldier, aiming to bring war into touch with architecture.[16] Indeed, his written style is more artillerist than theorist.

While the first two books of *Della architettura militare* are as pragmatic as would be expected from a military professional, the third book represents a radical shift in De Marchi's thinking. This treatise contains many examples of geometrically ordered cities on perfect sites, but among these is scattered a variety of wild and supple city plans in which the city seems to buckle under the pressure of the site itself. De La Croix describes the third book as having an "entirely different spirit," in which "the plodding reporter and chronicler suddenly turns into a most versatile and independent inventor."[17]

De Marchi's work is highly unique among the literature on military architecture abundant at the time. His deployment of a set of hypothetical problems arising from contextual imperfections was unprecedented. The heady array of non-platonic military plans pointed to a potential malleability and responsiveness embedded in the city plan.[18]

In his more tentative scenarios, De Marchi hypothesizes an ideal city undisturbed but adjacent to a contextual disruption—a harbor, for instance, as in the case of City 27. This twelve-bastioned city is symmetrical down to its radial interior planning. It is the site that exerted massive asymmetrical force to which the city, until now, had remained impervious.

A second step in the city's deformation is entertained when the city—both the exterior shell and the interior fabric—reacts to the pressure from the context. City 155 appears as a once-perfect circle, conceptually deformed by the force of the sea. De Marchi, in his nonchalant style, writes pragmatically and undramatically about this unconventional move:

> with great advantage, one can secure a maritime location, where the whole force of fleets can stand there safe from enemies, and there would be no fleet, however strong and large and well-armed it might be, neither galley nor battleships, that would dare to go amidst four towers where they could easily be hit and sunk. These towers could be constructed where there were intervals of rivers, lakes, ponds, canals, as can occur in some sites.[19]

In the plan, what one would expect to have been a convex western edge is instead a slightly concave curve, frontal with the shoreline, its supposed eighth bastion amputated to form a stumped 'launch platform.' The piazza is placed central only to this conceptual circle and not to the actual boundary: in fact, only one block surrounds its western edge, whereas four blocks line its eastern edge. Further, the entire grid of the city is deformed, widening both the block and street dimension toward the seawall in acknowledgment of the dominant force.

Finally, the contextual element forces itself through the walls and becomes part of the interior of the city and De Marchi's games began in earnest. In City 25, the

FIGURE 3.5 City 27. Francesco de Marchi, *Della architettura militare.*

harbor gate fits perfectly between two seaside bastions, protected just as the other flanks are—by cross fire. The harbor penetrates the walls to occupy a circular area within the radial whole. At the intersection of the center of the outer polygon and the tangent of the inner circle, a new central piazza is located (where it should be, both according to the outer circle and with respect to the harbor: stepping off the ship, one would be immediately in the center of the city). The circular harbor acts

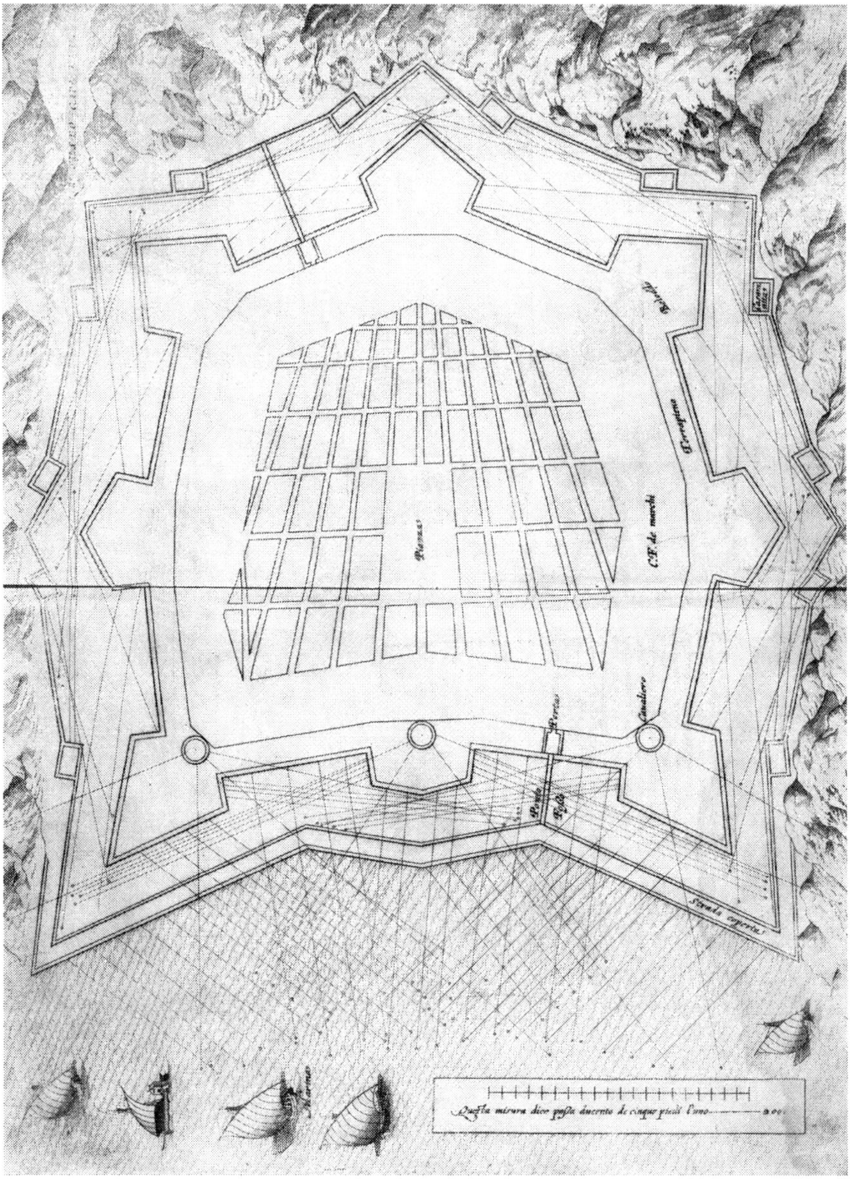

FIGURE 3.6 City 155. Francesco de Marchi, *Della architettura militare.*

as a cut-out in the city's radial military (center-to-bastion) fabric, but has no effect on the street pattern itself.

In a similar operation, De Marchi's City 60 is interrupted by the meandering course of a river. Again, the natural element enters and exits cleanly between bastions, its centerline aligned with that of the city, so that the location of the central piazza coincides with both the center of the river and the center of the city as a whole. Consequently, the axis of the city and its accompanying secondary piazzas coincide with the axis of the main bridge.

City 48 demonstrates another radical step beyond the already unconventional proposals displayed by its predecessors. This city contains a distinctly larger river, widening more markedly toward the south, with three bridges (two shown) and chains replacing the flanks at each wall-penetration. While the preceding plans acted simply as an imposition of the geometrical city form, with subsequent cut-outs and minor deformations, here the organic form of the river generates the entire city fabric. Most of the streets meander with the river's course, while some order is retained by the cross-streets remaining wide and straight. These major streets do not connect to the bastions and the bastions themselves are not aligned with each other but are (presumably) oriented according to local topography.

True to form, De Marchi justifies the entry of the river into the city on military grounds:

> when one part of the land is lost, all of it is not lost, as happened at Parma, when the French once took half the land, but since the river Parma divided nearly the whole land through the middle they could not take the other part, and so they were driven back outside where each side engaged in battle across the river.[20]

City 59 represents the most extreme struggle between nature and the artifice: here, the meandering river cuts first irregularly through a flank on entry and, on exit, intersects with a bastion. Three bridges cross the river, two on the north–south axis, which align with the east wall and its respective grid-lines, and one aligning with the only east–west axis of the city, which opens on to the central piazza at the intersection of the bridge axes. The city has seven bastions in total, three aligned and to the right, and those to the left of the plan which produce unequal flanking angles and distances seemingly related to factors other than the river. As with City 48, not all of the axial streets connect directly to the bastions, and consequently the circulation between bastions must be managed by the ring road in the discontinuous cases.

Legibility of Contextual Deformation

Aware of De Marchi's military priorities, one might attribute this meandering plan as emerging from a military logic, possibly as a result of Alberti's notion that the ancients used to design their streets to be narrow and winding, imagining that they could be defended better.[21] In justifying the curve of the river embedded so completely in the city, De Marchi writes, "I would not want the river to travel in a straight line in the fortification because that would increase the velocity of the water's course . . . "— an expectedly pragmatic explanation. However, he continues, " . . . it seems to me more beautiful to see; that this is the truth one can see in the ancient and famous city of Pisa, for whoever wishes

FIGURE 3.7 City 25. Francesco de Marchi, *Della architettura militare.*

to praise it says that Pisa is along the Arno, which creates a curve: a perspective that is most beautiful to see."[22] Beauty and identity, it seems, have now entered into the underlying logic. Additionally, De Marchi describes the meandering street pattern as offering variation and surprise. Walking along the main streets, he writes, the citizen will be "confronted with a new and different vista at every corner he passes."[23]

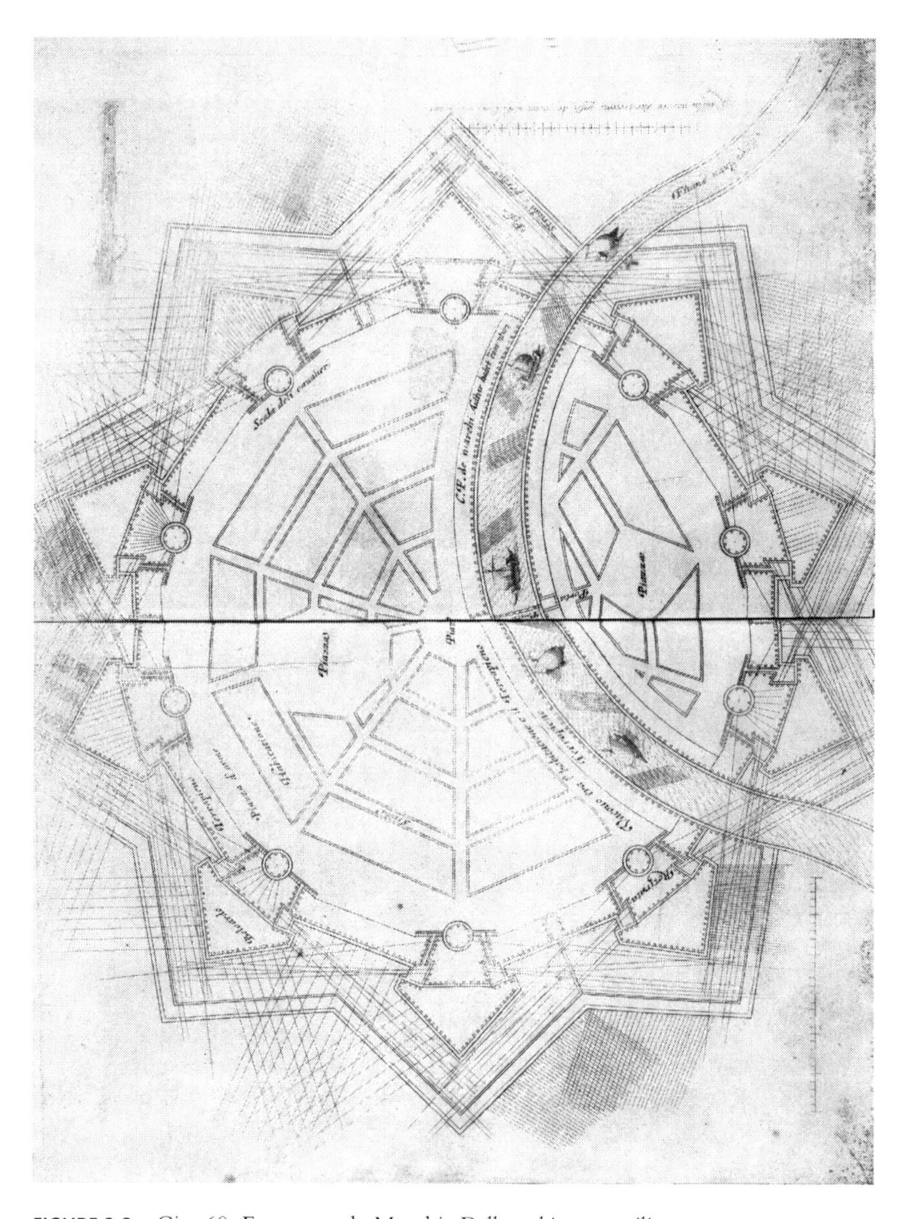

FIGURE 3.8 City 60. Francesco de Marchi, *Della architettura militare.*

In truth, it appears that De Marchi is not guided purely by utilitarian considerations, nor, as has been suggested, is he simply performing an exercise in pattern-making.[24] Rather, he is communicating the *meaning* of the city *in relation to its context*: by understanding one street, something much larger can be understood—the push and pull that occurs between nature's ideal order and the uncertainty of natural contingency. It is through this relationship that De Marchi's poorly concealed desires for beauty, identity, variation, and surprise are realized. Despite the

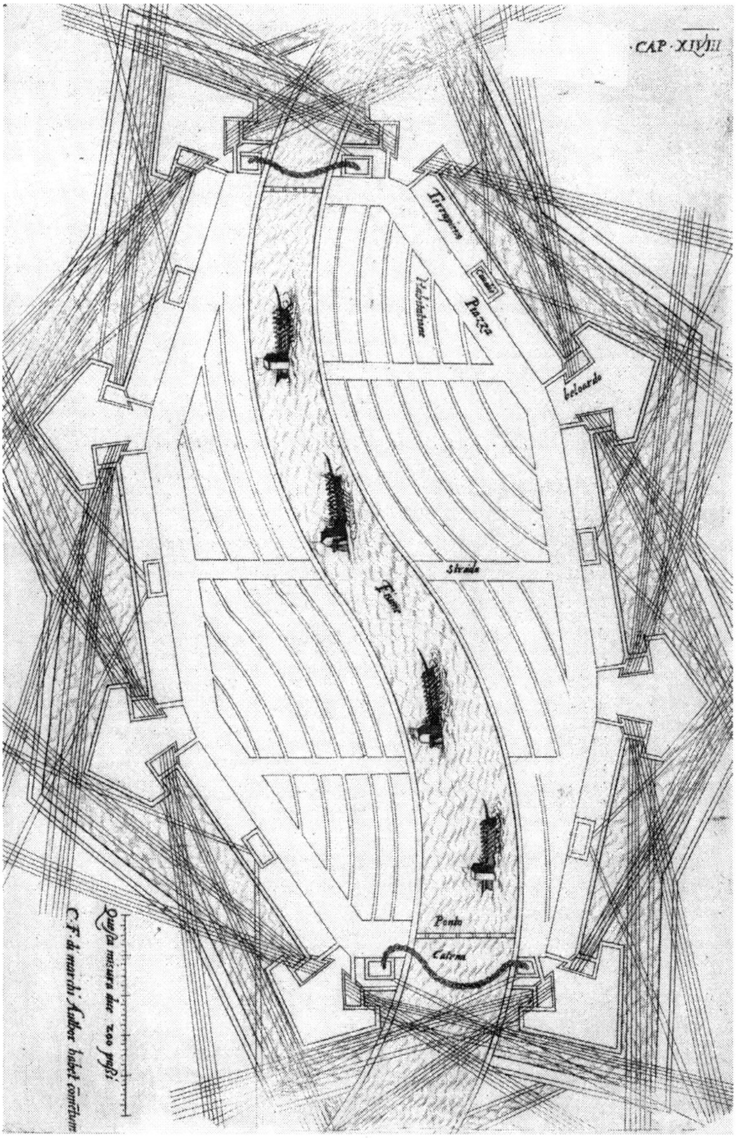

FIGURE 3.9 City 48. Francesco de Marchi, *Della architettura militare.*

dryness of De Marchi's writing, his drawings express, perhaps beyond any possible expression of words, the dynamism and reactivity that emerge from that incongruous relationship.

The resistance to malleable geometries that was rife in the idealistic context of the treatise in De Marchi's day has not necessarily waned over time. In World War II, as Jesse Reiser and Jason Payne have described, a similarly rigid military strategy had catastrophic effects on the British airborne division. While Her Majesty's Royal Air

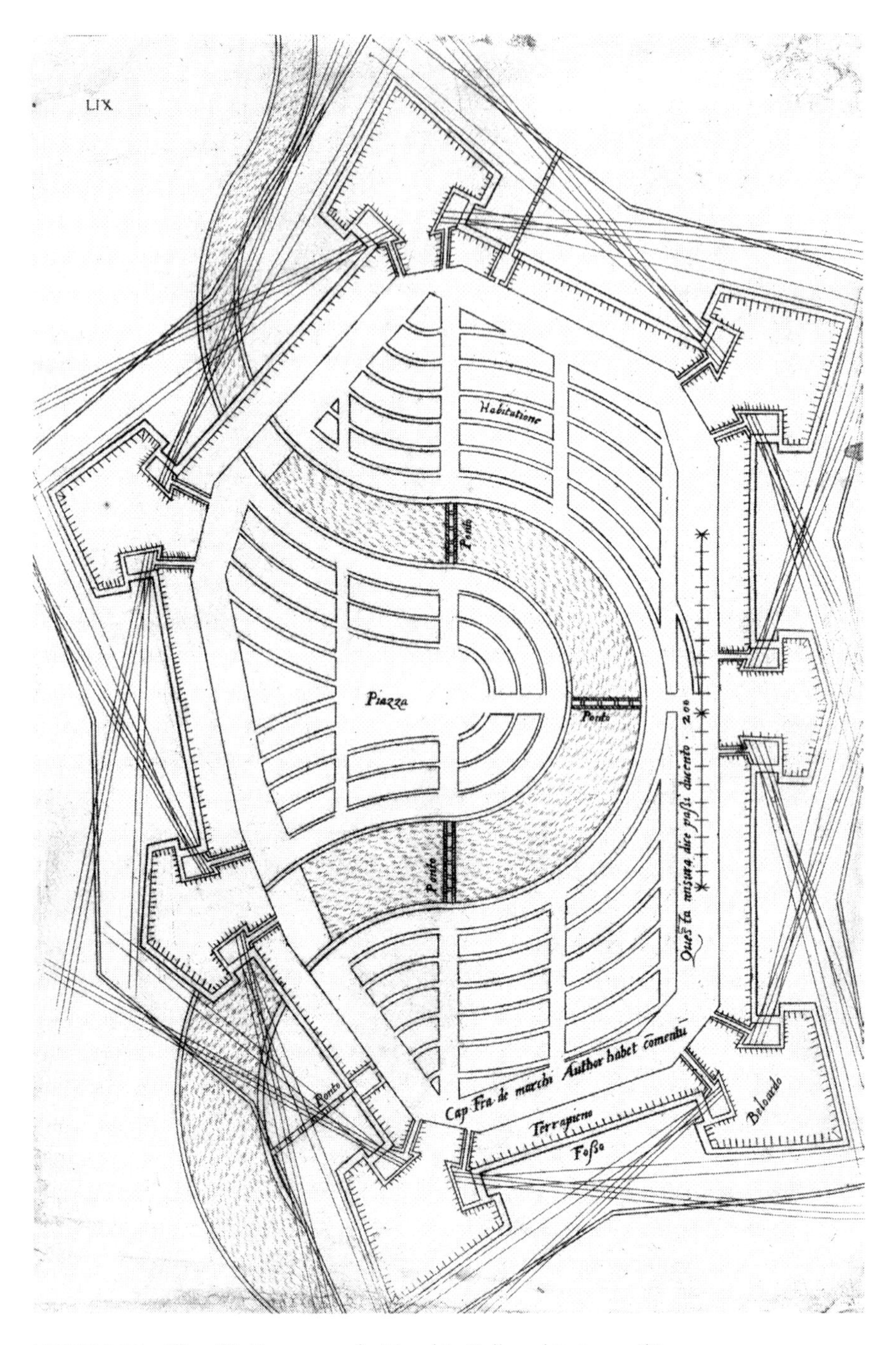

FIGURE 3.10 City 59. Francesco de Marchi, *Della architettura militare.*

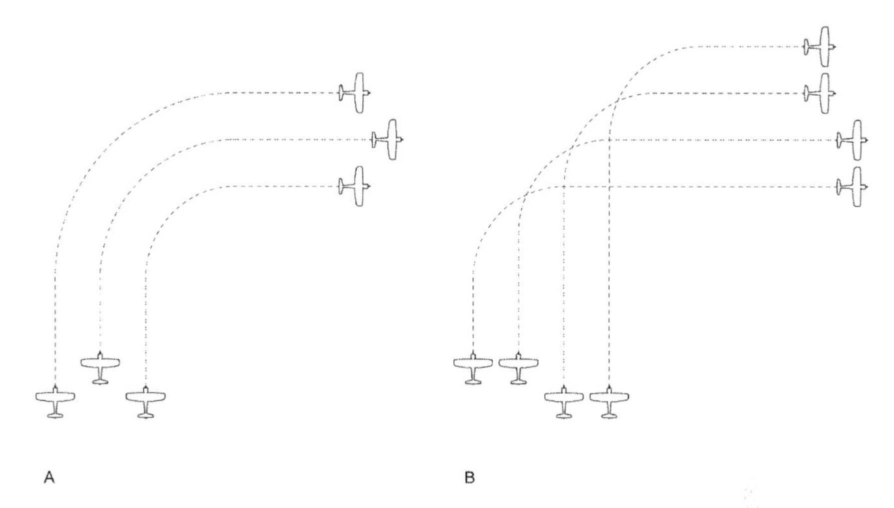

FIGURE 3.11 British (A) and German (B) air strategies. From Jesse Reiser and Jason Payne, "Chum: Computation in a Super-Saturated Milieu," in *Kenchiku Bunka* (Tokyo: Shokokusha Publishing, May 1998), 2. Redrawn by CODA.

Force flew in geometrically stable fixed formations, the German Luftwaffe's non-linear thinking allowed them to turn quickly and completely reconfigure their formation. Flexible geometry permitted necessary adaptability to changing conditions, while the lumbering British were ordered to maintain a rigid geometric formation that was easily out-maneuvered. In a mirror image of the ambivalence of military engineers in the Renaissance, these twentieth-century strategists remained fixated on pure geometries regardless of their poor performance in battle. As Reiser and Payne note: "the British insistence upon simple cleanliness of fixed formations, which really had more to do with the colonial aesthetics of pure geometries than the real business of air combat, is what led to their poor showing against the Germans."[25]

At the conclusion of what might appear a strictly historical phenomenon, then, consider that almost 500 years after De Marchi's treatise, many urbanists remain reluctant to admit context and circumstance into the design process. While the designed city is once again understood as a sign—from the regular geometries produced by architects, including Norman Foster's square city at *Masdar*, and Richard Rogers' circular *Compact City* in Lu Zia Sui, Shanghai; to symbolic forms produced by developers, such as Nakheel's *The Palm*, *The World*, and *The Universe* in Dubai—these contemporary urban forms reference geometric and symbolic figures inherently unresponsive to external forces. Moreover, the latter examples, as literal islands, isolate themselves from the disordered world, minimizing, as much as possible, the intrusion of the deformative potential of uneven and unpredictable surroundings. As in De Marchi's last city (City 57), where the sea penetrates the city completely, the tabula rasa condition is reinstated, with all the perfect symmetry, symbolism, and order—as well as the rigidity and muteness—that contextlessness implies.

FIGURE 3.12 City 57. Francesco de Marchi, *Della architettura militare*.

Notes

All De Marchi images are from Francesco de Marchi, *Della architettura militare* (Gaspare dall'Oglio, Brescia, 1599). Courtesy Avery Architectural and Fine Arts Library, Columbia University.

1 Plato, *Laws*, 360 BC, trans. by Benjamin Jowett, http://classics.mit.edu/Plato/laws.6.vi.html.

2 Vitruvius, *The Ten Books on Architecture*, trans. Morris Hicky Morgan (New York: Dover, 1960), 22.

3 Ibid., 14.

4 Leon Battista Alberti, *On the Art of Building in Ten Books*, trans. Joseph Rykwert, Neil Leach, and Robert Tavernor (Cambridge, MA: MIT Press, 1988), 196. Additionally, "Of all Cities, the most Capacious is the round One" (Alberti, *On the Art of Building in Ten Books*, 102).

5 Ibid., 94.

6 Filarete, also known as Antonio di Pietro Averlino, *Trattato di Architettura di Antonio Filareto* (Florence, 1465). Reprinted as *Filarete's Treatise on Architecture, Volume 2: The Facsimile* (New Haven, CT: Yale University Press, 1965).

7 And potential misinterpretations: Vitruvius mentions the eight directions of the winds but proposes that the plan of the city should work with the winds, not passively accept their abstract form. This reading of Vitruvius would have opened up another trajectory in Renaissance city design, and one that would have been more aligned with De Marchi's thinking.

8 S. Lang, "Sforzinda, Filarete, and Filelfo," *Journal of the Warburg and Courtauld Institutes*, 35 (1972), 392.

9 S. Lang, "The Ideal City from Plato to Howard," *Architectural Review*, 112, 668 (August, 1952), 97.

10 Niccolò Tartaglia's treatise on ballistics, *Nuovo Scientia* (1537), and his *Quesiti ed invenzione divers* (1538), concerning artillery, mathematics, mechanics, and fortification, mark the beginning of the shift from architect-artist to military engineer. Formerly, the architect was also a mathematician, astrologer, inventor, and artist.

11 Horst de la Croix, "Military Architecture and the Radial City Plan in Sixteenth Century Italy," *Art Bulletin*, XLII, 4 (1960), 281.

12 Martha Pollak, *Turin, 1564–1680: Urban Design, Military Culture, and the Creation of the Absolutist Capital* (Chicago: University of Chicago Press, 1991), 22.

13 In practice, many of the ideal cities of the fifteenth and sixteenth centuries, when actually implemented, were forced to deform due to site conditions, existing city form, and civilian needs. Even Palmanova, whose final form was very similar to its paper representations thanks to its siting on a perfectly flat and open plane, was significantly altered in its eventual implementation.

14 In De La Croix's synopsis, "Castriotto believed that mountain sites were stronger. De Marchi was undecided, but also seemed to favor the mountains, while Alghisi was a strong advocate of flat and open sites. Busca devoted nine full chapters to the problem, only to decide that a final choice between the two was most difficult." Horst de la Croix, "Military Architecture and the Radial City Plan in Sixteenth Century Italy," 283.

15 The *Elements* to which Euclid had dedicated his book were: the point, the line, and the area. The combination of these elements produced geometrical forms, and the purest of all of these was the circle. Whether attributed to the divine will of God or the indubitable laws of science, the form of the circle came to represent the geometric order of the world and the cosmos.

16 John R. Hale, *Renaissance Fortification: Art or Engineering* (London: Thames and Hudson, 1977), 33.
17 De La Croix, "Military Architecture and the Radial City Plan in Sixteenth Century Italy," 287.
18 In his treatise, De Marchi's city plans do not appear in the progressive order that they appear here. Rather, these examples appear sporadically throughout the treatise, intermingled with more conventional platonic forms.
19 Francesco de Marchi, *Della architettura militare* (Gaspare dall'Oglio, 1599), chap. 57, trans. by Ashleigh Imus for the author.
20 Ibid., chap. 48, trans. by Ashleigh Imus for the author.
21 "I notice that the ancients preferred to give some of their roads within the city awkward exits, and others blind alleys, so that any aggressor or criminal who entered would hesitate, being in two minds and unsure of himself, or, summoning up the courage to continue, would soon find himself in danger" (Alberti, *On the Art of Building in Ten Books*, 107).
22 De Marchi, *Della architettura militare*, chap. 48, trans. by Ashleigh Imus for the author.
23 De La Croix, "Military Architecture and the Radial City Plan in Sixteenth Century Italy," 288.
24 In her article, "The Ideal City: From Plato to Howard," Susan Lang refers to this plan as an example of the fifteenth century's tendency "to draw plan as an exercise in pattern-making." It is to this comment that Horst de la Croix responds with his article "Military Architecture and the Radial City Plan in Sixteenth Century Italy," arguing that the designs were "the products of practical men who were guided primarily by utilitarian considerations." Their feisty argument is printed in *Art Bulletin*, 43, 4 (December, 1961).
25 Jesse Reiser and Jason Payne, "Chum: Computation in a Super-Saturated Milieu," in *Kenchiku Bunka* (Tokyo: Shokokusha Publishing, May 1998), 2.

4

AN ECOLOGICAL APPROACH TO THE PICTURESQUE

While the Picturesque's very name implies a tendency toward the pictorial, the visual, and the aesthetic, theorists of the Picturesque have at times understood the irregular and chaotic forms produced in this movement as having a superior functionality. Nikolaus Pevsner, in fact, in a book written in England in the 1940s but published only recently, argues that the Picturesque was actually *functionalist* at its core.

The architectural understanding of function—as faithful translation of program[1]— however, seems inadequate to describe the radical forms advocated (if rarely realized architecturally) in Picturesque design. Functionalism expresses what the architecture *does*, whether literally or metaphorically, yet what architecture thinks of itself as *doing* tends to be rather self-centered: in the expression of its parts (stairs, structure), in the showing of its inhabitants (machines, workers), or in the production of signs of its own manufacturing in the building elements. Functionalism in the Picturesque sense is more complex. The function expressed is not limited to the object itself, but the object in specific and chaotic negotiation with the world around it.

A more appropriate model of function, in fact, might be found in ecological theory: specifically via perceptual psychologist James J. Gibson, who, as we have seen, offers the more complex term of *affordance*. By aligning the Picturesque not only with functionality, but with more nuanced ecological notions of affordance, this chapter considers a new approach to our over-used and under-thought terms of *function* and *program* when paired with behavior and site.

A Brief Overview of the Picturesque[2]

Before the Picturesque was officially named, aesthetic considerations of natural phenomena were much discussed in circles formed around the Newtonian ambivalence between nature-as-ordered and nature-as-wild. As the conversation evolved, the discussion of natural wilderness inevitably broadened to encompass the constructed landscape, and eventually challenged the popular standards for the ideal and geometric garden. In 1685, for example, William Temple proposed alternative garden designs that were "wholly irregular," and that would compose "many disagreeable parts into some figure."[3] He attributes his ideas to the Chinese concept of beauty, where the "greatest reach of imagination, is employed in contriving figures where the beauty shall be great, and strike the eye, but without any order or disposition of parts that shall be commonly or easily observed."[4] In the end, despite his clear appreciation, Temple cautions against experimentation with such difficult to achieve 'sharawaggi' in the garden in favor of more attainable designs.

Despite his warnings, by middle of the eighteenth century, ideas very close to those described by Temple and others were translated directly into garden designs and, subsequently, the relationship between landscape gardening and scenic painting was more clearly concretized.[5] Geometric layouts and organization in plan were rejected in favor of a montage of scenes along a path, from the perspective of the ambulatory body. This naturalness, however artificial, was a radical departure from the main continental trajectory at the time, which favored order and control.

In tandem with the shift in gardening design, new aesthetic theories departed from mainstream notions of beauty as ideal and harmonic, and favored instead the natural and the wild.[6] And, as philosophical writing became increasingly influential in both intellectual and design circles, so was the 'English' garden finally elevated to an upper-level form of art. Finally, in a flurry of publications around 1794, the two trajectories of aesthetics and gardening productively merged to form a Picturesque landscape garden theory.[7] Sir Uvedale Price, in his *Essay on the Picturesque*, wove together several previous versions of the Picturesque including Alexander Pope's ideas on curiosity, partial concealment, and intricacy, and Gilpin's observations of roughness, variation, irregularity, and even irritation.[8] Crucially, Price established the Picturesque as a third alternative to Edmund Burke's dialectic of beauty and the sublime. Picturesqueness, according to Price, is not beautiful by convention, but is pleasing to the eye because of its striking character. It other words, what it expresses is provocative and inevitably fascinating: therefore, while it is perhaps not beautiful, it is certainly not ugly. Price clarifies, defining the condition of ugliness as, "the *want* of form, that unshapen lumpish appearance, which, perhaps, no one word exactly expresses."[9] On the other hand:

> an ugly man or woman, with an aquiline nose, high cheek bones, beetle brows, and lines in every part of the face, is, from these Picturesque circumstances, which might all be taken away without destroying ugliness, much more *strikingly* ugly, than a man with no more features than an oyster.[10]

Price advocated, then, not just for that which is purely pleasurable for the senses, but rather a mixture of that which is pleasing and the deeply striking.[11] (Later, Ivor de Wolfe would credit Price with being "perhaps the first man in history to reveal that an object may be 'ugly' in itself and yet in a suitable context have aesthetic possibilities."[12])

These emergent evaluations and re-evaluations of the concept of beauty in nature effectively subverted the widely held position that the universe is necessarily expressive of an inherent order, and shifted attention to its uncontained variety and infinite intricacy. But while the possibilities for embracing the wilder side of the natural world were seriously entertained in landscape and scenic painting practices, the field of architecture lagged behind the cultural wave by nearly a century.

A prime example of this impasse between landscape and architectural thinking is to be found in Jacques Molinos' *Champs de Repos*. Here, features like stands of trees, clearings, and shadowy grottos are encountered along a meandering course. Points of reference are organic and inconsistent rather than geometric and measured. Experience is varied and scenic rather than ordered by an ideal plan. The texture of the rendering resists manicured lawns and hedgerows in favor of an aesthetic derived from Picturesque thinking. And yet the architectural elements oppose these qualities: a temple in the form of a monumental pyramid is located at the center of the serpentine network of paths and plantings, all of which is enclosed by a wall in the planometric form of a circle. While all around it appears to be wild and untamed, all that is architectural—the object and the wall—remains geometric and regular.

FIGURE 4.1 *Champs de repos* ("Field of Rest"), design for a picturesque circular cemetery by Jacques Molinos, Montmartre Quarries, Paris, 1799. From Blanche M.G. Linden, *Silent City on a Hill* (Library of American Landscape History, 2007), 71.

License to abandon classical order in English architecture had only begun to be considered a possibility. A decade earlier, Sir Joshua Reynolds had timidly written:

> It may not be amiss for the Architect to take advantage *sometimes* of that to which I am sure the Painter ought always have his eyes open, I mean the use of accidents, to follow where they may lead, and to improve them rather than to trust a regular plan . . . Variety and intricacy is a beauty and excellence in every other of the arts which address the imagination; why not in Architecture?[13]

Until that moment, the main thrust of architecture in England was, astonishingly, and despite the frenzy of writing and gardening practices enamored with wildness, Palladian revivalism. Even strong advocates of Picturesque architecture did not fully commit to the idea of a valid alternative to (neo)classical symmetry.[14]

Gilpin, earlier still (1776), had explained the Picturesque's relationship with Palladianism far more aggressively than Reynolds: "A piece of Palladian architecture may be elegant in the last degree," he admits, but "should we wish to give it a Picturesque beauty, we must use a mallet, instead of the chisel, we must beat down one half of it, deface the other, and throw the mutilated members around in heaps."[15] Despite the barely concealed enthusiasm of this statement for the violent destruction of all things Palladian, few works of Picturesque architecture (apart from the many ruins that appear in paintings) demonstrate such wild abandon.

FIGURE 4.2 *Brough Castle*, Westmorland, 1834. Engraved by William Alexander le Petit from an original study by the painter-architect Thomas Allom (London: Fisher, Son & Co., 1833).

Pevsner, however, understood the Picturesque agenda as architecturally more constructive than destructive and credits *Vanbrugh Castle* at Blackheath, London (1717–1725), with having been the first Picturesque, asymmetrical—and thus, anti-Palladian—house in Europe since the Renaissance.

Pevsner considered the varied composition—the balance across the diversified forms as they rose, fell, grouped, and then splayed across and embedded into the landscape—to be the epitome of Picturesque architecture. That Vanbrugh's residence at Blackheath was intended to "have the air of a castle"[16] was made clear by both description and design—complete with ramparts, turrets, and crenellations. Such a militaristic reference, of course, suggests both an incremental construction process, and one dominated by pragmatics: a functional Picturesque. However, while Pevsner's argument for this underlying functionalism is well supported in his urban examples, this architectural example is far from exemplary, partially, perhaps, due to the domineering castle-aesthetic. Unfortunately, in the years to follow, this aesthetic became unnecessarily and inextricably associated with the Picturesque movement, and thus stifled the potential development of other (functional) interpretations.

FIGURE 4.3 *Vanbrugh Castle*, wood engraving. Artist unknown. From *Old and New London* by Walter Thornbury and Edward Walford (London: Cassell, Petter and Galpin, *c.*1897).

Townscape and the Functional Picturesque

Perhaps encouraged by another set of ruins, the origins of the Picturesque resurfaced in Britain in the 1940s following World War II. As editor of the *Architectural Review*, Pevsner,[17] along with the magazine's owner Hubert de Cronin Hastings (under the pseudonym Ivor de Wolfe) and Art Director Gordon Cullen, fervently promoted the resurgence of Picturesque discourse and, along with it, the requisite aesthetics: irregular, compositional, and varied—an approach that was "no longer ideal, rational, or pure, but synthetic, mixed, and compromised."[18] From the 1930s until the 1970s, over 200 pro-townscape articles were published in *Architectural Review*,[19] including titles such as "Exterior Furnishing or Sharawaggi," "Townscape: A Plea for an English Visual Philosophy Founded on the True Rock of Sir Uvedale Price,"[20] and "Twentieth Century Picturesque,"[21] all elaborated in a series of eponymously named books by Cullen on issues of *Townscape*. As a whole, this onslaught intended to apply a specifically *English* Picturesque sensibility to urban post-war reconstruction.

This tendency marks a decisive rupture between England, mainland Europe, and, in particular, the United States. While the general post-war inclination in the U.S. was to turn to monumental and formal Modernism, England decisively favored *genius loci* over *tabula rasa*[22]—a preference that would form the basis for contextualism in architecture, per Pevsner's fellow Englishman, Colin Rowe. Rowe, however was a detractor of the Picturesque revival and, when the time came, he specifically sought to distinguish his own *Collage City* from Townscape.[23] Despite its many pro-Modernist assertions, Rowe characterized the Townscape movement as "nostalgic, placatory, and manipulative in its top-down populism . . . an open gaol conducted on compassionate principles."[24]

Despite Colin Rowe's best efforts, many critics have identified a strong connection between the Townscape and *Collage City* models. Macarthur writes that, although Pevsner does not use the term *collage* explicitly, "it is the collage-like overlay of distinct planning ideas, his 'set-pieces' adjusted to their sites and to existing features, that he praises in *Visual Planning*."[25] The term 'Picturesque,' he claims, was simply replaced by 'collage.'[26] More damningly, in a special issue of *AR*, respected historian and critic Reyner Banham claimed that the true author of *Collage City* was the original author of *Townscape*, Ivor de Wolfe.[27]

Pevsner, however, distinguished his particular approach from both the surge of pro-English Picturesque sentiment *and* from future contextualist movements when his findings revealed a functionalist agenda at the heart of the Picturesque movement. In fact, in "Twentieth Century Picturesque" (1954),[28] Pevsner refutes accusations of anti-Modernism in 1940s' English planning and goes so far as to locate Picturesque disorder and irregularity at the very foundations of Modernism's functionalism.

To further bolster his alignment of functionalism with the Picturesque, Pevsner draws on early Picturesque texts that grapple with the inherent struggle between aesthetics and function. In one very early text, for example, Francis Bacon displays an attitude that is decidedly functional. In his 1597 *Essay of Buildings*, he argues:

"houses are built to live in, and not to look on; therefore *let use be preferred before uniformity*, except when both may be had."[29] And observing the dual or complementary nature of aesthetics and use in all things Picturesque, Pevsner borrows from Charles Locke Eastlake, who advocates the "uneven distribution of parts which is at once necessary to convenience and the cause of Picturesque composition,"[30] to again clarify his own definition.

In short, the Picturesque according to Pevsner is simply: "the aesthetic potential of functional building planning."[31] If we can move beyond the obvious qualities of Modernism's cubic volumes, lack of ornamentation, large openings, etc., we find Picturesque qualities: "a mixture of materials, synthetic and natural, rough and smooth, and beyond that, the free planning of a whole quarter . . . interaction between landscape and building . . . and between different buildings of different shapes and heights."[32] In this way, Pevsner aligns Modernism's functionalism with the Picturesque movement and his own version of it in *Visual Planning*. "The qualities of the modern movement were not developed to please the eye," he argues, "but because without them no workable, no functioning, no functional architecture is possible in our age. Impose symmetry, impose axiality and grids, impose rules, even where the artist is feeling his way, and you reduce the usefulness."[33]

The pairing of functional with aesthetic irregularity is not as contradictory as it may seem. In fact, a truly Picturesque approach insists that the two support each other. That is to say, in responding purely to needs, Picturesque (or Modern) architecture will produce irregularity, disorder, and haphazard aesthetics *only as a pleasant side-effect*. And although it is questionable whether Modernism was ever a simple response to function as much as an aesthetic in itself, the idea of responding purely to needs returns us inevitably to the animal–environment relationship: the inescapable expression of that need-force through the form of the object.

The Ecological Approach to Function

In his definition of functionalism, historian and theorist Adrian Forty deftly charts the emergence and multifarious meanings of function from the eighteenth century. For our purposes, it is remarkable that in tracking a workable definition of functionalism for architecture, Forty finds a biological link to the term's eighteenth-century point of origin. Function, he notes, was a key concept of Lamarck and Cuvier's at the end of the eighteenth century. Rather than classify bodily organs by the criteria of appearance and position, these naturalists thought it more accurate to first identify a given organ's 'function' within the larger body of the organism and then determine its place in the system in order to understand the relationship of an organ to the sum of its parts.

Function was then translated into architectural terms by Viollet-le-Duc and understood similarly—as "the role played by each part within the structure."[34] This architecture–biology analogy is perhaps best expressed Leopold Eidlitz, who wrote:

> All natural organisms are possessed of the mechanical ability to perform certain functions. This ability we find more or less clearly expressed in their forms as a whole or in their crystallization. In this way, they convey to the mind an expression of these functions and thus they tell the story of their being. The architect, in imitation of this natural condition of matter, so models his forms that they also tell the story of their functions; and these functions are always mechanical conditions of strength, elegance, and repose, in combinations of various quantities of these properties. The fundamental principles of the modelling of architectural forms is therefore mechanical.[35]

Despite functionalism's early connection with biology, by the mid-nineteenth century, function had come to mean what we might today call program: "the activities designated for a particular building or part of building."[36] As function became architecturalized, especially in, and in the criticism of, the Modern movement, the possibility of further synergies between the two disciplines' understandings of the term slipped away.

One post-split strand linking the two trajectories of architectural functionalism and biology can, however, be found in James J. Gibson's theory of affordances, presented in *The Ecological Approach to Perception*, which describes a perceptual world in which functionality is primary. An affordance (as we have seen in "Niche Tactics") is a use-quality contained within both the perceived world and the perceiving animal that stimulates a process of simultaneously occurring projection and consumption that together produce meaning. The *function* of the encountered object, Gibson proposes, is perceived before the color, the form, or the shape of the object. For example, the physical properties of flat horizontal rigid and extended afford standing or walking: it is walk-on-able. Affordance, however, does not reside completely in the object but in the relationship of the object with the perceiving body. *Affordance*, Gibson posits, "cuts across the dichotomy of subjective-objective and . . . is equally a fact of the environment and a fact of behavior . . . is both physical and psychical, yet neither."[37] Furthermore, in Gibson's discussion of a given animal's living environment, or habitat, he makes a distinction between the *habitat* and the *niche*. The niche is precisely defined by the animal's set of affordances; while the term habitat defines where an organism exists, the term niche defines *how* it exists.

Gibson's theory is of course an elaboration of Gestalt theory, which argued that, rather than visual experience being a two-fold process whereby colors were sensed as a primary process and then "clothed with meaning"[38] to result in the perception of things, it was the thing itself that contained meaning, which could be readily perceived. In Kurt Koffka's words, "an object looks attractive or repulsive before it looks black or blue, circular or square."[39] Koffka's suggestion is that objects have a demand or invitational quality that is primary. Similarly, the terms 'valence' and 'invitation character' are two translations of the German term 'Aufforderungscharakter,' coined by Kurt Lewin to describe this intrinsic meaning of objects. A valence, according to Lewin, is the meaning that is perceived in an object, according to the needs of the observer. A mailbox, for example, has a demand character only when I need to mail a letter.

To an animal, the affordances contained within its niche are things that are eat-able, drink-able, breath-able, shade-able, conceal-able, and so on. These affordances are linked to specific perceptual and functional components within the animal: the animal's sense of smell as it relates to the affordance of eat-ability in an object, and that object relating to the shape and function of its mouth, stomach, and eventually to the entire organism, and back into the environment. In other words, this time Jakob von Uexküll's: "All the organs of plants as well as of animals owe their form and their distribution of materials to their meaning as utilizers of the meaning factors which come to them from the outside."[40]

If architecture is allowed to stand in for the animal, as has often been suggested,[41] it too requires a method of perceiving and adjusting to its affordances, and also to its systems of consumption. A series of questions that probe architecture's relationship to the environment encountered at its site emerge. For instance: What does sunlight afford architecture, for example, and how might architecture respond to maximize or minimize its affect? What does rainwater afford and how might architecture respond? What do views afford and how might they change architecture?

While this latter consideration—that of the vista— is given most attention in early Picturesque architecture, as well as in Pevsner's study of English town planning, climatic concerns are also addressed as a secondary concern. The irregular

FIGURE 4.4 *Luscombe Castle*, near Dawlish, Devonshire. Engraved by Le Petit; drawn by T. Allom. From John Britton, *Devonshire Illustrated, in a Series of Views of Cities, Towns, Public Buildings, Streets, Docks, Churches, Antiques, Abbeys, Picturesque Scenery, Castles, Seats of the Nobility, &c. &c.* Published by Fisher, Son & Co., London, 1829.

form of *Luscombe Castle* in Devon, for example, "enables the internal disposition of rooms and their relation to the landscape."[42] Here, the orientation of rooms and within them the orientation of doors is motivated not only by external landscape features but by climate: views to the north and west will often be "covered with wet, as to render the landscape hardly visible."[43] Most importantly, these Picturesque moves should not only do something, they should express that they are doing it. They should offer the possibility that, "functional equipage might become architectural expression and a culture of forms."[44]

This architecture, though, is not 'functional' according to the most common architectural usage. That is, the parts might not express the essence of their own utility: rather, the overall form of the building aggregates as its parts are arranged according to their relation with utilities beyond themselves, in their surroundings.

This expression, it is important to note, should not demand attention. Picturesque thinkers—most prominently Udevale Price—believed that the Picturesque should never force unplanned-ness for the sake of composition or aesthetics (the fundamental problem of the Picturesque castle-aesthetic). To reconcile this seeming impossibility, Price proposed that architecture should simply respond to the views and, by thus doing, a Picturesque architecture would be generated automatically. Price writes that:

> [if we], instead of making a regular front and sides, were to insist upon having many of the windows turned towards those points where the objects were most happily arranged, the architect would be forced into the invention of a number of Picturesque forms and combinations, which otherwise might never have occurred to him.[45]

This accidental but necessary composition is what John Macarthur has described as "unideal" and "weak form."[46] These terms suggest contingent and deformative external and internal forces acting on the form, as well as the legibility of those forces.

The Contemporary Ecological Picturesque

In the 1950s, the great British critic Peter Reyner Banham, a former student of Pevsner's, maligned Townscape as a "surrender to all that was most provincial and second-rate in British school and intellectual life."[47] Even so, Macarthur believes the style so often associated with Banham and his Independent Group—Brutalism—to be just as Picturesque as Townscape, and a stepping stone to contemporary Picturesque discourse and practice. "Where Townscape emphasizes the light pleasures of a kind of fortuitous sub-beauty in the spirit of Gilpin's travels," he argues, "Brutalism is anti-aesthetic, or rather, an aesthetic of the unpleasing."[48] Certainly, in its "valuation of materials as found,"[49] brutalism aligned with functionalist aspects of the Picturesque.

Despite a certain resurgence of brutalism today, however, Macarthur believes that it is not here that we might find a contemporary Picturesque, but in the practices that engage with the everyday user and the informal city, such as Atelier Bow-Wow and Lacaton and Vassal. In fact, Bow-Wow, specifically, align the key terms of our discussion quite explicitly. Their use of the term 'behaviorology' in place of 'function,' "positions projects within an ecosystem of behaviors as elements which participate in spatial production."[50] Contemporary Picturesqueness, then, might be described as architecture's *behaving* in a given situation, acting within a limited and abstracted set of possibilities that exist between the incoming architecture and the scene. It might deploy techniques of affordance, deriving function and meaning from outside and relating the potentials to its own body, a body that may need to contort as a response. As the organism reaches out and draws in (in both senses) those elements of the environment that afford something to it, so too Picturesque design reaches out into the landscape or the city to pull aspects of the world toward it and modifies itself as a consequence.[51]

Likewise, the Berlin-based office, SMAQ (Sabine Müller & Andreas Quednau), provides a model for practicing a contemporary Picturesque. SMAQ's research and built work operates on a beg-borrow-steal mentality: with minimal means and no predetermined aesthetic agenda, the work engages at the point of intervention only to immediately renegotiate the various systems present at the site and create a dialogue that reaches beyond the architecture itself.

The Picturesque in SMAQ's "BAD" in Stuttgart, for example, can be found less in the organic swirls of the screen, but rather in its operating system as it taps into a public water main using a standard hosepipe arrayed in a specific configuration with

FIGURE 4.5 SMAQ, Sabine Müller & Andreas Quednau, BAD, 2004, Solitude, Stuttgart.

the sun. BAD uses extant utilities and responds to natural resources so that it warms precisely enough water for one bath, and simultaneously provides privacy for changing. Its aesthetic is a side-effect—an identifiably irregular play of parts that are not sensible in themselves, but only in relation to the required functions of the architectural organism in dialogue with the site. In another project, City Boids—Molecular Urbanism, SMAQ describe the constantly fluctuating informal city, and their practice that learns from it, as a negotiation: a series of "combinatorial acts of setting needs and site in a tight relation."[52]

This mode of activity plays not only on identifiable elements but on the redundancies existing in the site (or in the object), which can grow or change in relation to needs and resources. This practice recalls Stephen Jay Gould's term 'exaptation'—an alternative to the term 'adaptation,' which implies the creation of something for some use—in order to define a misuse of the element produced by adaptation. Exaptation in nature describes instead "features co-opted for a current utility following an origin for a different function (or no function at all)."[53]

What the ecological approach to the functional Picturesque allows most importantly, then, and where this text most crucially hopes to build on Pevsner's functionalization of the Picturesque is twofold. First, that function is not necessarily something embedded in the architecture but exists as an affordance between the architecture and its environment, in the relationship between the two. And, second, that function is not a constant characteristic, but is something that is supple, and can be negotiated as environments and organisms change. The embedding of redundancy or of dynamism into the function of the object, the understanding of possible futures, of alternate interpretations, of re-labelling, of wit, guile, sneakiness, slyness, and cunning, is at the heart of the ecological approach to the functional Picturesque.

William Gilpin explained such preference for action over ideals and aesthetics with an animalistic metaphor:

> We admire the horse, as a real *object*; the elegance of his form; the stateliness of his tread; the spirit of all his motions; and the glossiness of his coat. We admire him also in *representation*. But as an object of Picturesque beauty, we admire more the worn out cart-horse, the cow, the goat, or the ass.[54]

Today, free from the preconceptions of ideals, order, and regulation that persisted even in *Collage City*, and motivated to respond tactically to a multitude of affordances, contemporary Picturesque practices probe the question of what result this function-oriented reaching out and drawing in might have. Certainly, in the Picturesque tradition, the results must be more like pack-donkeys, cart-horses, and other working animals that *do* more than just please the eye, and look like it too.

Notes

1 This definition was popularized by John Summerson in his 1957 lecture to the RIBA. John Summerson, "The Case for a Theory of Modern Architecture," *Journal of the Royal Institute of British Architects*, 64, ser. 3 (June 1957), 307–314.

2 Many excellent histories of the Picturesque movement and its resurgences exist. For a more complete synopsis of the Picturesque, see John Macarthur, *The Picturesque: Architecture, Disgust and Other Irregularities* (New York; London: Routledge, 2007).
3 William Temple, *Miscellanea, the Second Part . . . II. Upon the Gardens of Epicurious* (London: printed by T.M. for Ri. and Ra. Simpson, 1690).
4 Nikolaus Pevsner, *Visual Planning and the Picturesque*, ed. Mathew Aitchison (Los Angeles: Getty Publications, 2010), 112–113.
5 Chiswick, by William Kent, 1715, and Twickenham, by Alexander Pope, 1719, are two early, if tentative, examples.
6 Writers and theorists, including William Gilpin, William Hogarth, and Edmund Burke, began to write on topics of Picturesque aesthetics, beauty, and the sublime. Burke's widely accepted, *A Philosophical Enquiry into the Origin of Our Ideas of the Sublime and Beautiful* (1756), was a cornerstone of the discourse on aesthetics, perception, and sensation.
7 In particular, see Sir Uvedale Price's *An Essay on the Picturesque* (London: printed for J. Mawman, 1810), Richard Payne Knight's *The Landscape: A Didactic Poem* (London: Bulmer, 1795), and Humphry Repton's *Sketches and Hints on Landscape Gardening* (London: Bulmer, 1794).
8 Price borrows Gilpin's examples of the goat and ass, to which he adds the examples of gypsies and beggars, and a "building with scaffolding." Sir Uvedale Price, *An Essay on the Picturesque, as Compared with the Sublime and the Beautiful: And, on the Use of Studying Pictures, for the Purpose of Improving Real Landscape*, 3 vols (London: printed for J. Mawman, 1810), 1, 115.
9 Price, *An Essay on the Picturesque*, 1, 188.
10 Ibid., 1, 203.
11 Ibid., 2, 131.
12 Ivor de Wolfe (Hubert de Cronin Hastings), writing as The Editor, "Exterior Furnishing or Sharawaggi: The Art of Making Urban Landscape," *Architectural Review*, 95 (1944), 5.
13 Joshua Reynolds, *The Works of Sir Joshua Reynolds, To Which Is Prefixed an Account of the Life and Writings of the Author*, by Edmond Malone, 4th ed. (London: T. Cadell & W. Davies, 1809), 2, 134–135.
14 Pevsner, *Visual Planning and the Picturesque*, 139.
15 William Gilpin, *Three Essays: On Picturesque Beauty: On Picturesque Travel: And on Sketching Landscape: To which is added a Poem on Landscape Painting* (London: R. Blamire, 1792), 7.
16 Pevsner, *Visual Planning and the Picturesque*, 141.
17 Nikolaus Pevsner is perhaps one of the most recognizable figures in the discourse on the history of architecture—most specifically, Modern Architecture. His *Pioneers of the Modern Movement*, later retitled *Pioneers of Modern Design*, remains a reference when current questions around the emergence and parameters of Modernism in architecture arise. Nikolaus Pevsner, *Pioneers of Modern Design* (originally published as *Pioneers of the Modern Movement*, 1936, 2nd ed., New York: Museum of Modern Art, 1949; revised and partly rewritten, Penguin Books, 1960).
18 Pevsner, *Visual Planning and the Picturesque*, 20.
19 Identified by Mathew Aitchison, in John Macarthur, *The Picturesque*, 198.
20 Ivor de Wolfe, "Exterior Furnishing or Sharawaggi," 3–8; "Townscape: A Plea for an English Visual Philosophy Founded on the True Rock of Sir Uvedale Price," *Architectural Review*, 106 (1949), 354–362; as well as Gordon Cullen's various *Townscape* publications.
21 Nikolaus Pevsner, "Twentieth Century Picturesque," *Architectural Review*, 115, 688 (1954), 228–229.
22 Pevsner, *Visual Planning and the Picturesque*, 19.

23 Ibid. In his introduction to *Visual Planning*, Macarthur differentiates Ivor de Wolfe's townscape from Picturesque proper as a movement because townscape was "modeled on collage and not the unity of the subject that was the basis of eighteenth-century painting composition." The difference, he claims, lies in the original's harmonizing of a scene through elimination of discordant elements (as with the boundary in the haha wall) versus the production of unity through the incongruous relationship of different styles and periods in one scene.
24 Colin Rowe and Fred Koetter, *Collage City* (Cambridge, MA: MIT Press, 1978), 179.
25 John Macarthur and Mathew Aitchison, "Pevsner's Townscape," in Pevsner, *Visual Planning and the Picturesque*, 30.
26 Ibid.
27 Reyner Banham, "De Wolfe the Author?," letter to the editor, *Architectural Review*, 158 (1975), 322.
28 Pevsner, "Twentieth Century Picturesque."
29 Francis Bacon, *The Essays; or, Councels, Civil and Moral, and the Wisdom of the Ancients* (Boston, MA: Little, Brown, 1856), 207. Emphasis added.
30 Charles L. Eastlake, *A History of the Gothic Revival* (London: Longmans, Green, 1872), 143.
31 Pevsner, *Visual Planning and the Picturesque*, 24.
32 Pevsner, "Twentieth Century Picturesque."
33 Pevsner, *Visual Planning and the Picturesque*, 168.
34 Adrian Forty, *Words and Buildings: A Vocabulary of Modern Architecture* (New York: Thames & Hudson, 2000), 177.
35 Leopold Eidlitz, *The Nature and Function of Art, More Especially of Architecture* (London: Sampson Low, 1881), 223–224.
36 Forty, *Words and Buildings*, 179.
37 James J. Gibson, *The Ecological Approach to Visual Perception* (Hillsdale, NJ: Lawrence Erlbaum Assoc., 1986), 129.
38 Ibid., 140.
39 Kurt Koffka, *The Growth of the Mind* (New York; London: Routledge & Kegan Paul, 1928), 320.
40 Jakob von Uexküll, *A Foray into the Worlds of Animals and Humans*, trans. Joseph D. O'Neill (Minneapolis, MN: University of Minnesota Press, 2010), 151.
41 Since Vitruvius (see Introduction to this volume: "Bubbles Burst"). Le Corbusier too considers the architect a "creator of organisms." Le Corbusier, *Toward a New Architecture* (1927), trans. Frederick Etchells (New York: Holt, Rinehart and Winston, 1986), 103.
42 Humphry Repton, *The Landscape Gardening and Landscape Architecture of the Late Humphry Repton Esq.*, ed. John Cladius Loudon (London, 1840), 501–502.
43 Macarthur, *The Picturesque*, 129.
44 Ibid., 146.
45 Price, *An Essay on the Picturesque*, 2, 268–269.
46 Macarthur, *The Picturesque*, 157, 111. This comment comes from Macarthur's reading of Yve-Alain Bois's study of Richard Serra's work in his essay "A Picturesque Stroll around Clara-Clara," *October Files: Richard Serra*, ed. Hal Foster with Gordon Hughes (Cambridge, MA: MIT Press, 2000). In most general terms, Macarthur defines weak form as a building that effectively lacks an overall identifiable figure or gestalt and his analysis finds a direct correlation between weakened form and heightened phenomenal experience. This definition of weak form overlaps partially with Peter Eisenman's weak form, as "arbitrary, undecidable, excessive," but differs where Eisenman defines it as having "no strong relationship to narrative space or time." For more elaboration

on the concept of weak form, see Peter Eisenman, "Strong Form, Weak Form," in *Re:Working Eisenman* (London: Academy Editions, 1993).

47 Peter Reyner Banham, "The New Brutalism," *Architectural Review*, 118 (1955), 13.

48 Macarthur, *The Picturesque*, 106.

49 Banham, "The New Brutalism," 15. Banham defined New Brutalism as having three characteristics: memorability as an image; clear exhibition of structure; valuation of materials as found.

50 Yoshiharu Tsukamoto and Moyomo Kaijima (Atelier Bow-Wow) *Behaviorology* (New York: Rizzoli, 2010), 15.

51 Humphry Repton coined the term "appropriation" to describe this technique as applied to landscape. Where Repton's idea of appropriation is concerned with ownership and domination over the land, our alternative interpretation of the term might allow us to think of the drawing in of specific affording aspects of the world into the architecture.

52 Sabine Müller and Andreas Quednau, *City Boids—Molecular Urbanism*, Office Pamphlet (SMAQ, Berlin, 2004).

53 Stephen Jay Gould, *The Structure of Evolutionary Theory* (Cambridge, MA: The Belknap Press of Harvard University, 2002), 1232. Gould gives the examples of feathers, which, although now thought to assist in flight, may originally have served the function of thermoregulation; or the wings of a heron, which may have evolved for flight but which also function as a shading device to better see fish in the water. Function, Gould believes, evolves too. What he calls the "quirky functional shift" (p. 1224) is the tendency for unpredictable and recurrent change in the functional context that allows redundancies in evolved features to be used in new ways. Gould in fact uses architecture's enabling of changing program (from church to soup kitchen on his street) as a metaphor for the suppleness of the organism's own ability to reuse parts that were developed 'for' one function for another.

54 Gilpin, *Three Essays*, 13–14.

5

THE DONKEY'S WAY

Alternate Paths for Le Corbusier's *Plan Voisin*

The Pack-Donkey

Le Corbusier begins his 1929 publication, *The City of To-morrow and its Planning*, with a metaphorical comparison: between Man, who walks in a straight line, because he is goal-oriented and "governs his feelings by reason," and the pack-donkey, who instead meanders along, and who "mediates a little in his scatter-brained and distracted fashion . . . zig-zags in order to avoid the larger stones, or to ease the climb, or to gain a little shade . . . takes the line of least resistance."[1] The donkey's winding path, an analogy for the existing continental city, is derided as "the result of happy-go-lucky heedlessness, of looseness, lack of concentration and animality," in contrast to the ordered city of the straight line and the right-angle, which is "a reaction, an action, a positive deed, the result of self-mastery. It is sane and noble."[2]

This asinine comparison forms the basis of Le Corbusier's argument for the strict geometries of his *Ville Contemporaine (Contemporary City for Three Million Inhabitants)* and its subsequent implementation proposal in the *Plan Voisin*. Following man's path, the *Ville Contemporaine*, originally shown in November 1922 at the Salon d'Automne in Paris, is a hypothetical study, a "laboratory experiment," in which all special cases or accidents have been avoided, and an ideal flat and unoccupied site has been assumed.[3] The well-known plan shows a centralized grid-iron city which transitions from residential courtyard typologies at the edge to commercial cruciform tower typologies toward the center.

It is these cruciform towers at the center of the plan that dominate the eye-level perspectives and perhaps best demonstrate the intentions of this densified, yet decongested and green city. Le Corbusier describes the viewing of the towers as a sublime experience. He writes, "their outlines softened by distance, the skyscrapers raise immense geometrical façades all of glass, and in them is reflected the blue glory of the sky. An overwhelming sensation. Immense but radiant prisms."[4]

The *Ville Contemporaine* is a manifesto against the existing continental city, whose twists and turns stifle the air, the health, and the efficiency of the city. Yet beyond

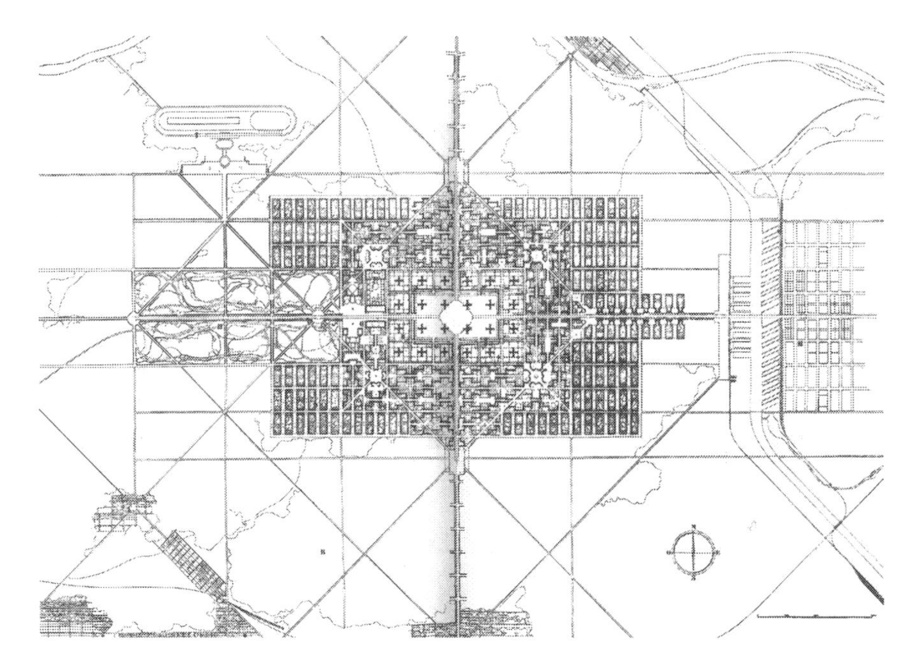

FIGURE 5.1 Le Corbusier, *Ville Contemporaine*: "The heavy black lines represent the areas built upon. Everything else is either streets or open spaces. Strictly speaking the city is an immense park. Its lay-out furnishes a multitude of architectural aspects of infinitely varying forms. If the reader, for instance, follows out a given route on this map he will be astonished by the variety he encounters. Yet distances are shorter than in the cities of to-day, for there is a greater density of population." Le Corbusier, *The City of To-morrow* (New York: Dover Publications, 1987, pp. 180–181), © F.L.C./ADAGP, Paris/Artists Rights Society (ARS), New York, 2014.

social or environmental concerns, the densification of the *Ville Contemporaine* into a series of repeatable vertical elements is fundamental to the intellectual and conceptual life of the new city. Le Corbusier explains: "The result of a true geometrical layout is *repetition*. The result of repetition is a *standard*, the perfect form (i.e. the creation of standard types). A geometrical layout means that mathematics play their part . . . It is the very essence of architecture."[5]

Order in the urban realm is advocated as a sign of the human being's transcendence of animality and nature, toward the abstract and ideal. Le Corbusier argues that although those elements that come into contact with the body are organic (and, presumably then, reactive to the form of the body), the ideal state of order occurs at a greater scale, more distant from the body:

> The further human creations are removed from our immediate grasp, the more they tend to pure geometry; a violin, a chair, things which come into close contact with the body, are of a less pure geometry; but a town is pure geometry. When man is free, his tendency is towards pure geometry. It is then that he achieves what we call order.[6]

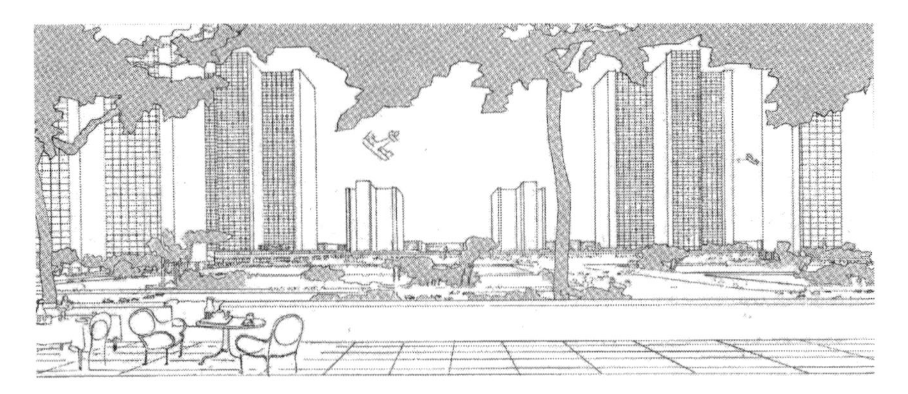

FIGURE 5.2 Le Corbusier, *Ville Contemporaine*: "The center of the city seen from one of the terraced cafés surrounding the Great Central Station square" (Le Corbusier, *Oeuvre complète*, vol. 1, p. 134). © F.L.C./ADAGP, Paris/ Artists Rights Society (ARS), New York, 2014.

In contrast, the "donkey's way"—the approach which is, by definition, reactive to its context, negotiating a responsive path—results in "erratic: lopsided abortions."[7]

Catherine Ingraham's "The Burdens of Linearity: Donkey Urbanism" notes that the donkey here is representive of "disorderly nature, of the chaotic and diseased body, of a barbaric architectural and urban past"[8] and that the opposition set up by Le Corbusier represents more than just a struggle between two geometrical or aesthetic possibilities, but becomes an argument for the separation of culture and nature. Ingraham explains:

> Orthogonality is Le Corbusier's theory about how to win architecture and the city away from the irrational forces arrayed within them. It extends beyond the (merely) rectilinear to any form that is erected against the monstrous, speechless, wandering, pathless incoherence of the genealogical "line" itself—the (chaotic) history of the city and architecture. Orthogonality keeps culture hegemonically superior to nature and attempts to obliterate the trace of nature in culture.[9]

The collision between nature and culture is foregrounded when Le Corbusier's *Ville Contemporaine* is given a real site. The *Plan Voisin* of Paris, shown in the Pavilion of the Esprit Nouveau at the Exhibition of Decorative Art Paris (1925) is the proposed implementation of this hypothetical plan into the existing fabric of Paris. The aggressive proposal is presented as "a frontal attack on the most diseased quarters of the city."[10] Like its predecessor, *Voisin* establishes a grid system, repeating every 350–400 yards, and punctuated by huge glass cruciform skyscrapers, liberating 95 percent of the ground and creating a vertical city abundant with light and air. Adjustments are made in the transition from the hypothetical to the real: the longitudinal streets of *Voisin* are skewed to align with the existing axis of the river and Rue de Rivoli, while the transverse streets retain their north–south orientation, creating parallelogram-shaped islands. The overall border is cropped so that the figure of the new city is an irregular cut-out in the fabric, rather than the perfect rectangle of *Contemporaine*. Perhaps the most enduring image of *Voisin* is the juxtaposition of the existing and the proposed plans, which demonstrates the violence with which it cuts through and erases the existing fabric with a seeming disregard for the existing architecture, culture, and urban condition. His confidence in the proposal's aggressive approach is clear in much of Le Corbusier's argumentation, for example, when he writes:

> Imagine all this junk, which till now has lain spread out over the soil like a dry crust, cleaned off and carted away, and replaced by immense clear crystals of glass, rising to a height of over 600 feet; each at a good distance from the next and all standing with their bases set among trees.[11]

Detour: The Grid

Such abrupt and totalitarian erasure is, perhaps, an inevitable consequence of the grid. Used as a standard for city planning for millennia, the grid has long provided

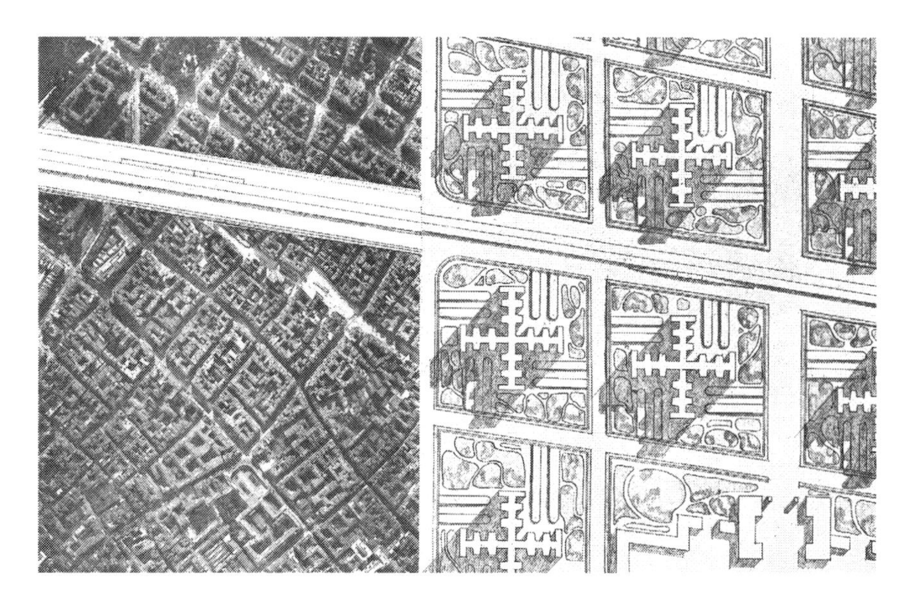

FIGURE 5.3 Le Corbusier, *Plan Voisin*: "Here is the solution proposed by the 'Voisin' Scheme. Here are the districts which it is proposed to demolish and those which it is suggested should be built in their place. Both plans are to the same scale." Le Corbusier, *City of To-morrow* (p. 289), © F.L.C./ADAGP, Paris/Artists Rights Society (ARS), New York, 2014.

a simple and repeatable strategy for equal distribution and accessibility of land. The Commissioners Plan of Manhattan of 1811, for example, claimed to "unite regularity and order with the public convenience and benefit and in particular to promote the health of the City."[12] Whether maligned for its "relentless monotony,"[13] or celebrated for its "undreamed-of freedom for three-dimensional anarchy,"[14] the grid is conceptually one of endless expansion with repetition, ignoring all accidents and discontinuities. The original version of the Commissioners Plan of Manhattan of 1811 shows exactly such a relentless grid, canceled upon the encounter of an edge or a river, but never bent or stretched.

However, there are instances in which the final realization of that grid *is* overwhelmed by an obstacle and, like the donkey, forced to deviate from the straight route due to, sometimes literally, a rock in its path. At certain moments in Manhattan's fabric, the rigid grid fails to resist the power of the landscape. Saint Nicholas and Morningside Parks, for example, sited in the steep and uneven topography of Harlem, demonstrate such instances of nature superseding the grid. In each case, a massive rock outcropping is impassable and the grid is forced to

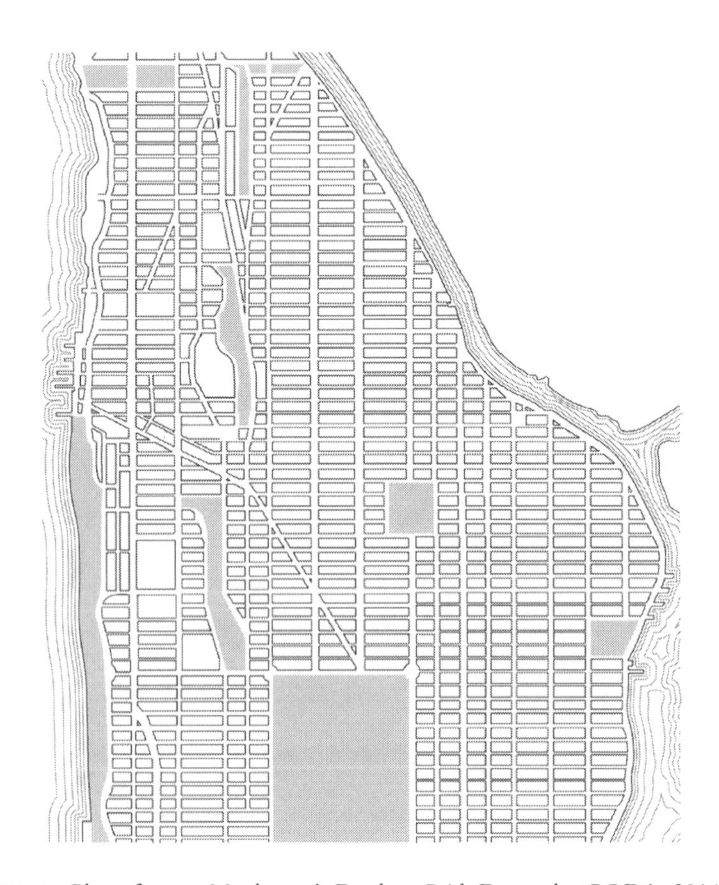

FIGURE 5.4 Plan of upper Manhattan's Donkey Grid. Drawn by CODA, 2014.

FIGURE 5.5 The Rock at St Nicholas Park. Courtesy of Friends of St Nicholas Park.

meander around its organic boundary. The existing and unmovable resists the linearity of Man's way and forces him, momentarily, to take the 'donkey's way.'

Resistances

While the *Plan Voisin* seems to march relentlessly across the existing flat site, demolishing everything in its path, a few flecks of resistance are visible in Le Corbusier's drawing: 18 in total,[15] which, like Manhattan's great rocks, are capable of resisting the power of the grid and so remain as fragments of resistance in the otherwise pure plan.

Why does Le Corbusier allow these fragments to remain in the plan? Returning to the *The City of To-morrow and its Planning*, we find a justification tucked away in the final chapter, called: "The 'Voisin' Scheme and the Past," in which Le Corbusier raises the issue of preservation and proposes that certain fragments of our common inheritance are to be "rescued." While admitting a tendency for nostalgia, the strategy is one of isolation, recontextualization, and reprogramming of significant historical buildings:

> Thus one might find, surrounded by green grass, an exciting and delightful relic such as, say, some fine Renaissance house, now to be used as a library, lecture hall, or whatnot . . . They would stand surrounded by Verdure: what could be more charming![16]

Le Corbusier argues that, even with these disorderly fragments, the scheme maintains the overriding aspiration for order, since the old is now bracketed within the

1. Église Saint Laurent
2. Église Saint Élisabeth
3. Archives Nationales
4. Notre Dame des Blancs Manteaux
5. Musée des Arts et Métiers
6. Église Saint Nicholas des Champs
7. Église Saint Merri
8. Église Saint Eustache
9. Palais Brongniart
10. Basilique Notre-Dame-des-Victoires
11. Palais Royal
12. Église Saint-Roch
13. Opéra de Paris
14. Place Vendôme
15. Église Saint-Louis-d'Antin
16. Église de la Madeleine
17. Église Saint-Augustin
18. Palais de l'Élysée

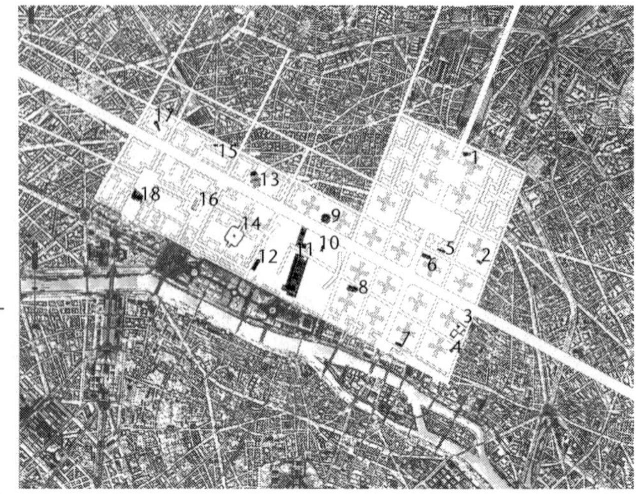

FIGURE 5.6 Redrawn after Le Corbusier's *Plan Voisin* on pp. 274–275, *The City of To-morrow and its Planning*. Image by CODA, 2012. Google Earth, © Landsat, 2007. Original image © F.L.C./ADAGP, Paris/Artists Rights Society (ARS), New York, 2014.

amorphous form of the park-scape. These proposals, seemingly in contradiction to earlier statements of intent in which "we are to forgo, or relegate to a minor place, pleasure arising out of picturesqueness or of what is merely pretty or willful, and to confine ourselves to sterner delights which severe and pure form can give us,"[17] and the more aggressive statement that "by this immense step in evolution, so brutal and so overwhelming, we burn our bridges and break with the past,"[18] provoke questions around Le Corbusier's incentives for such contradictions.

A more cynical motivation for this rescue mission has been suggested: Le Corbusier needed a phoenix symbol, and "in his concern to illustrate a new world rising above the ashes of the old, one may detect a reason for his highly perfunctory approach to major monuments—only to be inspected after cultural inoculation."[19] Considered in this way, the historic buildings become relics against which the new can be measured. Overlaying a certain language over another had already been a trope in Le Corbusier's architectural-scale work in which the curvilinear form is read against (but never without) the grid.[20]

However, Le Corbusier appears ambivalent as to whether or not these historic fragments are indeed present in the design. His text is both reverent and dismissive, both at the abstract scale (the soul vs. the mechanism) and specifically in relation to the relic.[21] While they appear very roughly in his preliminary plan, and blurrily in some aerial views, the architect does not present any line-drawing perspectives for this project as he does for the *Ville Contemporaine*. As such, the only eye-level perspectives that endure in the memory are the sanitized and empty views of that earlier prototype. Because matching perspectives were never produced for the *Plan Voisin*, it has not been possible to gauge the effect of the fragments within the city and, consequently, the impact of these fragments has been largely glossed over.

If we are to take seriously their presence, then we will first need to reimagine the missing perspectives. These images show the arresting and incongruous consequences of the fragments within the ordered city that stand in complete contrast to the stated ambitions of the project and begin to surreptitiously introduce the *Donkey's* obstacles into the project.

These images show a provocative tension that is set up at eye level between the historic dwarves and the modern giants. Not only in terms of scale, but in terms of material, ornamentation, orientation, and so on—the two object types could not be more opposed. Nevertheless, as part of the green system, the fragments fit into Le Corbusier's rules since donkey-behavior is both permitted and encouraged in the green space.

However, since the fragments pre-date the new system, there is every chance that they do not fit neatly into the parallelograms of verdure, but intersect, in fact, the infrastructural lines or the architectural pieces themselves. This logic begs the inevitable question of intersecting systems: but first, another detour is in order, as is the donkey's wont, into a second, less obvious, set of obstacles.

Detour: Invisible Forces

In the translation from the hypotheticality of *Contemporaine* to the reality of *Voisin*, there are other contextual pressures that go beyond the visible. The sun, for example, much discussed by Le Corbusier in his study of the solar day[22] and as an inevitable component of the lightness and airiness of the new living and working conditions, is now possessed with specific altitude and azimuth data. The environmental condition of the fully glazed wing on the north arm of the cruciform is extremely different from its south-oriented counterpart. Such data might cause the wings and their crenellations to deform, while the ground cover to the north of the towers may assume a function and form more accepting of its shadowy situation.

Although the forms remain unchanged in *Voisin*, the discrepancy did not go unnoticed by the architect: in 1933, he annotates an axonometric drawing of the *Plan Voisin* (drawn eight years earlier), describing the cruciform towers as "radiating light" but adding a crucial—and ambitious—note: "Later corrections will be introduced (in Antwerp) . . . henceforth *all* sides of the skyscraper will receive the sun."[23]

Indeed, in Antwerp, we see the early signs of deformation in the cruciform towers, now three-pronged space-invader shapes, symmetrical only along one axis, with an open south façade and a shriveled north-wing.[24] In a later description of this *Grate-Ciel Cartésien* (1938), Le Corbusier claims that this form was generated as part of the *Ville Contemporaine* project. However, since this form does not appear in the *Contemporaine* plan, it must be assumed that Le Corbusier is here implying

FIGURE 5.7 The reproduced view of "the center of the city seen from one of the terraced cafés surrounding the Great Central Station square" (Le Corbusier, *The City of To-morrow*, p. 246), now located at the Palais Royal, includes the *Basilique Notre-Dame-des-Victoires* (left) and *Église Saint Eustache* (right). CODA, 2012. Original image © F.L.C./ADAGP, Paris/Artists Rights Society (ARS), New York, 2014.

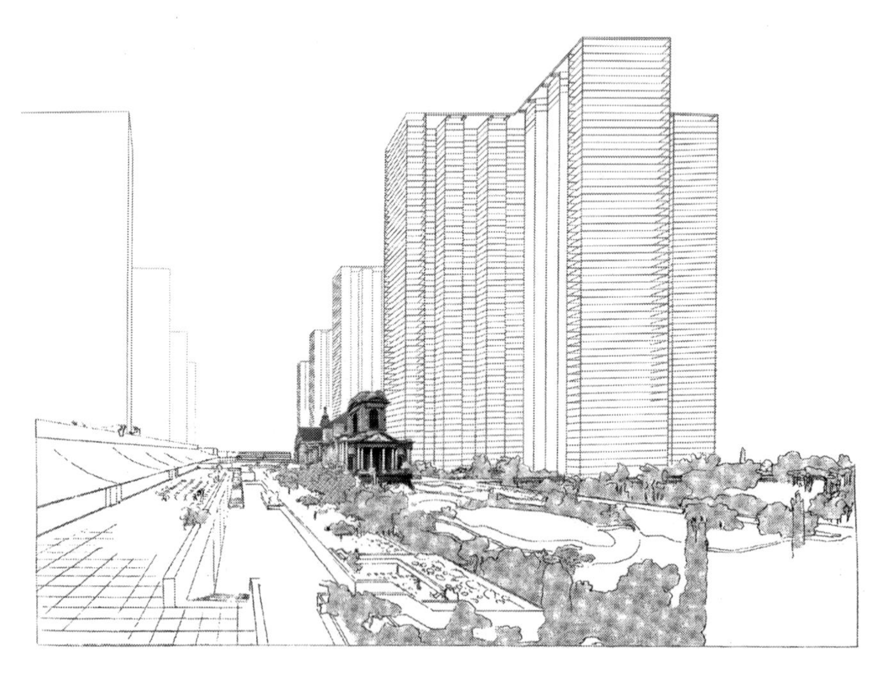

FIGURE 5.8 The reproduced view of "the center of the city seen from one of the terraced cafés surrounding the Great Central Station square" (Le Corbusier, *The City of To-morrow*, p. 245); the view of "the parks at the base of the skyscrapers" includes the *Église Saint Eustache*. CODA, 2012. Original image © F.L.C./ADAGP, Paris/Artists Rights Society (ARS), New York, 2014.

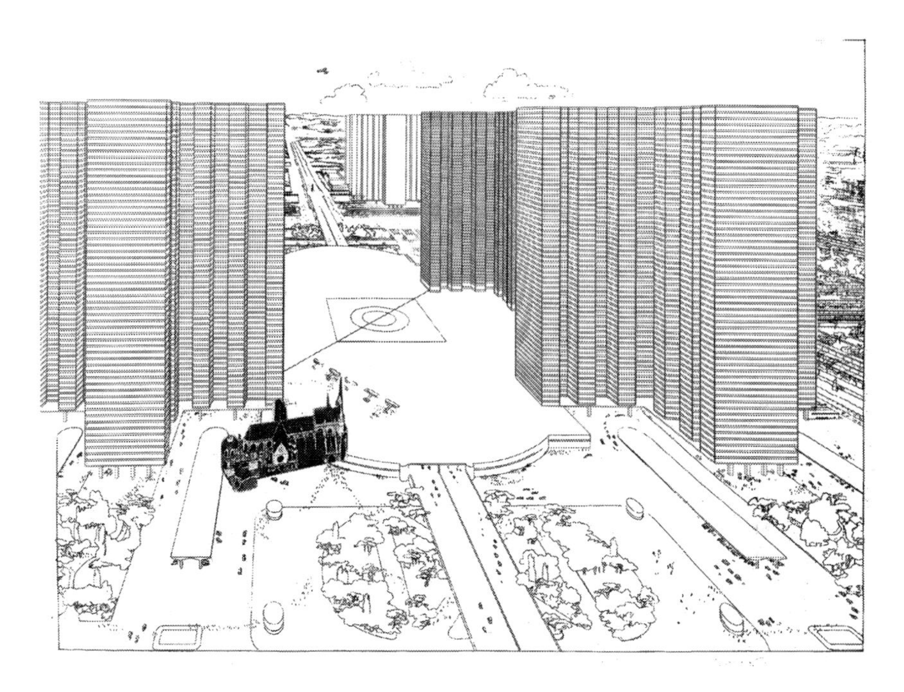

FIGURE 5.9 The city seen from one of the main tracks for fast motor traffic (Le Corbusier, *The City of To-morrow*, p. 243) includes *Église Saint Laurent*. CODA, 2012. Original Image © F.L.C./ADAGP, Paris/Artists Rights Society (ARS), New York, 2014.

FIGURE 5.10 Aerial view of Le Corbusier's scheme for Antwerp, 1933 (note the existing cathedral collaged into rendering) (Le Corbusier, *Oeuvre complète*, vol. 2, p. 159). © F.L.C./ADAGP, Paris/Artists Rights Society (ARS), New York, 2014.

FIGURE 5.11 Le Corbusier, *Grate-Ciel Cartésien*, 1938 (Le Corbusier, *Oeuvre complète*, vol. 3, p. 77). © F.L.C./ADAGP, Paris/Artists Rights Society (ARS), New York, 2014.

that the form was born *as an idea*, which at that time took the cruciform shape and only later mutated into the space-invader *Grate-Ciel Cartésien* shape.

This mutated and evolved form reappears in many projects[25] but, crucially, when the opportunity arises for a reconsideration of the *Plan Voisin* in 1937, the original cruciform towers are finally deformed into the *Grate-Ciel Cartésien* shape.

In this and in the final 1946 plan for Paris, the fragments are completely removed from the plan and, although they remain in some aerial perspectives, they are distant from the objects of Le Corbusier's design and less likely than ever to cause a reaction than previously.

Admission

Ten years after the initial proposal, Le Corbusier's work on "The Radiant City" forces a dramatic admission of wrong-doing:

> This takes me back to 1922 and the state of mind I was in while I was designing a *contemporary city for 3 million people*. My analyses, my calculations, and a powerful intuition convinced me that I must set up a new scale for the city . . . But how disturbed I was by the results! What anguished weeks I

FIGURE 5.12 Le Corbusier, Vision for Paris, 1937 (Le Corbusier, *Oeuvre complète*, vol. 4, p. 47). © F.L.C./ADAGP, Paris/Artists Rights Society (ARS), New York, 2014.

> lived through! . . . I was tortured by the thought that the great empty spaces of this imaginary city, everywhere dominated by the sky, would be so dead, so dull, that its inhabitants would be panic-stricken.[26]

The outcome of this remorse was (mis)guided into social and programmatic reform. Le Corbusier ruminated on solutions:

> What if I can manage to fill my modern man's 24-hour day completely; what if, moreover, I can manage to make his life more comfortable; what if, better yet, I can contrive to make him a gift of personal liberty within his collective organization.

His proposal, in *Ville Radieuse*, was to replace the towers with horizontal slabs that would float above the ground and allow a closer connection between inhabitant and nature in the city. Unfortunately, the raising of the buildings on pilotis served only to exacerbate the problem of connectivity with the ground, and certainly did not improve the enduring issue of dullness. And in demanding a "clean tablecloth" as a site,[27] the architect did not allow himself the opportunity to encounter the

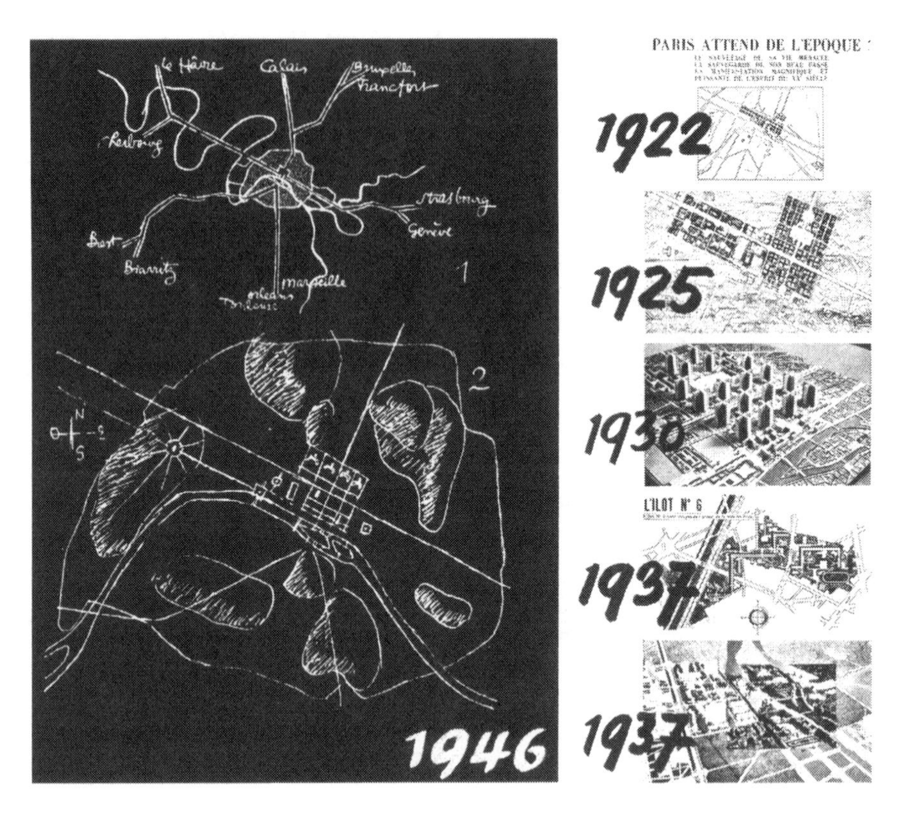

FIGURE 5.13 Le Corbusier, compilation of the various plans for Paris (Le Corbusier, *Oeuvre complète*, vol. 4, p. 144). © F.L.C./ADAGP, Paris/Artists Rights Society (ARS), New York, 2014.

contingencies that were right under his nose; contingencies that might have forced him into taking the donkey's path.[28]

Among many other condemnations, Le Corbusier's urban proposals have been criticized because they favor a model that responds to "the idea of a reconstructed society . . . largely unconcerned with local spatial minutiae," celebrating "generalities" rather than "specifics."[29] Returning to the original 1922 *Plan Voisin*: if each block were to be concerned with the spatial minutiae, we would notice that the fragments do not *only* fall fortuitously into the parklands of the plan. Indeed, there are many instances where rescue-worthy historic fragments fall *within* the footprints of the blocks themselves. Although many were rescued, many of the more inconvenient fragments were overlooked in Le Corbusier's plan, regardless of historic value. A new plan drawing, then, shows the possible locations of fragments that might have been included in the *Plan Voisin* had their value (and locations) been prioritized. Included here (and not in the original) are, for example, the Église Notre-Dame de Bonne Nouvelle,

1. Église Saint Laurent
2. Église Saint Élisabeth
3. Archives Nationales
4. Notre Dame des Blancs Manteaux
5. Musée des Arts et Métiers
6. Église Saint Nicholas des Champs
7. Église Saint Merri
8. Église Saint Eustache
9. Palais Brongniart
10. Basilique Notre-Dame-des-Victoires
11. Palais Royal
12. Église Saint-Roch
13. Opéra de Paris
14. Place Vendôme
15. Église Saint-Louis-d'Antin
16. Église de la Madeleine
17. Église Saint-Augustin
18. Palais de l'Élysée
19. Saint-Martin des Champs
20. Synagogue de Nazareth
21. Cloître et église des Billettes
22. Église Notre-Dame de Bonne Nouvelle
23. Église Saint-Leu-Saint-Gilles
24. Bourse de commerce de Paris
25. Eglise Réformée de l'Oratoire du Louvre
26. Église Notre-Dame-de-l'Assomption

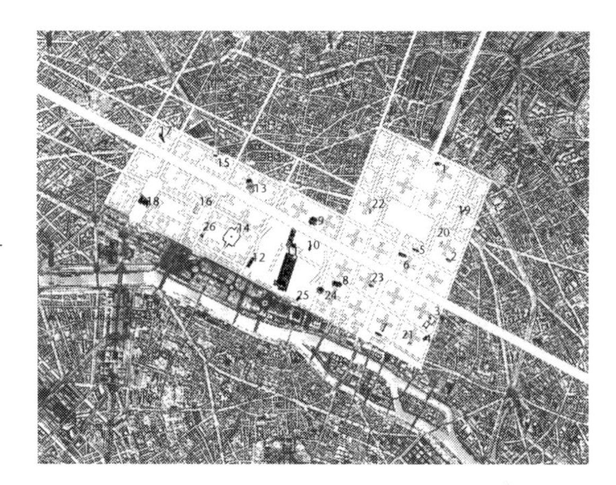

FIGURE 5.14 Le Corbusier, chosen fragments *and* the ignored fragments. Redrawn after Le Corbusier's Plan on pp. 274–275, *The City of To-morrow and its Planning*, but including eight additional 'missing' monuments that do not fit so comfortably into the project's boundaries. Image by CODA, 2012. Google Earth, © Landsat, 2007. Original image © F.L.C./ ADAGP, Paris/Artists Rights Society (ARS), New York, 2014.

Saint-Martin des Champs, the Synagogue de Nazareth, and numerous other historic buildings.

Were Le Corbusier to truly embrace his declaration of preservation, each tower, which we have now seen to contain a certain amount of mutational potential, would need to shift, adjust, and negotiate with its ground. By embracing the inevitable "animality" and "lopsided abortions"[30] that the incongruous presence of the fragment-intersecting-tower produces, the cruciform would need to deform to produce arches, bridges, and pockets that would give space to the existing monuments. In doing so, perhaps, these accidental collisions could create the sought-after difference within the monotony of the block.

Regardless of his subsequent work, which did take on a plasticity that overrode the grid, the *Voisin* proposal was to have an overwhelming effect on the production of architecture in the years to come. Had he respected the 'donkey's way' as a viable model of intelligent negotiation that creates difference through relationship, the effect on the city after Le Corbusier may have been radically different.

FIGURE 5.15 Intersection of cruciform tower and *Église Saint-Leu-Saint-Gilles*. CODA, 2012. Original image © F.L.C./ADAGP, Paris/Artists Rights Society (ARS), New York, 2014.

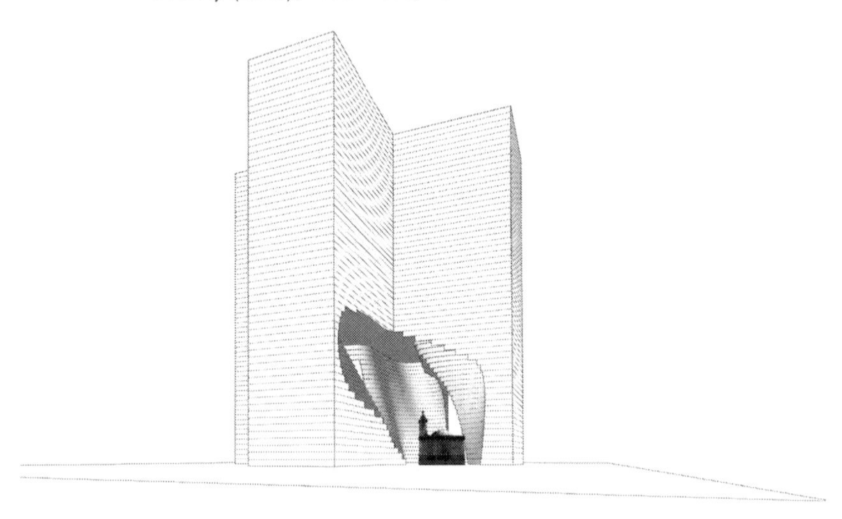

FIGURE 5.16 Intersection of cruciform tower and *Église Notre-Dame de Bonne Nouvelle*. CODA, 2012.

Notes

A note on the images: these images are to be understood as a provocation. Such donkey responses might occur at many levels and in many ways. The above examples show deformations of the towers but the urban plan itself is not deformed. This became the focus of this study since many of the new fragments intersected with the built forms, but should other fragments be considered, deviations in the street plan may add a second layer of deformation. Likewise, the interiors of the towers themselves are not considered here, but such violent cuts in the façade might suggest deformations at the level of the architectural plan.

1 Le Corbusier, *The City of To-morrow and its Planning*, trans. Frederick Etchells (New York: Dover Publications, 1987), 6.
2 Ibid., 12.
3 Ibid., 154.
4 Ibid., 178.
5 Ibid., 175.
6 Ibid., 22.
7 Ibid., 176.
8 Catherine Ingraham, "The Burdens of Linearity: Donkey Urbanism," in *Architecture and the Burdens of Linearity* (New Haven, CT: Yale University Press, 1998), 67.
9 Ibid., 68–69.
10 Le Corbusier, *The City of To-morrow and its Planning*, 280.
11 Ibid., 281.
12 Edwin G. Burrows and Mike Wallace, *Gotham: A History of New York City to 1898* (New York: Oxford University Press, 1999), 419–422.
13 Alexis de Toqueville, quoted in Sam Roberts, "200th Birthday for the Map That Made New York," *New York Times* (May 20, 2011). Sourced March 15, 2014.
14 Rem Koolhaas, quoted in Roberts, "200th Birthday for the Map That Made New York."
15 This number is an approximation due to the roughness of Le Corbusier's plan. There are 18 'flecks' in the plan that can be identified as notable buildings and monuments. However, there are at least eight other 'flecks' that do not have corresponding buildings and, conversely, at least eight buildings of 'historic importance' (mainly churches) that are ignored.
16 Le Corbusier, *The City of To-morrow and its Planning*, 287.
17 Ibid., vii.
18 Ibid., xxv.
19 Colin Rowe and Fred Koetter, *Collage City* (Cambridge, MA: MIT Press, 1978), 72.
20 For example, at *Cook* (1926), *Guiette* (1926), *Garches* (1927), *Savoye* (1929), and *MX* (1929).
21 The chapter "Classification and Choice" contains many contradictions between the soul of the city and the mechanism. Dismissive comments specifically related to the cathedral include: "Here we have the Cathedral, with its pointed forms and jagged outlines, its evident desire for order; but lacking completely that calm and balance which witness to a mature civilization" (p. 32) and " . . . the crocketed spires of the Cathedral reflect the agony of the flesh, the poignant dramas of the spirit, hell and purgatory; and forests of pine seen through pale light and cold mist. Our bodies demand sunshine. There are certain shapes that cast shadows" (p. 62). Le Corbusier, *The City of To-morrow and its Planning*.
22 In *Radiant City*, Le Corbusier brings up the issue of the solar day. He claims that the hours of the day have been misused and proposes that as a result of more proximate work and leisure, transport times can be eliminated leaving four hours of productive work and eleven leisure hours. The effect of the sun on the form of his architecture is not yet taken into account. Le Corbusier, *Quand les cathédrales étaient blanches* (Paris: La Librairie Plon, 1937; reprint 1965), 282.
23 Le Corbusier, *La Ville radieuse Paris: Editions de l'architecture d'aujord'hui*, trans. Pamela Knight, Eleanor Levieux, and Derek Coltman (New York: The Orion Press, 1967), 206.
24 Le Corbusier and Pierre Jeanneret, *Oeuvre complète 1929–1934* (Zurich: Les Editions Architecture, 1946), 283.
25 After Antwerp, this form returns in many projects: *Urbanisation d'Hellencourt* (1935), *Proposition for Manhattan* (1935), *Suburb of Rome* (1934), *Macia Plan for Barcelona* (1932), and of course again in the 1937 *Plan de Paris*.
26 Le Corbusier, *La Ville radieuse Paris*, 105.
27 Ibid., 97.

28 While the tension between the plastic and the orthogonal had long been a trope in his architectural work, Le Corbusier leaned more strongly toward the plastic and amorphous in some later urban plans. Architecturally, the two languages work in relationship with and reactively to one another. The curvilinear forms of the Algiers variations, for example, are justified as being designed "To respond to the landscape's invitation, an event of plastic creativity: response to horizons carries further; response to winds and sun is truer. A lyrical event. Of utmost importance, the climax of a rational procedure" (ibid., 237.) However, that potential reaction between his own forms and the existing forms never appears. Although the plan adjusts significantly through the many variations of the *Obus* project for Algiers, and parts of the city are left intact, especially buildings of significance such as mosques and the Kasbah itself, and although some of the adjustments may be related to the topography, the existing elements and the invisible context of culture, weather, or politics, the forms retain their autonomy and act inevitably as a second layer of the city, a figure that landed from above without adjustment to the existing site below. The curves continue to come from an internal aesthetic and not as a reaction to pre-existing obstacles.
29 Rowe and Koetter, *Collage City*, 72.
30 Le Corbusier, *The City of To-morrow and its Planning*, 176.

6

ALL DRESSED UP AND SOME PLACE TO GO

Modernism's opposition to site-specificity has taken many forms, from Le Corbusier's bubble analogy to Rosalind Krauss's leading question, which muses:

> Why did Le Corbusier lift his Dominos up into their stilt-like pilotis except to indicate that these houses-as-machines-for-living could be deposited *anywhere?* Why did Brancusi extend his formal attention downward to include the bases of his sculptures except to negate the convention of the traditional pedestal's function of tying a particular representation to a specific site, thereby producing a perfectly autonomous plastic body that can be located *anywhere*?[1]

As if to emphasize this opposition to site, Modern Architecture had already been largely redefined in the United States with the all-encompassing epithet: *The International Style*.[2] Originally the title of a book by Henry-Russell Hitchcock and Philip Johnson released on the heels of the *International Exhibition of Modern Architecture* at the Museum of Modern Art in New York City (1932), this dubious designation sought to define a motley collection of work that—despite many variations—had in common, according to its curators, a preference for volume over mass, for regularity over symmetry, and for an expression of function in place of frivolous ornament.[3] Coupled with similar strategies in other powerful institutions,[4] the term 'International Style' became somewhat bound to Modern Architecture. And though the originators were careful to clarify that this term does not imply "international in the sense that the production of one country is just like that of another," but in which "different innovators throughout the world have successfully carried out parallel experiments,"[5] the promise of the mechanical, of mass-production, and of massive urbanization in Western society produced a trend in thought that was globally scaled, preoccupied with the future of urban public life, deeply utopian, and was, by definition, set against the local.

This antagonism between the universal and the local was nothing new: it had been the subject of a series of altercations since the late eighteenth century.[6] At this particular moment, however, intense opposition to the new International Style, in what has been called the "American Regionalist Rebellion," fueled the debate.[7] The first inklings of revolt occurred between 1934 and 1945, a period during which Philip Johnson was temporarily away from his post at the Museum of Modern Art. A wave of regionalism surged up, facilitated in part through exhibitions and publications coming from MoMA's acting head of architecture and design, Elizabeth Mock, and later by Lewis Mumford's pro-regionalist article in the *New Yorker* (1947).[8] Following this publication, Johnson, who had returned to the helm, hurriedly organized a conference to address the question: "What is Happening to Modern Architecture?" Hitchcock and others attacked the regional movement for its backwardness and its so-called "Cottage Style."[9] These anti-historicist and anti-vernacular arguments were reiterated in the many retorts against regionalism throughout the twentieth century. Conversely, the same regionalist defense was repeated, citing Modernism's lack of respect for localized site conditions and insatiable desire to stand out.

Similar sentiments welled up in Italy in the 1950s. Ernesto Rogers, for example, criticized the globalization of style and called for an architecture that considered its environment. "Let us resist," he wrote:

> the affected cosmopolitanism which in the name of a still shallowly felt universal style raises the same architecture in New York, Tokyo, or Rio; identical architecture in both the country and the town. Let us seek rather to blend our works into the *preesistenze ambientali*, both the natural surroundings and those created historically by human genius.[10]

While this definition suggests an equality between the natural and the built, in another text, Rogers is clearer about his pro-historic tendency: "To consider the environment," he clarifies, "means to consider history."[11] This statement is in defense of his regionalist tower, *Torre Velasca* (1950–1958), which, as opposed to the typical Modernist tower, looks to local Milanese history, and in particular to the *Castello Sforzesco* for its aesthetic.[12] Rogers' contemporaries, especially Aldo Rossi and Vittorio Gregotti, reinforced this sentiment throughout the 1960s. Through prolific publications, they propagated the idea that "the task of the architectural project is to reveal, through the transformation of form, the essence of the surrounding context."[13]

In the same spirit, 'contextualism' emerged in opposition to Modernism's persistent disconnection and self-obsession. Stuart Cohen and Steven Hurtt coined the term in 1965 to describe the reactionary design work in Colin Rowe's graduate studio at Cornell University.[14] Like Rogers,[15] Rowe and his students opposed Modernism's utopianism, which, they believed, had "generalized and idealized even the most specific and particular requirements in relation to its millennial fantasies," and which insisted on "cultural, symbolic, and physical detachment from

FIGURE 6.1 Ernesto Rogers, *Torre Velasca*, Milan, 1950–1958; *Castello Sforzesco*, Milan, begun in the 1450s. Photographs by CODA, 2013.

aspects of an existing context."[16] Conversely, then, contextualism would derive form from local contexts and contrast what R.E. Somol called "internationalist utopia of nowhere" with the "contextualist nostalgia for somewhere."[17]

At its best, contextualism was a valiant effort to re-engage with the contingencies of the local—physically, culturally, and psychologically—to produce architecture in harmonious continuity with its surroundings. At its worst, however, despite pleas for pluralism and contrast, contextualism was understood as a conservative architecture of carbon copies; the subservient repetition of the building next door, and "ultimately," as Stuart Cohen laments, "akin to renovations, the successful renovation belying its newness to appear locked into and dependent on its specific physical context seeming to be that which it replaced."[18] In fact, in retrospect, Rowe remarked of contextualism that, "if not conservative, its general tone was radical middle of the road."[19] Even in *Collage City*, little mention of context or contextualism is made. By the 1980s, contextualism had left a bad taste in the mouth of the architectural avant-garde. Mark Wigley describes this moribund trajectory in no uncertain terms: "Contextualism," he laments, "has been used as an excuse for mediocrity, for a dumb servility to the familiar."[20]

To be fair, though, true contextualists had been careful to reject one-to-one readings of existing situations. In a retrospective defense of the movement in 1987, Cohen defines contextualism as "the design of buildings by *selectively* choosing to relate them to their immediate physical context."[21] That is to say: not mimicking but extracting from a context and responding to that extraction. Cohen claims that his main built case studies, Richard Meier's *Twin Parks* and Robert Venturi's *Guild House*, achieve this condition: that they both "successfully complete and replicate aspects of an existing physical context without implying the devaluation of existing social or cultural structures by suggesting the further replacement of buildings that symbolize them."[22] In Venturi's case, this effect is achieved by the continuity of material and window-type present in the existing context, but, at the same time, he writes:

> their effect is uncommon . . . because they are subtly proportioned and unusually big. The change in scale of these almost banal elements contributes to an expression of tension and a quality to these façades, which now read as both conventional and unconventional forms at the same time.[23]

Similarly, Meier's *Twin Parks* employs material continuity and exaggerated windows. In both cases, the projects borrow from their surroundings but retain a strong base in Modernism. It appears, in fact, that the positive tension in the examples is due to the observable presence of both Modern Architecture and existing built context; that there exists simultaneously an irresistible lure to an Internationalist aesthetic and at the same time a clear acquiescence to site materials and symbols. While the Modern tendencies pull the design in one direction, the contextualist forces hold it in place, and demand a certain amount of submission.

This point is reinforced by Cohen's use of Le Corbusier's *Plan Voisin* as an example of contextual design. Cohen writes: "Like the housing in Le Corbusier's Voisin, Meier's buildings are geometrically deformed in response to their context." Originally orthogonal, they both "undergo angular deformation to lock into the existing street pattern . . . suggesting a recognition of one aspect of their physical context."[24] That the simple realignment that occurs in the translation from *Ville Contemporaine* to *Plan Voisin*—a project otherwise, as we have seen, wholly detached from any relationship with site— is enough to be considered contextual, suggests that contextualism may be a wolf in sheep's clothing; that it is simply Modernism dressed in local garb. Stripped of their red-brick coats, the projects can barely conceal their underlying Modernist tendencies.

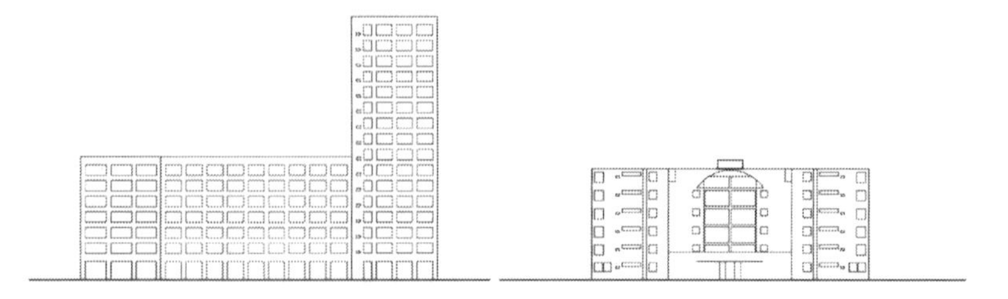

FIGURE 6.2 Richard Meier, *Twin Parks* Northeast Housing, Garden Street, The Bronx, NY, 1970; Robert Venturi, *Guild Hall*, Spring Garden Street, Philadelphia, 1964. Image of façade stripped of materials. Redrawn, CODA, 2012.

Critical Regionalism

With the original regionalism movement accused of blatant retrospection, and contextualism exposed as Modernism in disguise, its successor, *critical regionalism*, remains as perhaps the last possible bastion of resistance and a potential model for contextual thinking today.

Coined by Alex Tzonis and Liane Lefaivre in the early 1980s, critical regionalism aimed to uphold "the individual and local architectonic features against more universal and abstract ones."[25] Whereas contextualism respected the existing fabric, critical regionalism favored the vernacular, the cultural, and the traditional, even if it was, at times, dissociated from its immediate context. Tzonis and Lefaivre's addition of the word 'critical' to the older resistance movement of regionalism demonstrated a rejection of the potential oversimplification that was implied in regionalism: attempting to "pre-empt any imputation of regressive nostalgia."[26] It would appear, at first, that in *critical* regionalism, historicism and mimicry were rejected.[27]

However, Lewis Mumford, called—by Tzonis and Lefaivre—the "original critical regionalist," does not, in fact, oppose the global. He differentiates himself from those regionalists who believe in folk culture (whether Martin Heiddegger's phenomenological approach or Bernard Rudofsky's *Architecture Without Architects*[28]) by engaging regionalism and Modernism together. Mumford suggests, for example, that:

> it would be useful if we formed the habit of never using the word regional without mentally adding to it the idea of the universal—remembering the constant contact and interchange between the local scene and the wide world that lies beyond it.[29]

Mumford rejected historicism, but ironically, like the contextualists, took on another form of history in Modernism.

At the same time, Modernism was not so purely against the consideration of context. Certainly some of the CIAM figures, such as Josep Sert and Sigfried Giedion, supported respect for context and even Le Corbusier, in the 1930s, started to think of Europe in terms of "separate vernacular regional traditions,"[30] despite his earlier distaste for eclectic regionalism.[31] Mirroring regionalism's adoption of Modernism, Modernism, Colquhoun claims, adopts regionalism back.

Critical Regionalism 2.0

When Tzonis and Lefaivre's concept of critical regionalism was elaborated by Kenneth Frampton, the topic was again presented not as opposed to Modernism, but as a middle ground between two evils of the current state of architecture: what he considered, "on the one hand, a so-called 'high-tech' approach predicated exclusively upon production and, on the other, the provision of a 'compensatory façade' to cover up the harsh realities of this universal system."[32] Alas, then, critical regionalism too, despite its forceful admonishment, became more of

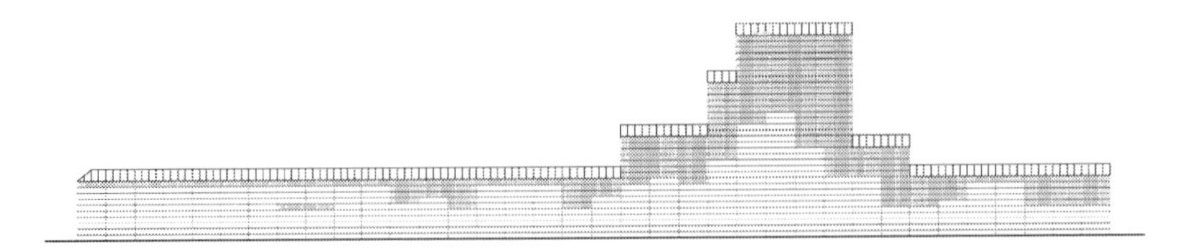

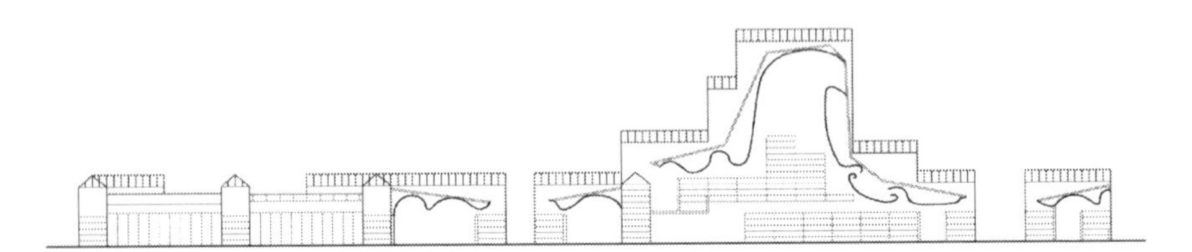

FIGURE 6.3 Jørn Utzon, *Bagsvaerd Church*, 1973–1976; elevation and section. Redrawn, CODA, 2014.

a middle ground than a radical alternative. This sentiment is perhaps best captured in the quote with which Frampton chooses to begin his essay, which, despite anti-universalist declarations, asks: "How to become modern and return to sources; how to revive an old, dormant civilization and take part in universal civilization?"[33]

Frampton takes as his exemplar Jørn Utzon's *Bagsvaerd Church* (1976), which, like Cohen's examples, combines both universal and site-specific desires, or what Frampton here describes as the "*rationality* of normative technique" with the "*arationality* of idiosyncratic form."[34] Frampton admits that the regular concrete exterior is one that has been manifested repeatedly in various locations globally. The non-universal in this example occurs only on the interior, however, as the voluptuous roof conveys a sense of spirituality, and what Frampton considers the "cross-cultural reference" of the pagoda.[35] This vernacular, it is worth noting, is programmatically—but not regionally—related to the project. While certainly normative and idiosyncratic, Frampton's example, with its mute exterior and interior reference to a distant vernacular, seems at odds with any notion of the local.[36]

Blending In

It may be this ambivalence between Modernism and site-responsiveness that is, at least in part, the reason why contextualism and regionalism in their various forms seemed to lack potency. Perhaps even more significant in this regard is the emphasis placed by both contextualism and regionalism on the familiar. While Frampton, for example, is careful to distinguish critical regionalism from other "simpleminded" attempts to "revive the hypothetical forms of a lost vernacular," his stance against "alien, exotic forms" and his description of the revolution as an "arrière-garde" articulate his opposition to radical or revolutionary tendencies.[37]

In fact, by Cohen's definition, contextualist works were "partial models for an architecture unassertive and antithetical to the revolutionary vision."[38] Warning against the tendency to become reactionary, Cohen called upon architects not to make work attempting to be anything "more than carefully considered architecture."[39] Instead, contextualism sought programmatic hierarchy. On the one hand, important public buildings were to be freestanding and should consequently possess greater license to distinguish themselves. Commonplace and ubiquitous buildings, such as apartment buildings that spread widely across the city fabric, were, on the other hand, designed to adhere more strictly to the rules of the existing city. Contextualist thought suggested that architects had a responsibility to produce an earnest reply to the following questions: "Am I really building the most important building in my block? Should my building rightfully differ from buildings around it in its urban type or should it continue the fabric of the city?"[40]

Along those lines, Cohen develops a key parable: "'blending in' does not mean that everyone should wear grey flannel suits; it means that if everyone has agreed that the occasion calls for a suit, to arrive in shorts and a t-shirt is either an act of ignorance or of arrogance."[41]

Strangely, this dress-code metaphor leads us, yet again, to Modernism. As Mark Wigley has shown, in his comprehensive article "White-out: Fashioning the Modern,"[42] on the intimate and repressed relationship between fashion and architecture from 1890 to 1920, the functional male suit was frequently upheld as a model for particularly *Modern* architecture—the style allegedly opposed by the contextualists.

Moreover, the suit had been used by Modernists as an example of anonymous and standardized architecture: on men's Modern fashion, Adolf Loos both asks and answers: "What does it mean to be well dressed? . . . it means to be dressed correctly . . . It is a question of being dressed in such a way that one is least noticeable."[43]

While Cohen's version of contextualism was certainly more expanded than the original, the suit metaphor reveals what is perhaps contextualism's greatest weakness: its moribund desire to blend in; to continue; not to make an arrogant fuss. Ironically, the shorts and t-shirt alternative, while not matching the common style, may have been a much more context-responsive choice of garment, depending on the weather. Nevertheless, so strong was Cohen's desire to blend in, that the aesthetic, once again, dominated over actual contextual response.[44]

Dress Detour

While Cohen's warning against the egoism of the 'starchitect' is certainly well taken, as in fashion, the alternative to blending in need not be the exhibitionist's apparel, but the simple and humble possibility of self-expression (beyond the constrained and repressed possibilities afforded by the tie).

An alternative to the shorts and t-shirt option, pedantic as it may seem, may point contextualism in another direction. In contrast to the welcome metaphor of the suit, dresses were criticized by early twentieth-century dress reformers/architects as being, for example:

> highly illogical constructions that, without a visible skeleton, allow a cloud of bows, puffs, flounces, and pleats to run amuck over all the contours of the body, and reconfigure it to an unformed mass of flesh, which doesn't permit the least inkling of the proportions of limbs and joints, and in which the beauty of the human figure has been completely lost.[45]

As such, Wigley describes the dress as Modern Architecture's "in the closet" embarrassment; what it "emphatically defines as its degenerate other," due to its femininity, ornamentation, and other similar concerns, "but from which it cannot detach itself."[46] Given its overriding desire for individuality, it may in fact be the dress that takes the place of the suit's opposite, desiring, as it does, never to find its copy.[47]

As such, the dress fits neither the Internationalist-Modern model of functionalism and standardization nor the contextual model of fitting in. Most importantly, the dress might be understood as being made for a specific occasion, and therefore it is, by nature, contextual. Whether couture or off-the-rack, the image of a fitting dress for a cocktail party, a wedding, a funeral, an interview, a picnic, a ball, or a day in the house, varies across a wide spectrum of possibilities, while the suit remains constant. Its effect is multi-dimensional. Endless variations in its construction enable and empower the dress as it necessarily inserts itself to add to both the material fabric and the atmosphere or scene to which it arrives as a representation of the designer and a personal reflection of the wearer. The dress slits, shortens, pleats, puffs, drapes, and plunges, according to the external constraints of occasion (program), climate, and location, as well as to the internal constraints of the exaggerated contours of the body. It may be silk, cotton, leather, fur, or plastic, and it may be any color or print. It does not look like its context: it is for it.

Architecture too can express itself in this way. And what it communicates can say something about more than itself: it can open a dialogue that welcomes and engages the many complex relationships that exist and are produced within its environment.

Questions for an Alternative Path

The following questions, then, while accepting the fundamental premises of both regionalism and contextualism (that is, to seek an architecture of the local versus the global), ask what is fundamental to retain of the original impetuses and what can be added and abandoned from the various manifestations of contextual (dress) thinking.

1 Can Contextual Thinking Occur Without The Dominating Image of History?

Colin Rowe asked a similar question: "How to be intelligible without involving retrospection?" He answers in the negative, however: that without retrospection, "it is difficult to see how any ideal of communication can flourish."[48] Rowe's dependence on precedent and its ambiguous legibility through distortion produces what R.E. Somol has called a "forever-now formalism," in which what Rowe hopes to be a timeless model is "ultimately co-opted by historicism."[49]

An alternative to this historicist approach is one that borrows from linguistic theory. In his 1996 article, "Prolegomena to a Rethinking of Context in Architecture," Val Warke sought to go beyond the understanding of context as the physical built environment and to seek to expand its meaning in order to enable a realignment of the by-then jaded arguments. Warke exposed the limitations of the common assumptions about contextualism and proposed instead a diversity and 'dialogability' of context. By deploying Roman Jakobson's structuralist linguistic theories in which all contexts are intrinsically unstable and boundless, Warke produces a list of ways in which architecture can be considered related to another work or event: beyond simple duplication, relationships might occur through rhythm, proportion, scale, metaphor, and so on. Contextualism, as a strategy of 'pointing,' may point to many more aspects of a context than a pre-existing architectural context. "History," Warke writes, "is only one contextualizing operation."[50]

Greg Lynn, perhaps, was on this trajectory until his focus was diverted by the digital project and a new formalism. Lynn combined evolutionary thinking with questions of meaning typically found in formalism and the conceptual project. Certainly, too, there is precedent for an ecological contextualism that arose in the 1960s with John McHale, etc., but that trajectory has also been diverted, this time toward sustainability. Today, it seems that the two strands of digital formalism and sustainability are well separated and continue to part ways.[51] New ways of thinking about context might instead borrow from both sides of the form–ecology abyss to generate a meaningful architecture in dialogue with its natural site, without Modernism or other historical styles dominating the production of form and expression.

2 Can Context Be Thought of as More (or Less) than Existing Built Form?

Val Warke has noted that one of contextualism's great failings was in its "direct formal translation of things to things," that is, from architecture to architecture.[52] Expanding our conception of context, how might architecture point to and engage in a dialogue with the non-architectural world?

Stuart Cohen took the first steps in expanding Rowe's definition of contextualism. As the title of his essay, "Physical Context/Cultural Context: Including It All," suggests, the original understanding of contextualism as "largely visual and spatial . . . to be intuited from an accepted local context, a site and its surrounding" is broadened to include the cultural context: the symbols and images, as well as the forms, of the site.[53] In this way, Cohen opened up the possibilities for more abstract thinking about what context might mean, and therefore what might be taken from context in order to produce new architecture. Nevertheless, Cohen's assumptions about the 'physical context' are limited to the existing built 'object.' He does not consider the 'physical' to include landscape, infrastructure, water, etc. and, further, the invisible and intangible environmental conditions of sunlight, wind, etc. Frampton is certainly more inclusive of the non-built, as evidenced in his subtitle: "Culture Versus Nature: Topography, Context, Climate, Light and Tectonic Form."[54] And although his examples do not completely support this suggestion, he certainly goes the furthest in opening up context to the non-built.

Context, in fact, beyond landscape and light, may be invisible. It may be energetic, kinetic, biologic, affordance-based in a Gibsonian sense, and many other things that are not revealed in either a Roweian figure–ground scan or a Cohenian inclusion of culture. It may be unbounded, in Warke's terms,[55] but also specific and measurable.

3 Can Reading Context Be a Process of Extraction?

The idea of extraction, as we have seen, is already embodied in contextualist thought when we are reminded by Cohen that context should be used *selectively*. This term is comparable to a similar statement that Kenneth Frampton also makes in the same decade, which describes critical regionalism as an attempt "to mediate the impact of universal civilization with elements derived *indirectly* from the peculiarities of a particular place."[56] In other words, the existing is not copied, it is used only as a reference, providing the possibility for new invention and interpretation.

Can we emphasize, through design, these terms 'selective' and 'indirect' (which appear in any true description of contextualism or critical regionalism)? The process of borrowing from the environment cannot function without the key component of extraction. Extraction, in this case, is the two-fold process of projection (of need or desire) on to the environment and the isolation of the elements highlighted by that projection (as discussed in the chapters "Bubbles Burst," "Niche Tactics," and "An Ecological Approach to the Picturesque"). In this way, it is not the context as a whole that is reacted to, but a distilled version of context specific to its user: its organism or, in our case, its architecture. Further, it is important that those elements that are extracted as dominant forces of the environment are not necessarily continued in the work; that they may instead be pushed against or protected from the work.

4 Can a Contexual/Regional Response Be Inappropriate?

As a result of contextualism's alignment with good behavior, a logical consequence in the discipline's progress was a counter-oscillation in which innovative and progressive architecture, by contrast, rejected any relationship with its context. As Val Warke has described it, after contextualism, "avant-gardism and radicality came from being as acontextual as possible."[57] Contexualism and the avant-garde became antonymous.

On the contrary, however, we might imagine a truly responsive architecture to produce unusual and unexpected forms. The 'revolutionary,' 'exotic,' and 'alien' might be generated, not for the sake of flamboyance, but because a response to exterior forces might *demand* that of the project. Such demands are likely as the exterior forces invariably are not symmetrically ordered and singular; they push and pull (or incite resistances) in different directions and inevitably result in something that does not 'look like' its neighbor. Thus, to a certain extent, we might claim that in order to be responsive, a certain disorderliness is *required*. A new way of thinking about and acting in context might, depending on the site, be composed of entirely discordant notes. Rather than feared and rejected, the radical might be embraced as a contextual necessity.

Near Escapes

Examples of inappropriate form that are responsive to site conditions exist. However, they are considered here imperfect examples as the context that they consider remains physical and visible. That is to say, while they satisfy questions of (1) ahistoricism, (2) extraction, and (4) inappropriateness, the context to which they are reacting remains, on the whole, a visible and tangible and architectural one. Keeping this in mind, let us consider some imperfect models.

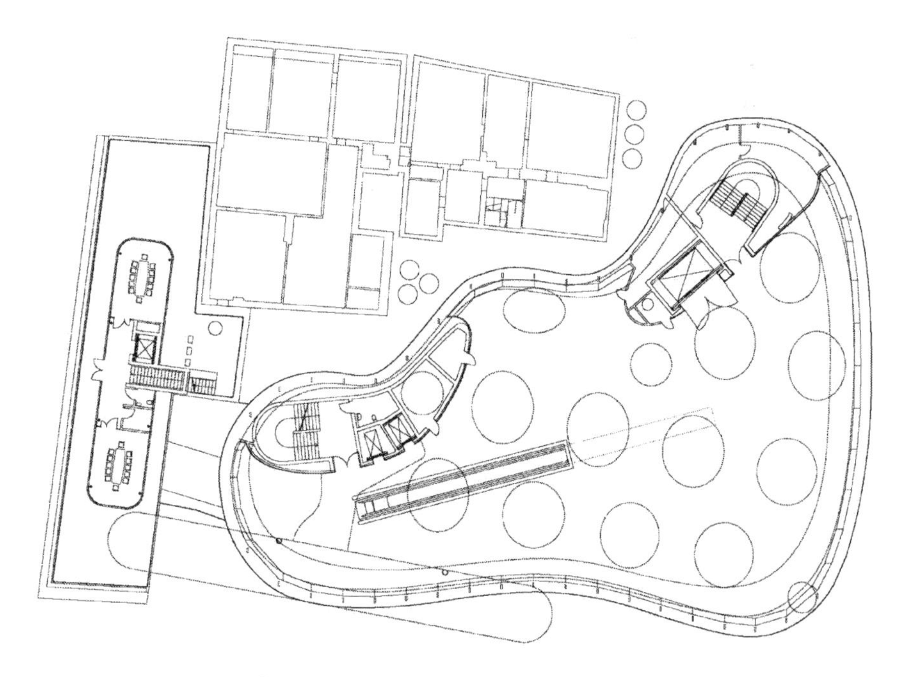

FIGURE 6.4 Peter Cook and Colin Fournier, *Kunsthaus* in Graz. © UMJ.

FIGURE 6.5 Peter Cook and Colin Fournier, *Kunsthaus* in Graz; rooftop view. Photo: Zepp-Cam. 2004/Graz, Austria © UMJ.

First is Peter Cook and Colin Fournier's *Kunsthaus* in Graz. The work can certainly not be accused of mimicking its neighbors: two adjacent listed baroque buildings and the nineteenth-century 'Eisernes Haus,' which was (like one of the architects) imported from England. Cook and Fournier's *Kunsthaus* loosely curves around the rectilinear contours of the existing ensemble, bulging on the elevated southern boundary, and retreating at the moment of entry. The roof is punctured by north-facing nozzles, which, despite their alien appearance in the cropped image, respond to the city's disheveled roof-scape and the topography beyond. Originally intended to shift positions to maximize light intake, the nozzles now all point north, except a single nozzle that breaks form and focuses on one of the city's main monuments: the Schlossberg.

Among other innovations cited by the architects, the *Kunsthaus* explicitly aims for a "provocative engagement with cultural/urban context."[58] This engagement is described as an analysis of the urban context "not only in terms of built form but also in terms of land use and urban life, demonstrating that a contextual approach based on affinities in terms of social activity may be more effective than one merely relying on visual references."[59] While the architects do not demonstrate any site analysis, they do provide a series of formal steps. Starting with a sphere over which a mesh of gravitational points is distributed, the form is then sculpted by means of 'pushing or pulling' on the points. These forces are, presumably, a combination of push from the interior, requiring certain area and volume, pull from the exterior requiring site coverage, and push from the exterior due to the presence of existing buildings and height regulations, with resultant smaller-level adjustments for entries and nozzles.

The project is generated through the non-standard analysis of and response to site forces, so that they may be legible in the final form, but without the suited-up goal of blending in. Like Greg Lynn's early precedents, this building is not afraid to be different; it is selective in its response to site issues; it takes into account the

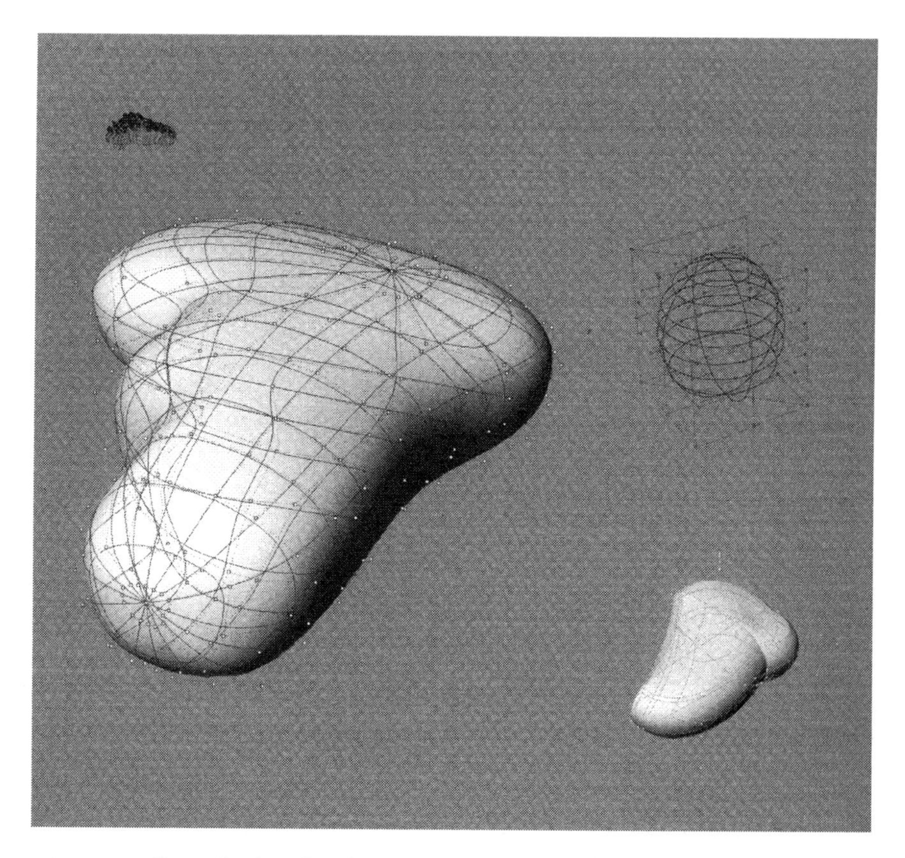

FIGURE 6.6 Peter Cook and Colin Fournier, *Kunsthaus* in Graz. © UMJ.

forces of the site (however visible and built); its result does not look like its surroundings but is *for* them. The material selection here is completely contrary to Cohen's choice of examples, both of which took on the red-brick garb of their neighbors. In this instance, clearly the *Kunsthaus* is not party to the continuity of the materiality of its surroundings. It does, however, originate in a platonic sphere, and thus inevitably refers, in a Roweian sense, to its idealized original form. In addition, the contextual forces that deform the original sphere are forces generated from the existing built environment and not an expanded notion of context. While escaping contextualism in many aspects, the *Kunsthaus* remains tethered to traditional contextual thinking in these two crucial ways.

The second imperfect example is from architects again not typically noted for their contextualism: the Office of Metropolitan Architecture (OMA). The design for the *Whitney Museum Extension* in New York (2008) is derived from tight site constraints: an extremely small footprint, the zoning envelope—which steps and slopes as it mediates between a commercial district on Madison Avenue and a residential district to the east—and the necessity that it, being an extension, both makes connections to and maintains appropriate distance from existing buildings.[60] The result is an expression of the given constraints as the building reaches up and over from one delicate and well-placed foot. The openings in the façade are a secondary map of the collision of structural stress and programmatic needs. The work

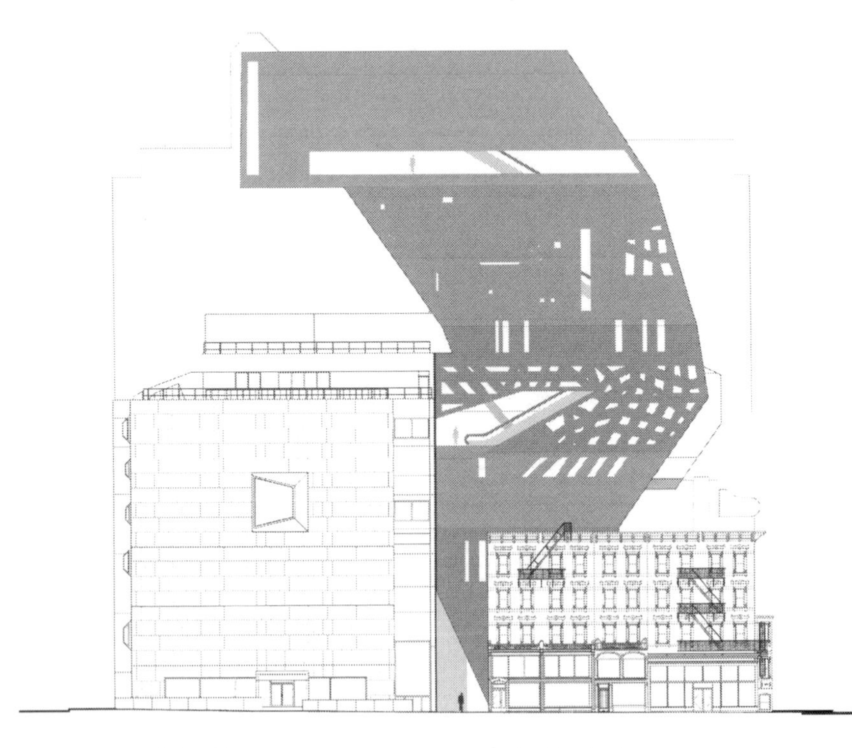

FIGURE 6.7 OMA, *Whitney Museum Extension*. © OMA, 2008.

as whole is a response to local needs and constraints and, crucially, the opportunities that the form takes in response to its physical, programmatic, and virtual site are legible. It is an awkward form that refuses to acquiesce to any preconceptions of 'museum' or of the architect's signature style. It shirks any responsibility to conventional notions of order, symmetry, or proportion. It is both part and part-of-whole. Its reasons for being the way it is are elucidated through understanding the specifics of its site. As with the *Kunsthaus*, this posture-shifting form cannot fulfill the criteria for escaping contextualism since it remains a deformation of a pre-existing type of the skyscraper as well as reacting mainly to existing built context.

While imperfect as models here due to their reliance on built form, these examples begin to get at an alternative to contextualism. These are bold works that stand out from the urban fabric, but could not be located elsewhere. Every move made is site-specific. Should these projects have been relocated midway through the design, they would have had to change significantly their form, materiality, and porosity. One might think of them, and others like them, as the very tentative beginnings of a new contextual trajectory; as dressed up, and with some place to go.[61]

Notes

1 Rosalind Krauss, "The Scantology of Anywhere: Modernism against the Grain," in *Anywhere*, ed. Cynthia Davidson (New York: Rizzoli, 1992), 252.

2 Similar terms had previously been used by Walter Gropius in *International Architektur*, and Ludwig Hilberseimer in *Internationale Neue Baukunst*.

3 Henry-Russell Hitchcock and Philip Johnson, *The International Style* (New York: W.W. Norton, 1995), 36. Certain architects fit less well into this description and were consequently edited by Hitchcock and Johnson. For example, as Val Warke has noted, "the pair cringed at having to include Aalto—included only to indicate true internationality—whose work was typically very rooted, very sited, so instead they tactically showed only an interior of the Turun Sanomat, which could appear to be un-situated." Email to author, July 29, 2014.

4 Institutions and associations beyond MoMA were on-board with the wide proclamation of the beauty and benefits of design for mechanized production and the regularity that would result in what was packaged for public consumption as *The International Style* (take the GSD and Gropius with the hire of S. Giedion and the Mechanization Takes Command lectures, or the abstract power of CIAM.)

5 Hitchcock and Johnson, *The International Style*, 20.

6 In addition to Chapter 4, "An Ecological Approach to the Picturesque," in this collection, for an overview of the rise of contextualism/regionalism Renaissance, through Picturesque, through Romanticism to Nationalistic Regionalism see "Critical Regionalism," in Arie Graafland (ed.) *The Critical Landscape* (Rotterdam: 010 Publishers, 1996), 126–148.

7 Liane Lefaivre, "Critical Regionalism: A Facet of Modern Architecture since 1945," in Liane Lefaivre and Alexander Tzonis, *Critical Regionalism: Architecture and Identity in a Globalized World* (Munich: Prestel, 2003), 28.

8 Lewis Mumford, "Skyline," *New Yorker* (October 1947) as referred to in Lefaivre, "Critical Regionalism," 265.

9 Ibid., 26.

10 Ernesto Rogers, "L'architettura Moderna dopo la generazione dei Maestri," *Casabella–Continuá*, 211, June–July, 1956, 3. Adrian Forty notes that Rogers did not use the term *context* or its Italian equivalent, which in fact was not in common use until after the contextualism movement; he used only *preesistenze ambientali* (Adrian Forty, *Words and Buildings: A Vocabulary of Modern Architecture* (New York: Thames & Hudson, 2000), 134).
11 Ernesto Rogers, "The Existing Environment and the Practical Content of Contemporary Architecture," *Casabella*, February, 1955.
12 Rogers' referential work is subsequently attacked by Reyner Banham and Robert Smithson, who considered it as, respectively, "regressive" and even "dangerous." Rogers' self-defense, which calls for an "evolutionary" approach to architecture, we must assume to mean evolution of historical form, rather than niche-thinking, which is being discussed in this collection. Ernesto Rogers, "L'Evolution dell'architettura," *Casabella-Continuá*, 228, June 1959. Trans. into English by Joan Ockman, *Architecture Culture 1943–1968* (New York: Columbia, 1993), 300–308.
13 Vittorio Gregotti's 1982 introduction to the French edition of *Le Territoire de l'architecture* (1966), French trans. from Italian by Vittorio Hugo (Paris: L'Equerre, 1982), 12.
14 While this is the claim that Cohen makes in his essay, "Physical Context/Cultural Context: Including it all," Jerry Wells in an interview with the author (February 27, 2014) suggested that the term was not developed until much later when Cohen was writing his essay. According to Adrian Forty the first significant appearance of the term 'context' is by Christopher Alexander in his *Notes on the Synthesis of Form* in 1964. This use, Forty proposes, is borrowed from the literary New Criticism movement. (Forty, *Words and Buildings: A Vocabulary of Modern Architecture*, 134.)
15 According to Adrian Forty, Rowe and Rogers opposed 'prodigy' architecture, as well as the expression of program, and used similar examples. However, Rowe was focused on form exclusively, and more interested in urban space than the architectural object. (Forty, *Words and Buildings: A Vocabulary of Modern Architecture*, 134.)
16 Stuart Cohen, "Physical Context/Cultural Context: Including it all," in *Oppositions Reader*, ed. K. Michael Hays (New York: Princeton Architectural Press, 1998), 66. Originally in *Oppositions*, 2, 1974.
17 R.E. Somol, "Speciating Sites," in *Anywhere*, ed. Cynthia Davidson (New York: Rizzoli, 1992), 94.
18 Cohen, "Physical Context/Cultural Context," 66.
19 Colin Rowe, *As I Was Saying: Recollections and Miscellaneous Essays*, vol. 3, ed. A. Carragone (Cambridge, MA: MIT Press, 1996), 2.
20 Mark Wigley and Philip Johnson, *Deconstructivist Architecture: The Museum of Modern Art, New York* (Boston, MA: Little, Brown, 1988), 17.
21 Stuart E. Cohen "Contextualism: From Urbanism to a Theory of Appropriate Form," *Inland Architect* (May/June 1987), 68.
22 Cohen, "Physical Context/Cultural Context," 85.
23 Robert Venturi, *Complexity and Contradiction in Architecture* (New York: The Museum of Modern Art, 1966), 116.
24 Cohen, "Physical Context/Cultural Context," 85.
25 Alex Tzonis and Liane Lefaivre, "The Grid and the Pathway: An Introduction to the Work of Dimitris and Suzana Antonakakis," *Architecture in Greece*, 15 (1981), 164–178.
26 Alan Colquhoun, "Regionalism 1," in *Collected Essays in Architectural Criticism* (London: Black Dog Publishing, 2009), 281. Originally published in *Postcolonial Spaces*, 1992.
27 Liane Lefaivre and Alexander Tzonis, *Critical Regionalism: Architecture and Identity in a Globalized World* (Munich: Prestel, 2003).

28 Bernard Rudofsky, *Architecture Without Architects* (Albuquerque: University of New Mexico Press, 1987). Originally printed in 1964.
29 Lefaivre, "Critical Regionalism," 35.
30 Colquhoun, "Regionalism 1," 281.
31 Alan Colquhoun, "Regionalism 2," in *Collected Essays in Architectural Criticism* (London: Black Dog Publishing, 2009), 288. Originally published in *Casabella*, January/February, 1996.
32 Kenneth Frampton, "Towards a Critical Regionalism: Six Points for an Architecture of Resistance," in *The Anti-Aesthetic: Essays on Postmodern Culture* (Seattle, WA: Bay Press, 1983), 17. Alan Colquhoun too, while acknowledging the contradiction, believes that the two are connected: that culture evolves with technology and universality (Colquhoun, "Regionalism 2," 287).
33 Paul Ricoeur, "Universal Civilization and National Cultures" (1961), in *History and Truth*, trans. Chas. A. Kelbley (Evanston, IL: Northwestern University Press, 1965), 277. Quoted at the beginning of Frampton, "Towards a Critical Regionalism," 16.
34 Frampton, "Towards a Critical Regionalism," 22; emphasis in original.
35 Ibid.
36 Warke argues that Bagsvaerd's exterior is anything but neutral. He considers the agricultural/industrial exterior to be "a reference to the blocky granaries strewn across the plains of Denmark, as well as to the tradition of exposed-timber frame farmhouses throughout Gladsaxe." Email to author, July 29, 2014.
37 "One thinks of the form-force aesthetics of Henri van de Velde or the 'whiplash-arabesques' of Victor Horta" (Frampton, "Towards a Critical Regionalism," 23).
38 Cohen, "Physical Context/Cultural Context," 86.
39 Ibid.
40 Cohen, "Contextualism," 69.
41 Ibid.
42 Mark Wigley, "White-out: Fashioning the Modern [Part 2]," *Assemblage*, 22 (1993), 6–49.
43 Adolf Loos, "Men's Fashion," in *Adolf Loos, Spoken into the Void: Collected Essays 1897–1900*, trans. Jane O. Newman and John H. Smith (Cambridge, MA: MIT Press, 1982), 12.
44 Today, we see in fact the same pattern in sustainable architecture: one that pacifies planetary guilt through its title, but whose primary goal is often a Modern or at least aesthetic goal. Any glass tower that is labelled sustainable is an example of such aestheticization.
45 Henry van de Velde, *Die Künstlerische Hebung der Frauentracht* (Krefeld: Druck und Verlag Kramer & Baum, 1900), 13.
46 Wigley, "White-out," 10.
47 In her book, *Fashioning Vienna: Adolf Loos' Cultural Criticism* (New York: Routledge, 2003, 122–123), Janet Stewart links two statements on the liberation and progressive abilities of the dress: first, Adolf Loos's comment that " . . . the leaders of fashion in men's clothing are those who hold the highest social position, while the leaders in ladies' fashion will be those women who have to show the greatest skill in arousing men's sensuality, namely the cocottes [prostitutes]," and, second, Georg Simmel's comment that while men's fashion is concerned with suitability to their place in the world, women's fashion is concerned with denoting social identity. Thanks to Val Warke for pointing out these connections.
48 Robert E. Somol, "Oublier Rowe," *ANY 7/8, Form Work: Colin Rowe* (1994), 11.
49 Ibid., 14.
50 Val Warke, "Prolegomena to a Rethinking of Context in Architecture," *Cornell Journal of Architecture*, 5 (1996), 13. In a 2014 guest lecture in the seminar "Contexts: Niche Tactics and the Possibility of Ugliness," Warke elaborated these literary contextual

tropes. His categories can be summarized as: Deictic (pointing to context), Elenctic (pointing but lying), Exophoric (pointing to another context) Endophoric-Anaphoric (pointing to a past context), and Endophoric-Cataphoric (pointing to a future context). Warke's architectural examples are, respectively: *Palazzo della Cassa di Risparmio*, Pistoia; Georges-Henri Pingusson's *Mémorial des Martyrs de la Déportation*, Paris; OMA's *Milstein Hall*, Ithaca, NY; Peter Eisenman's *Wexner Center for the Arts*, Columbus, OH; and Einar Jónsson's *Einar Jónsson House/Museum*, 1916, Reykjavik. (Val Warke, guest lecture in the seminar "Contexts: Niche Tactics and the Possibility of Ugliness," Cornell University, Dept. of Architecture, March 13, 2014.)

51 If we need reminding of this separation, we might consider Peter Eisenman's quip comparing sustainability to motherhood (paraphrasing): It's great that some people do it but I am not physically capable of it myself. (Presumably, the 'sustainablists' would feel the same, if less positive, about his genre of work.)

52 Warke, guest lecture in the seminar "Contexts: Niche Tactics and the Possibility of Ugliness." Cornell University, Department of Architecture, Spring 2014.

53 Cohen, "Physical Context/Cultural Context," 67.

54 Frampton, "Towards a Critical Regionalism," 21.

55 Warke, "Prolegomena to a Rethinking of Context in Architecture," 13.

56 Frampton, "Towards a Critical Regionalism," 23. Emphasis added.

57 Warke, guest lecture in the seminar "Contexts: Niche Tactics and the Possibility of Ugliness." Cornell University, Department of Architecture, Spring 2014.

58 Colin Fournier, "Kunsthaus Graz," http://eprints.ucl.ac.uk/13132/ (accessed January 5, 2014).

59 Colin Fournier, "Kunsthaus Graz, Research Outputs 1 and 2," http://discovery.ucl.ac.uk/13132/1/13132.pdf (accessed January 5, 2013).

60 Office of Metropolitan Architecture, "Whitney Museum Extension, USA, New York, 2001," http://oma.eu/projects/2001/whitney-museum-extension (accessed January 5, 2014).

61 From the song: "When You're All Dressed Up And No Place To Go," Benjamin Hapgood Burt and Silvio Hein.

7

SANTA MARIA DEFORMATA

The Predicament of Precedent

For Colin Rowe and Fred Koetter, as we have seen, contextualism often begins with its opposite: the ideal. Both Wittkower's twelfth villa diagram and Rowe's mathematical ideal are, by definition, acontextual. The strategy advocated in *Collage City* is one that takes a perfect and contextless object and inserts it into a context, which deforms it just enough so that both the original pure form and the deformation imposed by its adjustment to its new site are legible at once. Thomas Schumacher, Rowe's student at Cornell (along with Fred Koetter), clarifies the mutually dependent nature of the relationship between the ideal and context when he writes: "It is precisely the ways in which idealized forms can be adjusted to a context or used as a 'collage' that contextualism seeks to explain."[1] While *Collage City* does indeed explain the transformation between ideal and adjusted states, the emphasis is on the transformation and the adjusted, while the ideal itself remains uninvestigated.

Rowe, of course, had already made his name through the presentation of the pairing of Palladio's *Villa Foscari (Malcontenta)* and Le Corbusier's *Villa Stein*, in *The Mathematics of the Ideal Villa* (1947), in which the notion of ideal form is developed. This pair is sandwiched between more cursory comparisons of Palladio's *Villa Rotonda* and Le Corbusier's *Villa Savoye* and Schinkel's *Altes Museum* and Le Corbusier's *Palace of the Assembly* at Chandigarh. The crucial shift, of course, is that the comparisons almost thirty years later in *Collage City* are no longer between like forms with a shift in time, but between historic and approximately contemporaneous forms, with a shift in context.

Kicking off the line-up of comparisons between the deformed and the perfect in the chapter "The Crisis of the Object: The Predicament of Texture" in *Collage City*, Gunnar Asplund's *Royal Chancellery* (1922) and Le Corbusier's *Plan Voisin* (1925) are presented as one possible yet imperfect distorted/ideal pairing. To Schumacher, the *Chancellery*'s design allows site to dominate, arriving at a solution that is not mimicking but "both responsive and assertive, both figure and ground, both introverted and extroverted, and both idealized and deformed."[2] Rowe's comparison, albeit clearly against the relentless demolition and renewal of *Voisin*, nevertheless criticizes the *Chancellery* for being *too much* a part of an established urban continuum and therefore merely a simulation of a past.[3] Instead, Rowe and Koetter propose a middle ground, more in the spirit of Schumacher's description than the evidence at hand. Their strategy—one that they admit is an "ancient technique,"—is one of "deliberately distorting what is also presented as the ideal type."[4]

Having set the stage for their sequence of transformations, Rowe and Koetter continue to propose distorted/ideal pairs: twins separated at birth, and raised in pure and dirty habitats: *Palazzo Borghese*, for example, acts as both a response to its site and a characteristic palace of the Farnese type. The *Palazzo Farnese*'s perfect cortile deforms into the highly imperfect and elastic site boundary, combining "both archetype and accident," and creating "an internal situation of great richness and freedom."[5] This transformation, however, does not go far enough, since Borghese and Farnese exist in relative proximity in the center of Rome. While Farnese sits squarely in its urban space, set back from its well-behaved and orthogonal neighbors, and Borghese is forced into contortions and elongations, both exist within the comparable medium-pressure of the urban fabric.

The ultimate comparison between the perfect and the contextually compromised is presented via two tightly cropped photographs: the façade of *Santa Maria della Consolazione* at Todi (1508–1607), which, despite so-called provincial

FIGURE 7.1 *Santa Maria della Consolazione* in Todi, 1508–1524, Ambrose of Milan, Ambrogio Barocci, Cola di Matteuccio de Caprarola, Francesco de Vita; and *Sant'Agnese* in Piazza Navona, Rome, 1653–1657, Francesco Castelli Borromini. © Alinari Archives, Florence: from *Collage City*, by Colin Rowe and Fred Koetter, published by The MIT Press.

detailing, is selected to represent the "perfect building in all its pristine integrity,"[6] and the façade of *Sant'Agnese* (1652) in Piazza Navona, Rome,[7] which exists in a state of in-betweenness: "sometimes an ideal object and sometimes a function of the piazza wall," "simultaneously 'compromised' and intact."[8]

The façade of the ideal form at Todi unravels in Rome to become a hybrid contextual entity—between singular object and urban façade. This unfolding is both controlled and compounded by the constricted urban site, and so the site and the object enter into a productive dialogue.

The play between the two states allows for the possibility of keeping the original meaning intact while allowing local contingencies to be simultaneously legible, as

FIGURE 7.2 Pablo Picasso (1881–1973), *Violin*, 1912. Charcoal and newspaper pasted on paper, 62 × 47 cm. Musée National d'Art Moderne, Centre Georges Pompidou, Paris, France. © CNAC/MNAM/Dist. RMN-Grand Palais/ Art Resource, NY, © 2014 Estate of Pablo Picasso/Artists Rights Society (ARS), New York.

is the case, Rowe and Koetter propose, in the practice of collage. Such a strategy, employed city-wide, would act as a series of stitches that sew together traditional urban fabrics with Modern objects: the *Collage City*.

In collage proper, developed more than fifty years earlier in the field of Art, although the fragment is cropped out of its former context, it is deformed only perceptually, not necessarily physically, in its new context. Take Picasso's *Violin*, for example. Two pieces of newsprint, cut from the same page, make up at once part of the figure of the instrument and part of the background on which it sits. It is this perceptual ambiguity that is the key to the work: as Rosalind Krauss has described it, "the magic of the whole collage, indeed the brilliance of the game it plays, is that the two opposite meanings—*light* on the one hand and *opacity* on the other—are generated from the 'identical' scrap of paper, the 'same physical shape.'"[9] The constant form of the newsprint is given new meanings through fluctuating associations with its surroundings. Krauss continues: "Each newsprint fragment forms the sign for a visual meaning; then as it butts against another, the sign re-forms and the meaning shifts . . . for the same piece in another location, constellates another sign."[10]

Rowe and Koetter use this same language to discuss their borrowed version of collage: for example, when the perfect church of *Santa Maria della Consolazione* is collaged and morphed into a site on Piazza Navona, the result, *Sant'Agnese*, "continuously fluctuates between an interpretation of the building as object and its reinterpretation as texture."[11] And again, at the end of their book, a series of black-on-white urban scale figure–ground plans are presented as a series of *amuse-bouches*, described as: "an abridged list of stimulants, a-temporal and necessarily transcultural, as possible *objets trouvés* in the urbanistic collage."[12]

However, it is important to note that, in collage proper, the fragments are not pure, idealized forms but already existing products of their own messy contexts. Indeed, while the term 'ideal' has been taken at face value, Colin Rowe knew that the true ideal was a fiction. He wrote: "the absolute idealization of any useful building is logically impossible, because, if no other pressures influence its design, at least entrance and orientation must act as deforming pressures."[13] For Rowe then, the ideal architecture is not a platonic ideal but something inevitably already deformed to some extent itself. Taking this statement at its word, let us then return to *Santa Maria* at Todi, to investigate what other "deforming pressures" might be already present in this allegedly perfect form.

Santa Maria della Consolazione re-examined

Santa Maria della Consolazione at Todi is generally regarded as an ideal within its species, as "perhaps the most perfect and uncompromising example of its theoretically desirable type."[14] As a domed cross, it recalls Leonardo da Vinci's designs for a centrally planned church (1506), which is not, in fact, one perfect model itself but a series of iterations that enable the conception of a perfect form, created by overlaying a square and a Greek cross in plan. Variations on the fundamental design become embellished with articulations at the corners of the square, which leads to the multiplication of octagonal and embellished octagonal plans. The version chosen for development is a relatively simple variation in which the square and

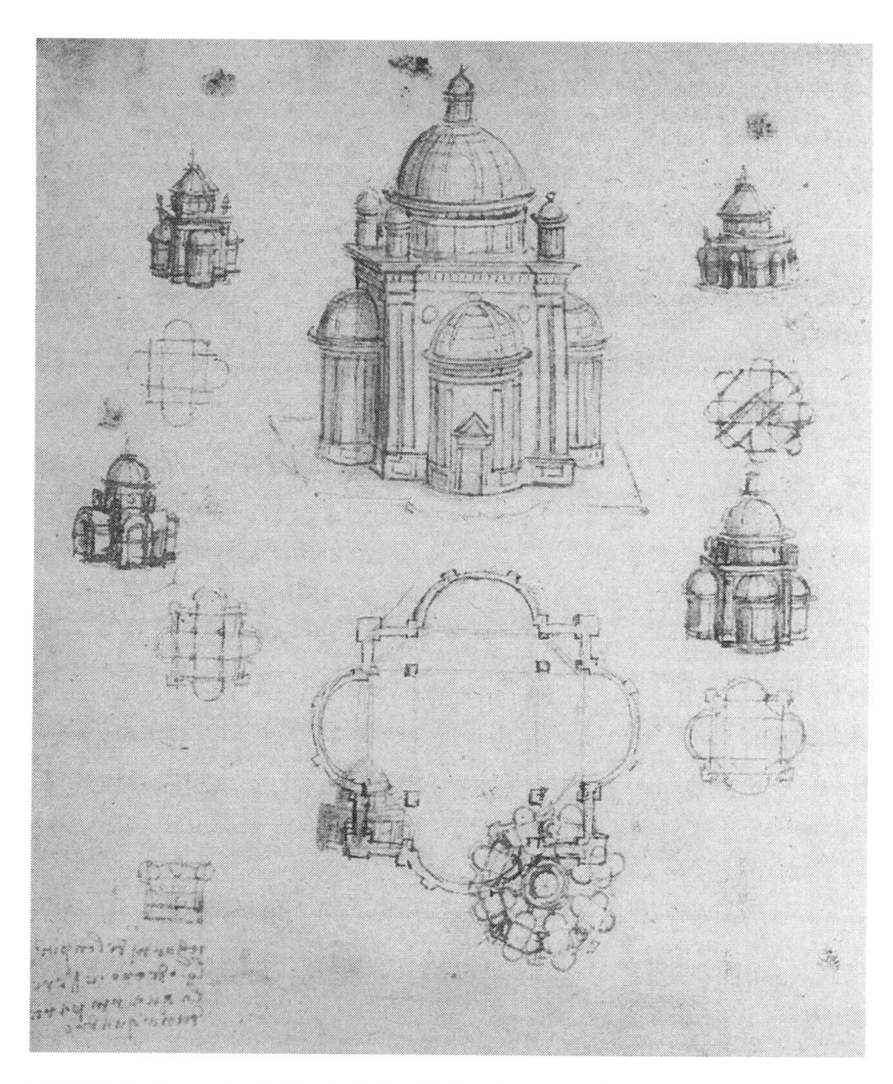

FIGURE 7.3 Leonardo da Vinci, *Codex Ashburnham*, complement to Manuscript B, 1487–1490. Fol. 93 verso: Plan and elevation of a church. Fol. 94 recto: Plan and elevation of a church. © RMN-Grand Palais/Art Resource, NY.

cross overlay remains legible, and the corner embellishments are ornamental rather than spatial. Common to all of Da Vinci's drawings is a symmetry and all-sidedness that does not take into account any of the variety of conditions found within the adjacent environment. As a series of siteless sketches, rather than a built work of multiple authorship, Da Vinci's drawings retain the all-round symmetry and repetition that the very act of building (or contextualizing) seems to eliminate.

Indeed, as soon as Rowe and Koetter's cropping-mask is removed, it becomes clear that *Santa Maria della Consolazione* does not exist in an ideal site, and is, in fact, through its entry and orientation, beginning a trajectory of radical deformation itself.

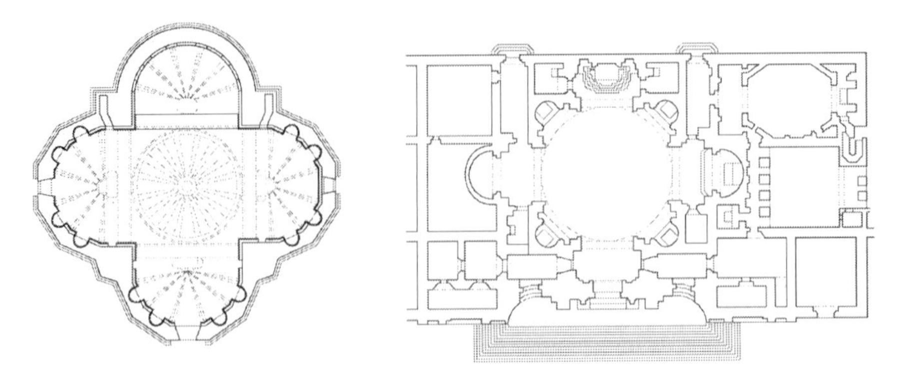

FIGURE 7.4 Plans, *Santa Maria della Consolazione* at Todi and *Sant'Agnese* in Piazza Navona, Rome. Redrawn, CODA, 2012.

One apse, occupied by the altar, is semi-circular in form, while the others are polygonal. This formal disparity—from curved to faceted—affects many aspects of the façade at a finer scale of detail, in particular the articulation of the pilasters and their capitals. The columns that articulate the edges of the polygonal sides, and their associated details, are folded along their centerline into two parts. Acting

FIGURE 7.5 Two pilasters on the north and west façades of *Santa Maria dell Consolazione*. Photograph: CODA, 2012.

FIGURE 7.6 The three doors of *Santa Maria della Consolazione*. Photograph: CODA, 2012.

as more than a line of symmetry, the entablatures along these lines become non-uniformly reduced and doubled: two narrow eagles instead of one, their bodies now produce secondary lines of symmetry.

Proceeding around the façade, there is no entry on the curved north (altar) side, and each of the doors on the other façades is decorated with a spectrum of ornamentation from the highly decorated east door, which faces the approach, to the stark west façade, where the door is merely a punctuation without pediment. This arrangement highlights a hierarchy at work: not all sides are equal.

Finally, while the altar should (according to tradition) face the east, the locations and orientation of the church within the landscape—the topography, the sunlight, and the presence of the historic city of Todi to the northeast—cannot accommodate an east–west axis and so the axis of prayer is reoriented north–south. The congregation turns its back on the vast landscape to the south, and the sun arcs across the altar wall before their eyes.

These anomalies, present in the 'perfect' form, should be of no great surprise, given Rowe's warning. In nature, as Georges Bataille reminds us, *everything* contains mutations: monstrous incongruities are present in all real forms, but are, for the most part, barely perceptible.[15] In line with this anti-ideal approach, *Santa Maria* begins to lose its foothold as a perfect model. Moreover, the information contained within these anomalies provides insight into the motivators of these latent deformations and opens up possibilities for further deformation.

Oedipal Progenies

Thoughts of deformations and deviations inevitably call to mind some progenies of Rowe's who, each in his own way, criticized his forefather's strategy as limited and closed, and sought instead to use the fundamentals of his thinking to open up alternative design strategies that might emerge from Rowe's original thinking.

For instance, Greg Lynn, in his essay "New Variations on the Rowe Complex," picks up Rowe's technique of formal analysis, which, Lynn claims, "illustrates

FIGURE 7.7 The four interior façades of *Santa Maria della Consolazione*. Photograph: CODA, 2012.

the intricate linkages between genetic and architectural theory," but which Rowe abandons in *Collage City*. Advocating the continuity of Rowe's early evolutionary thinking, Lynn argues that an interest in deformation does not preclude mathematical thought, and thus does not need to represent a rupture in Rowe's logic in the way that it does. For Lynn, this erroneous assumption leads to Rowe's abandonment of analytic formalism in favor of collage aesthetics, and inevitably to a closed set of systems that prohibit innovation. Lynn seeks an alternate path that allows *Collage City*-like deformations, but, as in evolution, *without* an ideal model.[16]

Much of Lynn's subsequent body of work was dedicated to this alternative mathematics,[17] completing, in a sense, Rowe's unfulfilled formalism through experimentation with digitally generated reactive forms that favored variation and difference over any notion of an ideal. The blobs with which we associate Lynn and many other non-blob projects take on precisely those contextual deformative forces that are present in *Collage City*. In *Stranded Sears Tower*, as we have seen, Lynn takes the precedent of the Sears Tower and lays it horizontally into its site, "entangling its monolithic mass with local contextual forces."[18] In a footnote, Lynn is careful to differentiate his use of the term "context" from the familiar use meaning the "evolution of a building from the general characteristics of an urban fabric," that is, from a Roweian and contextualist meaning of context. Instead, he claims, his contextual responses are formed out of "connections by vicissitude and alliance."[19] Such 'affiliations' promote local differences and exploit possible connections with program, structure, form, and culture rather than repressing these differences as fixed orders inevitably do.[20]

Similarly, R.E. Somol criticizes Rowe's complete dependence on pre-existing types, writing that Rowe inevitably "constrains difference to an internal and framed articulation within a system, a previous identity, rather than a process of perpetual differentiation."[21] Somol's alternative is what he calls the "difference machine": the production of a set that diverges rather than converges. This deviationist technique employs a strategy of "maintain and subvert," versus "erase and replace"—or what ultimately amounts to the amnesia of form.[22]

To replace, or at least expand, Rowe's outmoded strategy, Lynn and Somol both seek to multiply the inputs. Lynn is open-ended about the source of these transformations, citing program, structure, form, and culture, as well as the urban,

FIGURE 7.8 *Santa Maria della Consolazione*, aerial view. Photo courtesy of Roberto Marinoni.

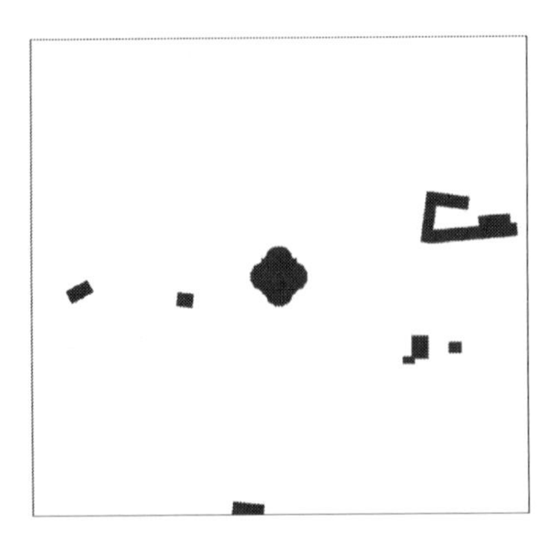

FIGURE 7.9 Figure–ground comparison of *Santa Maria della Consolazione* and *Sant'Agnese*. CODA, 2012.

the institutional, and the temporal.[23] Somol, too, offers a broad range of possible sources, "program, structure, material, the body, context . . . the earth, the ground, and gravity," as well as "an investigation of new sciences, aesthetics, and politics, or via alternative rearrangements of private subjects and public objects."[24] While both allude to a range of external transformative sources, the question remains: which forces to engage and deploy at any given moment?

A return to the source, as laid out above, reveals that the information might already be contained *within* the original object itself. Lynn comes close to prophesying this when he suggests that one "looks to mutation as a potential source of order."[25]

Santa Maria Deformata

Returning to the scene of the crime, then, the crucial omission in Rowe's and Koetter's version of the image and potential motivating source of any future deformation is the site that surrounds *Santa Maria della Consolazione*. It is not the tabula rasa condition that the tightly cropped image from *Collage City* implies. The church sits at the edge of the city, beyond its walls, on an asymmetrical terrace at one edge of a great and non-uniform valley.

It becomes clear, from this expanded perspective, that it is not simply the building's prototypical form that makes *Santa Maria della Consolazione* a suitable protagonist in Rowe's argument, but also its seeming isolation in plan. Rowe's rationale for deformation in *Sant'Agnese* required the presence of other material fabric (the city) with which to merge. *Santa Maria*'s singularity, its seemingly minimal relationship with its context, makes it a plausible member in the category of the ideal. Certainly, when the situation is redrawn as a figure–ground plan (in the style employed in *Collage City*) and set against the site conditions at Piazza Navona, the disparity between object and texture is apparent.

However, the forces that exist *beyond* the physical can be considered to be potentially *more* powerful and enabling of deformation than the static forms of the pochéd

FIGURE 7.10 Expanded context of *Santa Maria della Consolazione*: sun, wind, topography, visibility. CODA, 2013.

city plan. It is the softer systems at work that are so often missed by the figure–ground technique, a system of thought that relies upon poles of either/or rather than an endless plane plotted with possibility and contingency. All becomes solid or void. While useful in many ways, such an analytic and representational technique over-reduces elements of both site and form to fixed and inflexible categories, and as a result reduces the significance of subtler or less-visible contextual forces.

Situated within its site and liberated, then, from its role as an ideal form, *Santa Maria della Consolazione* might itself be allowed to deviate as freely as its urban twin, but instead of moving in the direction of similitude with its built context, may be forced, due to the lack of built fabric, to acquire another language.

Ironically, while the 'corrupted' *Sant'Agnese* is held in place by the tight constraints of its urban frame, the new form of *Santa Maria Deformata* acknowledges the non-built and invisible as powerful forces in themselves and allows for considerably more deformation.[26] While its base remains grounded, the volume of the church twists northeastwards toward the gravity of the city. On its major (north–south) axis, the axis of prayer, along which the break between curved and faceted exists, and the major topographical difference occurs, the dome opens, expands, and lollops to the south, and openings on the south become larger so as to bathe the altar in light. The north side shrivels and subsides, melting due to the smoothness of that façade, while all other sides retain their linearity and are controlled by the facets. On the east side, the side of the main entry door, ornamentation is exaggerated to become a narthex space as a mediator (a function of in between-ness performed

FIGURE 7.11 Five views of *Santa Maria della Consolazione* and *Santa Maria Deformata*. CODA, 2012.

by the steps in *Sant'Agnese*), while the west side, with its minor door, shrinks. The shifting environment's influence has the potential to produce more extreme deformations than the static fabric of the city and, as such, allows a more clear communication of struggle between the basic form and its response. The east side acquires an increased amount of ornamentation, which fades continuously toward the south and west.

The *Santa Maria Deformata* experiment takes the challenge—as set out by Lynn and Somol—of finding information for subversion-deviation/mutation-force, but finds it *already contained* within the church of *Santa Maria* itself. This information points to and links to the site's energetic, topographic, and cultural specifics: the invisible site forces that are already partially revealed by tiny anomalies in the original structure.[27]

Deformata illustrates the seed of a design strategy that is (indirectly) derived from the idiosyncrasies of the site, but one not bound by either a physical historic context or an ideal to be respected and revered. Such mutant and bulbous forms communicate that things are not ordered and symmetrical in the world. Further, the various protrusions, concavities, humps, bulbs, and spikes point to the sources of the world's disorder and begin a dialogue between object and site. In this way the reading of the architecture can involve not only the thing itself, but the thing *and* its context.

In short, *Santa Maria* does not *need* Piazza Navona or any other urban context to provoke a transformation: they are already latent in the architecture. Once they have been identified, *Santa Maria* can be transformed in her own impure site, just as much as *Sant'Agnese* can in hers. This realization is neither to admonish *Santa Maria* for her impurities, nor to criticize *Sant'Agnese*'s digestion into the city, rather to identify the context at Todi as being potentially *as* rich and powerful as the context of Piazza Navona in Rome. If this is achieved, the small shifts that have begun already might be allowed to proliferate to provide a new deformed model in the same context as the original almost-pristine form. The difference, of course, is that while the *Sant'Agnese* transformation is inevitably influenced by and inevitably mimics its urban surrounds, *Santa Maria*'s transformation cannot take on the physical characteristics of its environment because they are non-architectural. A different language of reaction, then, must emerge.

The undertaking of this exercise, therefore, seeks to find alternative ends (or beginnings) to the transformative possibilities of 'collage' as interpreted and then deployed by Rowe and Koetter, as well as to rationalize the enormous range of potential deformative motivations offered by both Lynn and Somol. The aim is to find another outcome that is not about reading memories of ideal form morphed into an adjacent site, nor about randomly formless yet self-absorbed objects, but to *make visible* the site—both visible and invisible—*through* the transformed object.

Notes

1 Thomas L. Schumacher, "Contextualism: Urban Ideals + Deformations," *Casabella*, 359–360 (*The City as an Artifact*) (1971), 84.

2 Ibid., 86.

3 Fred Koetter and Colin Rowe, "The Crisis of the Object: The Predicament of Texture," *Perspecta*, 16 (1980), 127.
4 Colin Rowe and Fred Koetter, *Collage City* (Cambridge, MA: MIT Press, 1978), 77.
5 Ibid., 140.
6 Koetter and Rowe, "The Crisis of the Object," 129. Rowe and Koetter, *Collage City*, 77.
7 *Sant'Agnese* was commissioned in 1652 by Pope Innocent X as a chapel for his family palace, the *Palazzo Pamphili*, which faced on to Piazza Navona. The church was worked on by several prominent architects, including Carlo Rainaldi and Borromini.
8 Koetter and Rowe, "The Crisis of the Object," 129. Rowe and Koetter, *Collage City*, 77.
9 Rosalind Krauss, *The Picasso Papers* (Cambridge, MA: MIT Press 1999), 28.
10 Ibid., 25–26.
11 Rowe and Koetter, *Collage City*, 129.
12 Ibid., 151.
13 Schumacher, "Contextualism: Urban Ideals + Deformations," 85.
14 Sir Banister Fletcher, *A History of Architecture*, ed. John Musgrove (London; Boston, MA: Butterworths, 1987), 872.
15 Georges Bataille, "The Deviations of Nature," in *Visions of Excess*, trans. Allan Stoekl (Minneapolis, MN: University of Minnesota Press), 1985.
16 Greg Lynn, "Multiplicitous and Inorganic Bodies," *Assemblage*, 19 (1992), 34.
17 "What is necessary for a rigorous theorization of diversity and difference within the discipline of architecture is precisely an alternative mathematics of form; a formalism that is not reducible to ideal villas or fixed types, but is in its essence freely differentiated." Greg Lynn, "New Variations on the Rowe Complex," in *Folds, Bodies and Blobs* (Brussels: La Lettre Volée, 1998), 201–202.
18 Ibid., 42.
19 Ibid., 49. This issue is elaborated in Greg Lynn, "Architectural Curvilinearity: The Folded, the Pliant and the Supple," in *Folding in Architecture* (London: Architectural Design, 1992).
20 Ibid., 39.
21 Colin Rowe, as quoted in Robert E. Somol, "Oublier Rowe," *ANY 7/8, Form Work: Colin Rowe* (1994), 16.
22 Somol, "Oublier Rowe," 16.
23 Lynn includes the urban, institutional, temporal, cultural, as components of the context to be responded to and is also careful to avoid the reproduction of the existing—attempting to transform "the indigenous information of its context into alien novelty." Greg Lynn, "The Renewed Novelty of Symmetry," in *Folds, Bodies and Blobs* (Brussels: La Lettre Volée, 1998), 65.
24 Somol, "Oublier Rowe," 10.
25 Lynn, "New Variations on the Rowe Complex," 214.
26 *Santa Maria Deformata* is a study by CODA.
27 Lynn already went some way with his own tests in projects such as the *Stranded Sears Tower* and *Cardiff Bay Opera House*. Here, Lynn explores the relationship between architecture and evolution and considers these explorations "new concepts and techniques in contextualism." Lynn, "The Renewed Novelty of Symmetry," 65.

8

KULESHOV EFFECTS

The Premature Burial of Montage Architecture

After several strikes, collage architecture was dealt a terminal blow by Jeffrey Kipnis in his 1993 article, "Toward a New Architecture," where he described it as an "exhausted tool." Kipnis believed collage moribund as a technique that could only ever reconstitute remnants from the past without the ability to look forward. He claimed that, as a design methodology, collage was "incapable of generating a projective architecture given its reliance on recombinatorial tactics applied to existing contexts."[1] While still prolific in architectural representation,[2] collage as a *design tool* seems indeed to be all but dearly departed today.[3] Unfortunately, however, buried alongside collage for reasons of association rather than exhaustion was the parallel but distinct theory of *Montage*.

Like collage, montage emerged in circles outside architecture in the nineteen-teens. Their common emphasis on the combination of fragments perhaps best explains why the two modes of production have often been misleadingly conjoined, particularly within architectural discourse. Kipnis pairs the two automatically, describing both "collage and montage," as a "giddy logic of play, of reiteration and recombination," that "supplant Modernism's sober self-serious search for the Brave New."[4] Or, as Stan Allen observed at the turn of the century: "collage and montage acquired force through the collision of distinct orders and the generation of tension across seams of difference . . . today the disjunctive play of difference has lost its power to shock."[5] That is, collage *and* montage—the latter if only by association, were found to be mutually at a loss for use or effect.

Looking back to the origins of montage, rather than collage, may then facilitate a reconsideration of some of the ideas, in particular notions of gestalt and of the scenic background, that are fundamental to niche-thinking as it applies to architecture. The reapplication of early film hypotheses to architectural rather than filmic scenarios, readdresses the possibility of the influence of an object's context on the perception of its meaning.

Montage

The origin of the potential synergy between architecture and montage is often associated with the work of Russian filmmaker, Sergei M. Eisenstein. In his "Montage in Architecture" (*c.*1938), Eisenstein acknowledges architecture's cinematic potential, citing the Acropolis of Athens as "the perfect example of one of the most ancient films."[6] Eisenstein takes up Auguste Choisy's nineteenth-century text, *Histoire de l'architecture*[7] as a film script and draws a parallel between the prescribed physical path of passage through the Acropolis and that of the shots captured by the filmmaker's camera. The montage effect, he writes, is made of "the sequential juxtaposition of those shots."[8]

A comparable re-examination of Choisy is present in a much more familiar text: Le Corbusier's *Vers une architecture*, originally published in 1920, pre-dating Eisenstein's version by around twenty years. Le Corbusier reiterates Choisy's imperative, that buildings should be organized according to the principles of the Greek Picturesque, or what he famously translated as the "promenade architecturale" in

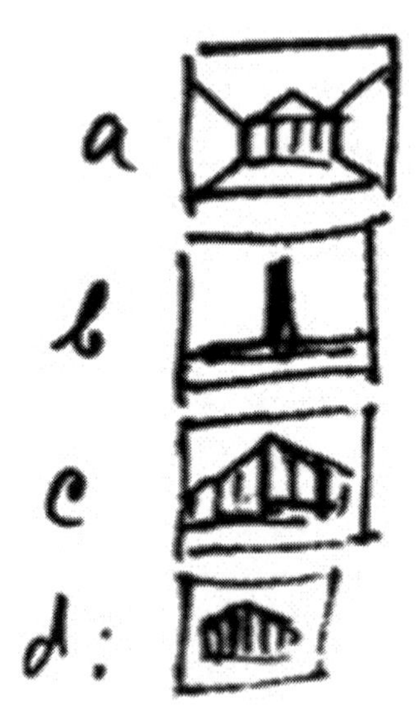

FIGURE 8.1 From Sergei M. Eisenstein, "Montage and Architecture," in *Assemblage* 10, December 1989, pp. 111–131 (orig. *c.*1938). Reprinted from Eisenstein's original essay. Used with permission of the State Cinema Museum and the International Eisenstein Center.

which " . . . the architectural spectacle offers itself consecutively to the view; one follows an itinerary and the views develop with great variety."[9]

Of course, the experience of montage differs fundamentally from the experience of architecture, in that montage in film is not a path followed by the body, but is instead, as Eisenstein notes, "the path followed by the mind across a multiplicity of phenomena, far apart in time and space, gathered in a certain sequence into a single meaningful concept; and these diverse impressions pass in front of an immobile spectator."[10] In this distinction, the concept of montage for architects is largely usurped by the Corbusian idea of promenade.

Although many texts exist on montage,[11] those written by Eisenstein and Le Corbusier in the early to mid-twentieth century mark the first moments when the principals of montage were seriously considered in relationship to the experience and production of architecture. Left to history, montage's role in our understanding of architecture might have remained merely the conception of a viewer's movement through a sequence of architectural 'shots.' However, the re-publication of Eisenstein's essay in a 1989 issue of the architecture journal, *Assemblage*, created a new point of entry for montage in architectural discourse, fueled, to some degree, by the by-then fraught relationship between collage and architecture. It may be, to some extent, the reprinting of this text that leads to the confusion of the terms in the 1990s. As Eisenstein's text unfolds, the role of the static image becomes increasingly dominant. According to Eisenstein, both religious shields and Soviet magazine covers are but 'montages' that take on entirely different meanings when back and front covers are juxtaposed. These descriptions steer his discussion closer and closer to collage.

However, the *origins* of montage one generation earlier, with fellow Russian filmmaker and mentor to Eisenstein's generation, Lev Kuleshov, focus on issues quite distinct from promenade and collage. By examining the whole image and not just the foregrounded subject, he investigates the process by which his audience understands meaning through film. Kuleshov eventually uncovers a dynamism in the relationship that exists between an object and its background that, reconsidered today, could propel the role of montage in architecture in an entirely new direction.

Moscow, 1919

Lev Kuleshov began his inquiry into the art of film in the packed Russian film theaters themselves. His intention was to observe the crowd, preferring low-cost venues where the public's reaction was not as controlled as in the more sophisticated alternatives. The result was a hypothesis that would become the basis of his experimentation with montage and its role in the manipulation of meaning.

Kuleshov produced a series of experimental shorts that were shown to a test audience. After the screening, he questioned audience members about their perception of the film. In one case, a long close-up of the expressionless face of

FIGURE 8.2 Stills from one version of the Kuleshov Effect as posted by EsteticaCC. See www.youtube.com/watch?v=_gGl3LJ7vHc&feature=kp.

well-known actor Ivan Mozzhukhin was inter-spliced with various extra shots: a bowl of hot soup, a woman in a coffin, and a child playing with a toy bear. Understanding Mozhukhin's facial expression differently depending on the shot with which it was intercut, test audiences were impressed by the actor's subtlety and range.[12]

In truth, the footage of Mozzhukhin's face was identical, and it was simply repeated between changing background shots. Nevertheless, it was perceived as subtly different because of associations made by viewers who projected a new meaning with each new background. Kuleshov arrived at the conclusion that meaning is invoked by juxtaposition rather than directly imposed by isolated shots or objects. Furthermore, the meaning associated with the film's primary object was established from a point outside the film itself, and indeed from a projection of the viewer on to the film as he or she made meaningful connections between the foreground and background.

In an inverse study, Kuleshov switched two pieces of footage. The first showed an imprisoned man's response to soup and, the second, his (different) response to freedom. In the switched version, the actor's reaction to soup was presented as his reaction to freedom and vice versa. The audience did not detect any switch, however, attributing the meaning appropriate to one background to the facial expression belonging to the other. Kuleshov concluded that "the viewer himself will complete the sequence and see that which is suggested to him by the montage,"[13] and thus meaning would be communicated as intended.

Through these experiments, Kuleshov argued, as Eisenstein would later reiterate, that the interrelationship of the shots was fundamental to film: "The content of the shots in itself is not so important as is the joining of two shots of different content and the method of their connection and their alternation."[14] Indeed, Kuleshov believed that montage itself was the irreducible source of film's artistic value, that content and narrative were irrelevant, and that the way in which the shots were assembled was more significant than the shots themselves.[15]

Kuleshov's "primacy of celluloid" bears more than a rudimentary resemblance to Formalism.[16] His position was likely influenced by the formalist group Opoyaz,[17] who claimed that the true material of literature was not plot, character, or theme, but language—a crucial compositional vehicle for comprehension and meaning.[18] Similarly, Kuleshov talked about his work as an alphabet, an organization of inarticulate material, working with syllables, not words.

The conclusions of Kuleshov's experiments, applicable to both film and language, go far beyond the notion that montage is simply a sequential combination of pieces. They suggest that meaning lies just as much with the context as it does the focal subject, or, in fact, between the two. Moreover, they suggest that meaning found there will be projected on to the object in order to re-inform its meaning. The effect he provoked, known today as the *Kuleshov Effect*, demonstrated the power of montage, in which "the spectator perceives the intentionally created *gestalt* in which the relationship of shot to shot overrides the finer aspects of any actor's performance."[19]

While incredibly important to our consideration of the context in relationship to the object, and gestalt has been described as precisely this, it is perhaps this term that, in fact, further blurs the distinction between montage and collage, especially because the term was also used to support Rowe and Koetter's *Collage City*. Here, gestalt ideas were cited as a perceptual inevitability, in the consideration of the urban condition: "Certainly," write Rowe and Koetter,

> in considering the modern city from the point of view of perceptual performance, by *Gestalt* criteria, it can only be condemned. For, if the appreciation or perception of object or figure is assumed to require the presence of some sort of ground or field, if the recognition of some sort of however closed field is a prerequisite to all perceptual experience and, if consciousness of fields precedes consciousness of figure, then, when figure is unsupported by any recognizable frame of reference, it can only become enfeebled and self-destructive.[20]

FIGURE 8.3 Rubin (Zissovici) Vase. CODA 2013.

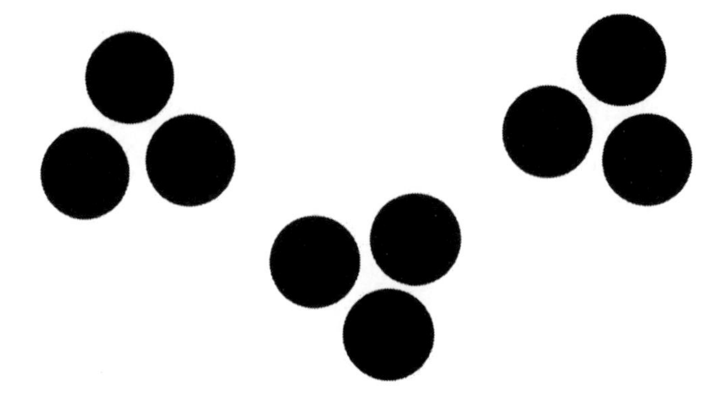

FIGURE 8.4 Proximity Gestalt. CODA, 2014.

Rowe and Koetter's solution to this destructiveness is not an unreasonable proposal. They propose a scenario in which figure and background are in dialogue in the urban context. They argue for an ambiguous reading of the architectural object at one moment as an object, and at the next as part of a background. The well-known *Rubin Vase*, developed by Edgar Rubin around 1915, illustrates the phenomenon of the rapid back-and-forth visual perception that occurs when the white vase is viewed as figure on black background or, alternatively, black silhouettes foreground a white background. Each condition exists separately as our perception fluctuates between two states, and regardless of how quickly the image appears to flip, the two are never viewed at once.

As noted, Kuleshov found that the audience inevitably groups together the shot of Mozzhukhin and the shot of the larger scene. Mozzhukhin, close-up, becomes the focal subject (as the buildings of the Acropolis would later become in Eisenstein's theory) and the changing scene becomes the background by which he is surrounded. In essence, while Rowe's and Kuleshov's differing interpretations of gestalt are at odds, what they mean is actually the same: the co-digestion of subject and object into one whole.

Pudovkin refers to a yet different genre of gestalt in Kuleshov. While acknowledging the inevitable figure–ground gestalt reading, Pudovkin believes that the Kuleshov Effect operates more pointedly in relation to the gestalt phenomenon called 'proximity.' In this branch of the theory, a number of objects (or sounds) are not read as individual parts but are perceptually grouped into a smaller number of elements due to their relative proximity. Thus, the observer of Kuleshov's film clips perceives scene one and scene two as related due to their quick succession. As demonstrated in the example shown in the above figure, the typical perception is an image of three groupings, rather than of nine separate fragments.

In psychological terms, the Kuleshov effect, whether due to figure–ground or proximity gestalts, is attributable to the function of 'assimilation,' that is, when meaning is given to or projected on to the object by the subject. Assimilation is at work "when the symbol '+' looks like adding, when a coffin appears imbued with the horror of death, and when a flag seems to have absorbed the particular virtues of a country."[21] Kuleshov's breakthrough was to locate the stimulus of that projection in the background.

Architectural Kuleshov Effects

Situated within his larger evaluation of montage and film, Kuleshov's filmic triad—subject, context, viewer—can be translated in architectural terms for experimental purposes. In place of Ivan Mozzhukhin: a building. In place of the background (soup, woman, or child): a varying context. The question for the audience is the same: are subtle changes in the unchanging expression of the faç(ad)e perceived as the context changes, resulting in a change of meaning?

An architectural Kuleshov experiment, rather than editing film, then, requires occurrences of shifting contexts in relation to a constant architectural object. Thus, we require a work of architecture that has moved or that exists in two or more locations.

Our first candidate bridges the gap between actor and architecture, a colossus that spans the Atlantic in her early life: the Statue of Liberty. Liberty was conceived

FIGURE 8.5 Colossal Hand and Torch, Bartholdi's Statue of "Liberty." Date issued: 1876. Courtesy of New York Public Library Photography Collection.

in Paris, on soil that was never intended as her permanent home, yet neither the sculptor nor the French public dissociated themselves from the undertaking of her construction. The Paris International Exhibition of 1878 featured Frédéric Auguste Bartholdi's statue—if only her head—as a point of pride for France. So great was this pride, in fact, that a quarter-sized replica, also built by Bartholdi, was produced to be retained in Paris. Sited on the Île des Cygnes, on the river Seine, the miniature statue was oriented toward her New York sibling, a move that translates to some, including Victor Hugo, as a sign that "bears witness to the union of two great peaceful lands."[22]

Two years prior to the Paris Exhibition, a counter-narrative was already forming around the partial monument. The Philadelphia Centennial had already set the stage for a claim to both American national and intellectual ownership over the

FIGURE 8.6 Head of the Statue of Liberty on display in a park in Paris. Date issued: 1883. Courtesy of New York Public Library Photography Collection.

incomplete statue. In the United States, it stood for decidedly American freedom, solidarity, and unity following the American Civil War.

Ten years later, as the finished statue was erected at its intended site on United States' soil, its meaning was again reconstructed, deviating greatly from its creators' intentions, not least because of its adjacency to Ellis Island and the gateway into the United States for millions of immigrants. As Edward Berenson has described:

> Never did Laboulaye and Bartholdi intend it to symbolize an open US door to immigration as many Americans would eventually come to see it, nor did the two Frenchmen understand the statue as representing the United States itself. For them, it stood for American liberty, a universal ideal that stemmed from the US experience but applied everywhere.[23]

Even within the United States, doubt surfaced over the statue's ability to radiate liberty in a country of such great public and institutional inequity. For many, the

FIGURE 8.7 Statue of Liberty—French pier. Courtesy of New York Public Library Photography Collection.

FIGURE 8.8 Statue of Liberty, 2013. Photo by Ryan Paxton/Caroline O'Donnell 2014.

statue symbolized the problem of state hypocrisy. The African American community considered the idea "ridiculous in the extreme" given the lingering racial violence and inequality still rife in the nation,[24] and at the inauguration event, a boatload of feminists condemned the embodiment of liberty as a woman "in a land where no woman has political liberty."[25]

As well as her early replication in Paris, hundreds of Lady Liberties have been built worldwide. Interpretations inevitably vary for scenarios from Liberty in the church to Liberty in the parking lot, but perhaps the most arresting change of context occurs in Charlton Heston's final scene of *Planet of the Apes*.[26] As Heston's character, George Taylor, famously rides his horse along the beach of what both he and the audience believe to be a distant planet, a jagged and alien shape passes closely in front of the dollying aerial camera. Its form is hardly recognizable until Taylor dismounts, incredulous: "Oh my God. I'm back. I'm home! All the time it was . . . We finally really did it. You maniacs! You blew it up! Damn you! God

FIGURE 8.9 *Planet of the Apes*, 1968. TM and © 20th Century Fox Film Corp. All rights reserved. Courtesy: Everett Collection.

Damn you all to hell!"[27] Finally, a beach-level shot shows the audience Heston's view: the Statue of Liberty, buried up to her midriff in sand, tarnished, but clearly recognizable. Fade to black. The statue itself does not change: in principle, her complete form is present. She is buried. Only her context has changed. The meaning generated by her new location on a wholly transformed planet Earth implies a global catastrophe of unknown origins in Earth's past (our future), one certainly not founded on ideals of friendship, equality, or liberty.

Admittedly, by reverting to film here, we have cheated in our architecturalization of the Kuleshov Effect. Such dramatic juxtapositions and large-scale movements are uncommon in architectural reality. What does occur frequently, however, and can serve our experimental purpose from here on, is an active and accurate copying. Our second example, then, is another Franco-American exchange: the American *White House*, home for the presidential first family, which

FIGURE 8.10 Children and parents on lawn of the *White House* for the Easter Monday egg roll, 1944. From the Library of Congress Prints and Photographs Division Washington, D.C.

FIGURE 8.11 *Château de Rastignac.* Courtesy of Michel Chanaud.

was first finished in 1800, expanded under instruction of Thomas Jefferson from 1806 to 1809 and then reconstructed in 1817; and the *Château de Rastignac*, which was begun just before the French Revolution in 1789, interrupted for about twenty years and finally completed between 1812 and 1817.

Beyond their physical context in the city versus the countryside, the radical difference in political contexts is glaring. The *White House* is understood even today as a bold symbol of power, purity, and the promise of new democracy for the nineteenth century. The latter, designed pre-Revolution, is reminiscent of several neoclassical monarchic precedents (*Maison Carrée d'Arlac*, in Mérignac, France, 1785–1789, *Leinster House*, in Dublin, Ireland, and other Georgian-era Irish country houses). Alone, either reading of the façade may be sensibly permitted and validated, but their direct relationship to their comparative contexts reveals the flexibility of its meaning. The intentional placement of the *White House* into the context of pre-Revolutionary France would make it possible to perceive the building as a country home for the French aristocracy. Or, place the *Château* in the *White House* image and it becomes a symbol of democracy because of the way that the building is mentally grouped with, or assimilated to, its context. Either interpretation of either building is possible, but both are ultimately determined by the larger scenario in which they are placed. We, a variation of Kuleshov's moviegoers, simply construct the meaning of the building with the information we are given. In the famous image of sheep on the lawn, the context is ambiguous. Whether this is now the rural context of Rastignac or the urban and democratic context of the *White House*, the audience is less certain.[28]

FIGURE 8.12 *White House* background, *Château de Rastignac* object. CODA, 2014.

FIGURE 8.13 *White House*, sheep on lawn, 1916–1919. From Harris & Ewing Collection, Library of Congress.

Such copying by the newly formed nation of the United States of America was common, even, improper as it seems, the copying of monarchic architecture (and urbanism) to represent the democratic regime. Ivy League universities copied the Gothic architectural style and campus layouts of their English predecessors, and wealthy immigrants such as the Rockefellers built in the revivalist style of their homelands.[29] Copying was accepted, celebrated even, during the nation's early phase, and again in the 1970s and 1980s, as postmodernism dominated architectural production, copies and pastiches abounded. This fact has been well documented in architectural essays on both Las Vegas and Disney World. However, in the last twenty years copies, in the West, have been increasingly condemned.

Ashton Raggatt McDougall's (ARM) *National Museum of Australia* (2001) demonstrates a contemporary case of direct architectural citation and, with it, a change of meaning. The museum complex, notoriously 'samples' many works of global architecture, including Jørn Utzon's *Sydney Opera House*, James Stirling's *Neue Staatsgallerie*, Le Corbusier's *Villa Savoye*, and most flagrantly a slightly scaled down and dematerialized but very recognizable version of Daniel Libeskind's *Jewish Museum* in Berlin. ARM's project attracted accusations of plagiarism from Libeskind himself,[30] but other architects insist that the context—particularly the presence of multiple other samples—clearly identifies the work as a quote.[31] The borrowed elements are strung together to a stylistically referential yet entirely different, if unapologetically eclectic, effect. Certainly a visitor would not be expected

FIGURE 8.14 Daniel Libeskind, *Jewish Museum*, Berlin. Google Earth, © 2014 GeoBasis-DE/BKG (7/24/2012); and Ashton Raggatt McDougall, *National Museum of Australia*. Google Earth, © 2014 DigitalGlobe (2/29/2008).

to feel the sorrow and disorientation expected of a visitor to Libeskind's *Jewish Museum*, and it is the context that frames that quotation. Instead, the visitor should understand something of the culture of Australia, which itself is an eclectic mix of imports from other cultures, although the fact that this wing houses the Aboriginal exhibition is not insignificant. The context provides the quotation marks that dissociate the architectural object from its original meaning and reframe it into a meaning of immigration and a subtle reminder of the atrocities in Australia's own history.

Paul Celan describes the anxiety in the *Jewish Museum* as coming not from the form itself but as arising in the spectator as he or she "becomes aware of the historical trauma configured in the materiality of Libeskind's architecture."[32] Whether through form, materiality, or other means, the background here is not necessarily the physical background but the ominous presence of the historical context of the Jewish people in Germany. As in many of the above cases, the physical context is not mute; it is itself rich with associations of historic, cultural, economic, and social affiliations that cannot be dissociated from its own meaning and consequently from the meaning of the architectural object.

Most recently, China has been maligned for its proliferation of copies. Architectural replication is nothing new here either: in fact, China has a strong history of replication that dates to its unification in the late third century BCE. When outlying states were conquered, a double of its main palace (sometimes reduced in scale) was built in Xianyang, the Capital City of Emperor Qin Shihuangdi, as a sign of victory. Duplication was still equated with domination in the 1950s, when the appropriation of Soviet architecture "served in the Chinese mind to vault China into leadership of the international socialist movement."[33]

Given the enormous growth in the country today, copies, especially of European origins, have abounded. Typically, complete historic old towns (Dorchester, England, Venice, Italy, or Hallstatt, Austria, for example) or historic buildings (Amsterdam Train Station, the Eiffel Tower) have been copied. In 2001, a fairly accurate copy of Le Corbusier's *Chapel at Ronchamp*, in Zhengzhou, capital of the northern central Henan province, was demolished at the insistence of the Corbusier Foundation, sparking discussions of architectural plagiarism laws in China. While most copies have been of historic buildings, recently the debate has been refueled by a case of "duplitecture"[34] concerning Zaha Hadid's *SOHO Wangjing Tower* and its near replica by the Chongqing developer Meiquan 22nd Century. And, as was the case with the White House, the copy may be completed before the original. Although the copy comprises two volumes instead of the original three, the formal similarities are difficult to deny. The smooth pebble-like forms are striated in horizontal bands and composed non-orthogonally on an urban island. In an interview in *Der Spiegel*, Zaha Hadid remains positive, hoping that the clones could exhibit some degree of mutation.[35] Unfortunately for her, this alleged copy, like many others, more likely sees its success in its replication rather than its evolution. Even so, we might also consider that Hadid's notion of mutation is one whose success is not judged, as it is in nature, through its relationship with its environment.

For our purposes, the in-situ renderings of both are hardly worth comparing, since both exist on island sites surrounded by wide streets with a backdrop of generic towers, but we might assume that the two cities consider themselves significantly different. In a debate, representatives from Meiquan cleverly attempted to shift the meaning of the alleged copy by using a contextual link: whereas the SOHO project supposedly referenced the Koi fish, their project, they claimed, was inspired by the cobblestones from the Yangtze River that pave the streets of

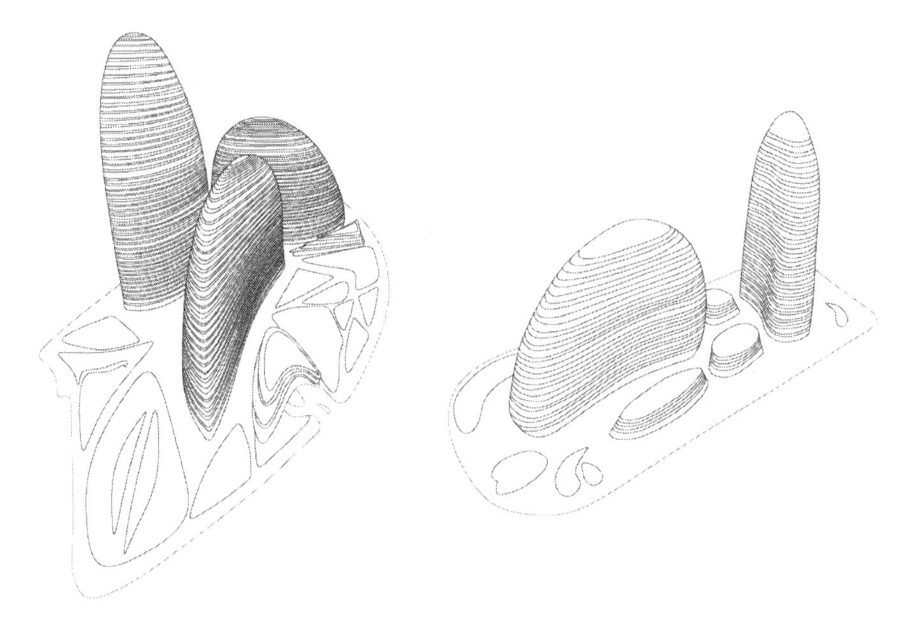

FIGURE 8.15 Zaha Hadid, *SOHO Wangjing Tower*, Beijing (left); and the Meiquan 22nd Century development, Chongqing (right). Redrawn by CODA, 2014.

Chongqing.[36] This presumably post-facto meaning given to the project is one that comes from its background: intuitively, the developers strengthened the connection between background and subject, in order to validate its originality.

The consequences for the meaning that becomes legible in these buildings and their different backgrounds remains to be seen, but the stage is now set. In tracing montage back to its origins in Kuleshov (and not in Eisenstein as has so often been the case), the role of the background in the perception of the meaning of the whole becomes crucial. The reintroduction of the term *montage architecture* and, in particular, of the *Kuleshov Effect*, allows the emphasis to perhaps bring the background to the fore. How might we design differently, given the Kuleshov hypothesis that the background is as effective and active in the reading of the work as the work itself? If we acknowledge a change of meaning through a change of contexts, how can our architectural output acknowledge the power of the background—both physical and invisible—in the construction of meaning within the architectural object?

Notes

1 Jeffrey Kipnis, "Toward a New Architecture," in *AD: Folding and Pliancy* (London: Academy Editions, 1993), 98.
2 As evidenced by the 2013 MoMA Exhibition, *Cut 'n' Paste: From Architectural Assemblage to Collage City*, July 10, 2013–January 5, 2014. Curator Pedro Gadanho describes his selection of work as "seamless digital collages that dominate contemporary architectural practice," www.moma.org/visit/calendar/exhibitions/1369 (accessed March 3, 2014).
3 For an in-depth discussion of collage and architecture see Andrea Simitch's "Re-Collage," *The Cornell Journal of Architecture*, 8 (2011).
4 Kipnis, "Toward a New Architecture," 98–99.
5 Stan Allen, *Practice: Architecture, Technique and Representation* (New York: Routledge, 2000), 168.
6 Sergei M. Eisenstein, "Montage and Architecture," *Assemblage*, 10 (December 1989), 116.
7 Auguste Choisy, *Histoire de l'architecture* (Paris: Gauthier-Villars, 1889).
8 Eisenstein, "Montage and Architecture," 116.
9 Le Corbusier and Pierre Jeanneret, *Oeuvre complète 1910–1929* (Zurich: Girsberger, 1964), 60.
10 Eisenstein, "Montage and Architecture," 111.
11 Of particular interest to architects may be Gilles Deleuze's explanation of montage as "the determination of the whole . . . by means of continuities, cutting and false continuities . . . " (*Cinema 1: The Movement-Image* (Minneapolis, MN: University of Minnesota Press, 1986), 30). Deleuze cites both Eisenstein and well-known filmmaker Dziga Vertoz but does not include Kuleshov in his discussion of cinema.
12 Ronald Levaco, "Introduction," in *Kuleshov on Film: Writings of Lev Kuleshov*, trans. Ronald Levaco (Berkeley, CA: University of California Press, 1974), 200.
13 Lev Kuleshov, "Art of the Cinema," in *Kuleshov on Film*, 46–47.
14 Ibid.
15 Lev Kuleshov, *Iskusstvo Kino: Moi opyt* (Moscow: Teakino-Pechat, 1929), 16–18. Sourced from Kuleshov, "Art of the Cinema."
16 Kuleshov, "Art of the Cinema," 26.
17 The Society for the Study of Poetic Language, founded in Petrograd in 1915 by Viktor Shklovsky, Boris Eichenbaum, and others.

18 Krystyna Pomorska, *Russian Formalism Theory and its Poetic Ambiance* (The Hague: Mouton, 1968), 23.

19 Vsevolod Pudovkin, *Film Technique and Film Acting*, trans. Ivor Montagu (London:Vision, 1954), 140.

20 Colin Rowe and Fred Koetter, *Collage City* (Cambridge, MA: MIT Press, 1978), 64.

21 Wolfgang Köhler, *Gestalt Psychology: An Introduction to New Concepts in Modern Psychology* (New York: Liveright Publishing, 1947), 219.

22 Robert Belot and Daniel Bermond, *Bartholdi* (Paris: Perrin, 2004), 361.

23 Edward Berenson, *The Statue of Liberty: A Transatlantic Story* (New Haven, CT: Yale University Press, 2012), 76.

24 *Cleveland Gazette*, November 27, 1886, quoted in David Glassberg, "Rethinking the Statue of Liberty: Old Meanings, New Contexts," paper prepared for the National Park Service, December 2003, 4, https://archives.iupui.edu/bitstream/handle/2450/678/RethinkingTheStatue-Glassberg.pdf (accessed March 9, 2014).

25 Berenson, *The Statue of Liberty*, 101.

26 Coincidentally enough, the 1968 film by Robert Schaffner was based on a 1963 French science-fiction novel, *La planète des singes*, by Pierre Boulle.

27 Spoken by the character George Taylor in *Planet of the Apes*, directed by Franklin J. Schaffner. APJAC Productions/Twentieth Century Fox, 1968.

28 A McMansion replica of the White House has been built by Fred Milani in Atlanta, Georgia. Its suburban context and possible foreclosure add yet another contextual background to the list.

29 Bianca Bosker, *Original Copies: Architectural Mimicry in Contemporary China* (Honolulu, HI: University of Hawai'i Press; Hong Kong: Hong Kong University Press, 2013), 6.

30 Deyan Sudjic, "Australia Looks Back in Allegory at its Inglorious Past," *The Guardian*, March 4, 2001, www.theguardian.com/theobserver/2001/mar/04/featuresreview.review2 (accessed March 3, 2014).

31 Matthew Rimmer, "Crystal Palaces: Copyright Law and Public Architecture," *Bond Law Review*, 14, 2, Article 4 (2002), 320–346, http://works.bepress.com/matthew_rimmer/30 (accessed March 3, 2014).

32 Paul Celan, *Sites of the Uncanny: Specularity and the Visual Arts* (Berlin: Walter De Gruyter, 2007), 241.

33 Jerome Silbergeld, "Foreword," in Bosker, *Original Copies*, ix.

34 Steven Heller, "Duplitectural Marvels: Exploring China's Replica Western Cities," *The Atlantic*, February 21, 2013, www.theatlantic.com/entertainment/archive/2013/02/duplitectural-marvels-exploring-chinas-replica-western-cities/273366/ (accessed March 3, 2014).

35 Kevin Holden Platt, "Zaha Hadid vs. the Pirates: Copycat Architects in China Take Aim at the Stars," *Spiegel Online International*, December 28, 2012, www.spiegel.de/international/zeitgeist/pirated-copy-of-design-by-star-architect-hadid-being-built-in-china-a-874390.html (accessed March 3, 2014).

36 Sian Disson, "Wangjing SOHO/Meiquan 22nd Century: The Sincerest Form of Flattery?," *WorldArchitectureNews.com*, January 7, 2013, www.worldarchitecturenews.com/wanmobile/mobile/article/21660 (accessed March 3, 2014).

9

DUCK JOKES

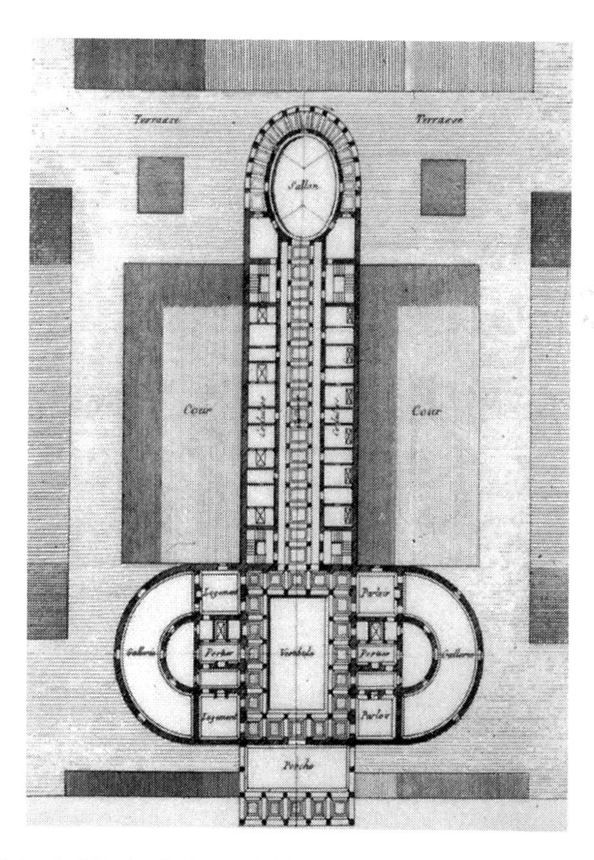

FIGURE 9.1 Claude-Nicolas Ledoux, Oikèma, 1789.

"You forgot to say 'away,'" says *Arrested Development*'s Michael Bluth, talking on the phone to a colleague who has called to report on his sister's first day at the office. Soon after, Michael repeats, "You mean 'away,' though, right? Because, otherwise, it sounds a little different." Hanging up the phone, Michael says: "Nellie has blown them all away."[1]

The set-up of expectation, followed by a surprising twist, is a common comedic tool. In Michael's case, the omission of the word 'away,' as in 'to blow away,' results in a new infinitive, 'to blow,' whose new meaning is too fallacious a truth for him to consider. This joke is a transformation of an earlier joke, in which an ambiguity of the same verb in the past tense is exploited as the character Tobias, covered in blue body-paint, responds to Michael's assumption that he is in the Blue Man Group. Tobias corrects: "I'm afraid I just blue myself."[2] This time, of course, blew/blue is the ambiguous object. These twist of expectation jokes are part of a larger grouping of jokes that rely upon the mental process of *incongruity resolution*.[3]

Albeit in less racy usage, Immanuel Kant was the first to propose a theory of incongruity resolution. "Laughter," he wrote, "is an affection arising from the sudden transformation of a strained expectation into nothing."[4] From the outset, then, the twin phenomena of expectation and transformation were on the table. Arthur Schopenhauer, who developed Kant's theory, substituted perceptual terminology, but the essence remains the same. To paraphrase Schopenhauer: when a correct perception overrides our incorrect preconception, humor occurs.[5]

The set-up of an intentionally ambiguous scenario is, as Edmond Wright explains, one of the primary methods of the construction of such a joke. A context is first established, and then replaced. The shock of being fooled, if only for a moment, and the subsequent acknowledgment of the error are, simply put, funny.

In his analysis of incongruity resolution, Wright deconstructs these jokes through diagramming out the parts of the ambiguous elements into their before (above) and after (below) contexts.[6] He begins with a simple knock-knock joke:

> *Knock, knock.*
> *Who's there?*
> *Toby.*
> *Toby who?*
> *Toby or not Toby, that is the question.*[7]

Wright's diagram of this joke centers on the two possible meanings of the object Toby/to be (a boy's name/a line from *Hamlet*). It demonstrates how the ambiguous element is interpreted differently depending on the contextual clues.

In the same way, a joke diagram could be drawn for our original *Arrested Development* joke, in which the infinitives to blow/to blow away are the ambiguous elements.

Wright, extending the logic of both Kant and Shopenhauer, emphasizes the elemental importance of contextual ambiguity:

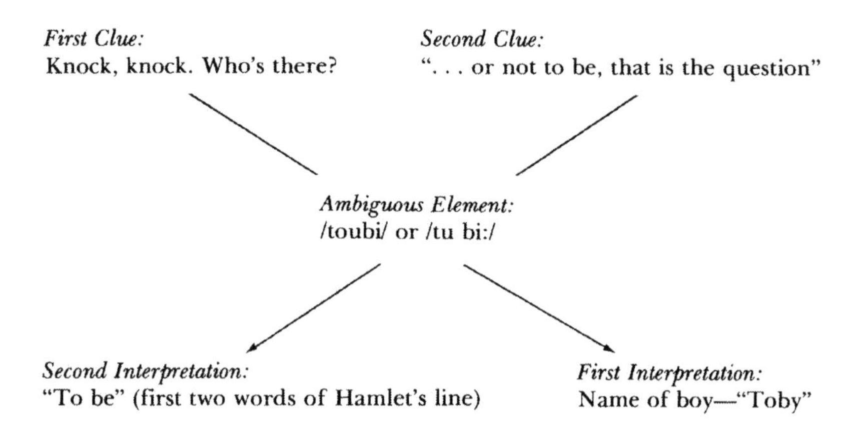

FIGURE 9.2 Edmond L. Wright, "Derrida, Searle, Contexts, Games, Riddles," in *New Literary History*, vol. 13, no. 3, "Theory: Parodies, Puzzles, Paradigms" (Spring, 1982), pp. 471–472 (463–477).

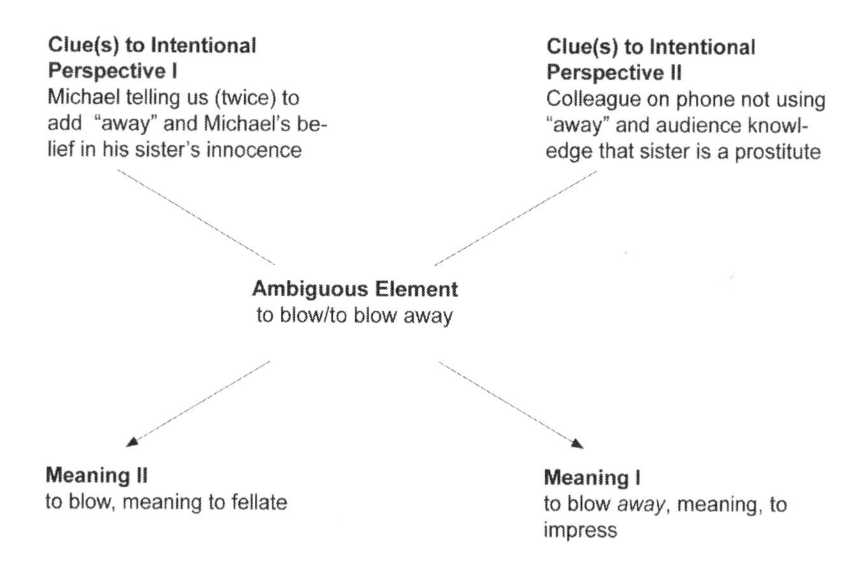

FIGURE 9.3 *Arrested Development* Blown Away joke diagram, after Edmond L. Wright's Joke Diagrams, CODA, 2014.

Jokes are made either (1) by establishing First Clue and Ambiguous Element, thus encouraging the First Interpretation, then providing the Second Clue, which forces the gestalt switch onto the Second Interpretation, as in the example above; or (2) by establishing First Clue and Second Clue, then providing the Ambiguous Element, thus forcing the two interpretations simultaneously (as in, "*What did the chimney-sweep say when he was asked if he liked his work?—It soots me.*").[8]

In a subset of incongruity resolution jokes, it is the shift of context—called 'frames' or 'scripts' by joke theorists[9]—that produces the resolution, and thus the humor. Take, for example, the following joke:

> *Two goldfish were in their tank.*
>
> *One turns to the other and says, "You man the guns, I'll drive."*[10]

Here, the second sentence forces a reconsideration of the context in which the scene is taking place (through the ambiguous object: tank), and it is this forced recontextualization that produces the comedy.

Wright explains this effect via a self-penned script of a series of Monty Python-style comedy sketches, in which the exclamation "*What a bore!*" is repeated in different settings. The word *bore* takes on different meanings as a result of the various different objects that can be called that word's various homophones (*boar* in a pig-farm in England, *boer* working on a farm in South Africa, *bore* (wave) in a boat, etc.). The humor, in this case, exploits the ambiguity of the object in question as it is repeatedly set into a new context.

In order to demonstrate the way in which the ambiguous sign may be given meaning through context, Wright employs the duck–rabbit illusion, which first appeared as a joke in the nineteenth-century German humor magazine *Fliegende Blätter*.[11] The illusion is well known for its ambiguous perception as a duck on the one hand or as a rabbit on the other. Never both at the same time, the figure

**Welche Thiere gleichen ein-
ander am meisten?**

Kaninchen und Ente.

FIGURE 9.4 The original Duck–Rabbit joke in *Fliegende Blätter*, 1892.

exists in a state of perpetual uncertainty between the two certain animal states. In psychologist Joseph Jastow's words:

> When it is a rabbit, the face looks to the right and a pair of ears are conspicuous behind; when it is a duck, the face looks to the left and the ears have been changed into the bill. Most observers find it difficult to hold either interpretation steadily, the fluctuations being frequent, and coming as a surprise.[12]

Wright, building on Ernst Gombrich's notion of rival contextual clues causing ambiguity in a sensory presentation,[13] argues that the ambiguity of the creature is greatly reduced by setting it in context: either the context of lettuce and a hutch, or of a pond and ducklings. While it remains *possible* to generate different perceptions in the one object, the addition of context to the image, Wright believes, strongly guides these identifications one way or another.[14]

By understanding the logic behind the construction of these jokes more completely—as a play between ambiguous object and context—it would seem to be of interest, to us, the makers of ambiguous objects embedded in contexts, to consider what is at stake for architecture when we play with that relationship.

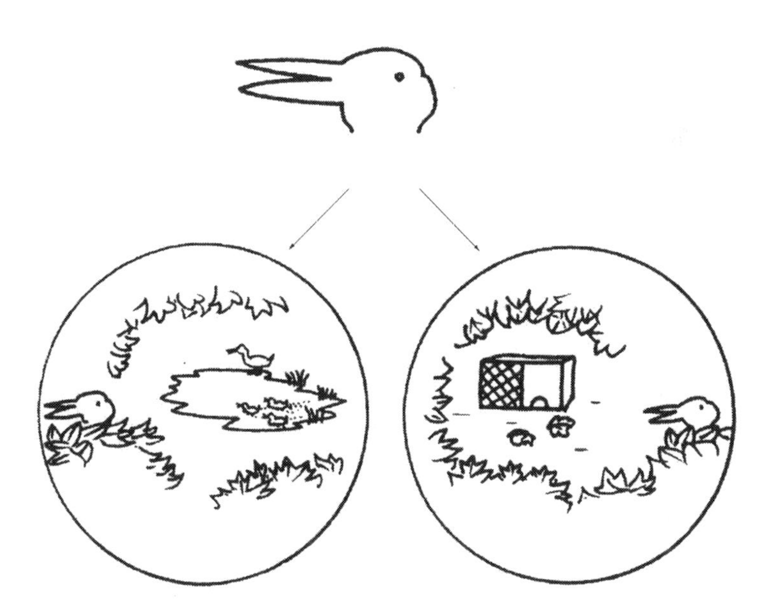

FIGURE 9.5 Edmond L. Wright, "Arbitrariness and Motivation: A New Theory," in *Foundations of Language*, vol. 14, no. 4 (July, 1976), pp. 506–508 (505–523).

The Architectural Joke

Perhaps like the human animal, architecture's ability to make a joke came more or less contemporaneously with the recognition of its ability to speak.[15] The term *architecture parlante*, coined in 1852 in an anonymous critique of the work of Claude-Nicolas Ledoux,[16] referred to an expression of programmatic meaning through form in a humorous and sometimes provocative way. The shape of the river inspector's house as an inspection tube and the hoop-maker's house as a hoop-shape might have incited chuckles, while the phallic form of the brothel perhaps provoked a more restrained snigger.

Ledoux's predecessor, Germain Boffrand, insisted that buildings should not only *have* meaning, but that they should *express* that meaning.[17] Emil Kaufmann took this idea one step further, describing *architecture parlante* as a kind of form that intended to "speak to the spectator's mind rather than appeal to his eye."[18] However, Boffrand and Kaufmann both reduce and imply the Vitruvian statement on the construction of meaning that preceded them by more than a millennium:

> Both in general and especially in architecture these two things are found; that which signifies and that which is signified. That which is signified is the thing proposed about which we speak; that which signifies is the demonstration unfolded in systems of percepts.[19]

Ambiguity, then, is present in one of architecture's earliest documents, and with it the possibility of the joke.

FIGURE 9.6 Claude-Nicolas Ledoux, *House of the Supervisors*, 1804.

FIGURE 9.7 The Big Duck, Flanders, Long Island. The Architectural Archives, University of Pennsylvania, by the gift of Robert Venturi and Denise Scott Brown. Photograph by Peter Blake, courtesy of the Peter Blake Estate.

By the nineteenth century, these inside jokes demonstrated architecture's unexpected ability to express something about itself—and in particular about its program—through formal language. More recently, of course, *Learning from Las Vegas* (1971) presented a similar typology: an architecture that communicated its function through its form: the *duck*. The duck idea originated not in Vegas but in Long Island, in a duck-shaped shop that sold, as the text-sign confirmed, "Fresh Killed: ducks and other fowl." The exterior form expressed the program (selling duck) of the building. The *duck* was explained through its comparison to the *decorated shed*, a nondescript and functional volume with a highly representational and two-dimensional façade: whereas the decorated shed "separated sign and enclosure, both were conflated in a 'duck' type: the architecture *was* the sign."[20]

Unlike the decorated shed, however, the duck is also *funny*. It is a building in the shape of an oversized duck, when a building should be a building and a duck should be a duck. This kind of humor is a kind of visual pun or double-entendre,[21] the result of the conflation of two familiar objects into one, rather than a switching of context. That is to say: this duck joke, like the original duck–rabbit, functions without context. The Long Island Duck is funny no matter what place it is in. Likewise, the structures selected by Venturi, Scott Brown and Izenour in Las Vegas were stand-alone gestures. Each sign of the Strip (whether literal or architectural) was independent from its surroundings. Signs negated the need for any context in the traditional sense. In fact, say the authors: "If you take the signs away, there is

FIGURE 9.8 Robert Venturi, Denise Scott Brown, and Steven Izenour, drawings of duck and decorated shed. From *Learning From Las Vegas*, pp. 88–89, revised edition. © 1972 Massachusetts Institute of Technology, by permission of The MIT Press.

no place."[22] The duck joke is semantic: it does not rely upon a context shift, but is instead self-contained within the object itself.

This is by now, thanks to postmodernists' copious use of the conflation of image and form, a familiar kind of architectural joke, from Frank Gehry's *Fish* (1986) to Kengo Kuma's *Doric Column* in his Mazda Showroom (1991). Looking back to Wright and Gombrich, however, we find another less-traveled path for the architectural joke: one that plays not just with the duck, but with the duck-in-the-duckpond.

Inside Jokes

Even before the duck's heyday, anti-duck Peter Eisenman had rallied against the semantic understanding of the architectural text in favor of the syntactic—a reading that was abstractive, organizational, and, most importantly, relational. Funnily enough, he was unintentionally laying the groundwork for the possibility of a new kind of contextual incongruity resolution joke in architecture.

Eisenman's syntactical thinking was founded on Colin Rowe's notion that architecture was like a code that could be deciphered. Rowe too understood architectural form as ambiguous: as "a continuous dialectic between fact and implication."[23] That is to say that, beyond the *real* building, there was a *virtual* building—*literal* and *phenomenal*, in Rowe's own terms—a phantom, constructed by the reading subject (a theory that echoes Vitruvius's original statement on the sign and the signified).

Following Rowe's thoughts on ambiguity and critique of claims to absolute legibility, Eisenman, in his early experiments, sought to 'unload' meaning from architectural elements: for example, his horizontal mirroring of a stair (rendering it inaccessible), or his use of the column for purposes other than structure. Alongside these practical experiments, Eisenman analyzed what seems at first glance to be the most parched of diagrams: Le Corbusier's *Maison Dom-ino*: consisting of no more than three horizontal slabs, six columns, six footings, and one staircase.

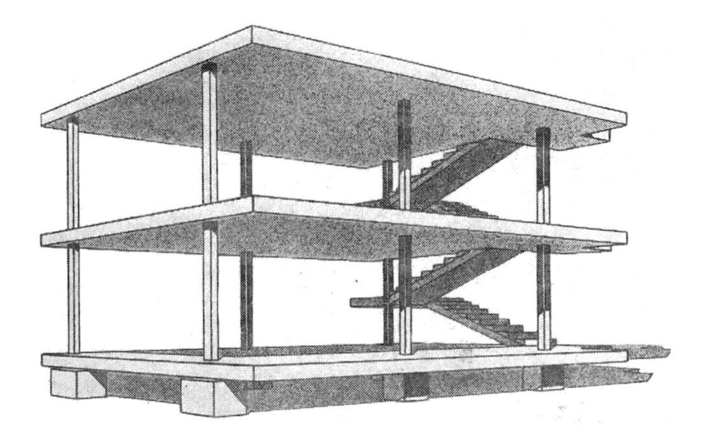

FIGURE 9.9 Le Corbusier, *Maison Dom-ino*. From *Oeuvre complète*, vol. 1, p. 23. © F.L.C./ADAGP, Paris/Artists Rights Society (ARS), New York 2014.

Despite the diagram's apparent dryness, Eisenman finds that the precise placement of elements such as columns and slabs allows the diagram to suggest "an idea . . . about itself."[24] He demonstrates the intentionality of Le Corbusier's design by redrawing the design not as it is, but specifically as it is not.

Eisenman diagrams four possible alternatives, from left to right: six columns placed at a greater distance from the sides than the ends (as in the original); four columns placed at a greater distance from the ends than the sides; four columns equidistant from all edges; and six columns in which the distance between centers is equal in either orientation.

This exercise in the production of fictional alternatives is repeated for *Dom-ino*'s other elements: the connection of the stair with the slab, the footings in the slabs, and the proportional spatial relationship between the slabs. The meaning of the diagram, then, comes from understanding the design decisions as precise articulations of the elements with each other, each alternative generating potentially

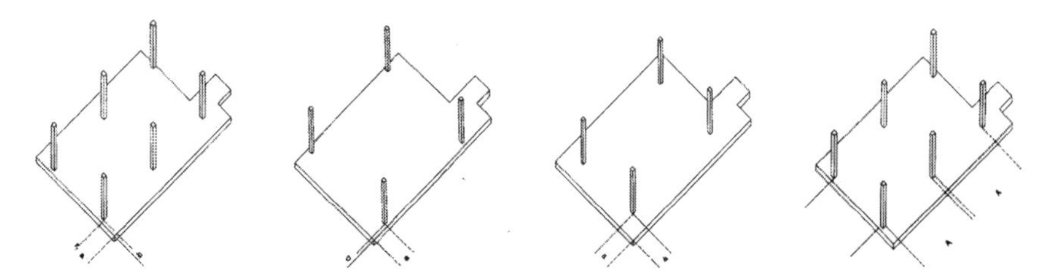

FIGURE 9.10 Peter Eisenman, analytic drawings from "Aspects of Modernism: Maison Dom-ino and the Self-Referential Sign." Drawings by Jay Johnson.

different meanings and the final selected set of conditions meaning something quite intentional. Through these miniscule but precise moves, *Dom-ino* expresses its dominant horizontality, differentiates between ends and sides, and suggests that while the sides are complete and will not grow, the ends are extendable (an idea reinforced by the diagram's title). As such, Eisenman sees *Maison Dom-ino* as a syntactical system distinct from the semantic understanding of the sign. In his own words, *Dom-ino* is a "sign system which refers to this most primitive condition of architecture, which distinguishes it from geometry, or from geometry, plus use, plus meaning."[25] That is to say: architecture's raw material is signs.

This analysis leads to his early house experiments, in which column grid and wall become separated by only a few feet, establishing an ambiguity as to which

FIGURE 9.11 Eisenman Architects, *Wexner Center for the Visual Arts*, The Ohio State University, Columbus, Ohio. Completed 1989. Column suspended over entry stair. Photo: D.G. Olshavsky/ARTOG. Courtesy Eisenman Architects.

system is structural, and which is representing structure. This ambiguity is perhaps best articulated in one moment of the *Wexner Center for the Visual Arts*, Columbus, Ohio, in which a column-like element is suspended over the entry stair.

The set-up is well planned; grids of structural columns and beams frame the interior and a skeletal corridor that projects from the entry into the interior warns of this system even before the visitor has entered. Their regular placement and identical white forms make for a familiar scene in which both the structural and organizational system are comprehended. Yet the attribution of 'structure' to the columns is called into question when, in the atrium, one column clearly hangs freely above the floor as if unfinished. By functional standards, this column is purposeless. This provokes reconsideration of the meaning of the column (and potentially those around it that in fact do meet the floor) and thus, possibly, the reaction of the laugh. This architectural joke can be diagrammed just as Wright diagrammed the knock-knock joke.

Rosalind Krauss comments on the role of the context in this set-up: "The non-supporting column is understood as a signifier ('a signal or notation') whose significance depends, at least in part, on the knowledge of everything that it is not."[26] Eisenman's process, and indeed his point, hinges upon the ambiguity in the preconceived role and performance of the column that is assumed as a result of its placement in the context of other similar columns. The relationship of the non-supporting column to the supporting columns that surround it is at once broken and intact. The incorrect preconception of the viewer is revealed as the observer perceives its non-supporting function and its meaning is called into question. Resolution of the incongruous column reveals what Eisenman set out to

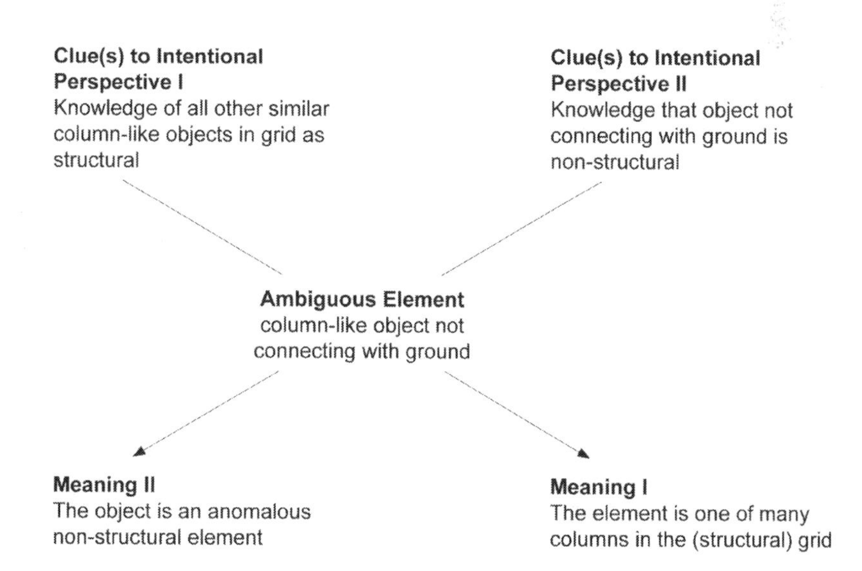

FIGURE 9.12 *Wexner Center* joke diagram in the style of Edmond L. Wright. CODA, 2014.

demonstrate: a syntactical understanding of architecture is one that refuses to consume the object in one complete optical bite and instead as a series of interrelated and meaningful pieces, or "traces" of its own "process of becoming."[27]

In and Out of Context

The impurity of the sign, its openness to becoming ambiguous, is at the heart of Eisenman's *Dom-ino* study. Each element does not mean one thing, it means different things depending on its context. Every diagram charts precisely the contextual relations existing in this emaciated diagram—the relation between the columns and the edge of the floor plane, the relation between the floor and stair, and so on. These elements are meaningless until drawn into relations with the others, at which time they together impart their meaning. For instance, as we have discussed, the distance of the columns from the side versus the ends implies a continuity or repeatability of the element in the longitudinal direction only. This meaning is only legible because of the relation between the two. Each is a supportive element of the other that, read together, produces meaning in architecture.

It is well known that Eisenman's architectural theory is influenced by Jacques Derrida, whose work builds in part on Ferdinand de Saussure's idea that words derive meaning from their context. In Saussure's words, "The idea or phonic substance that a sign contains is of less importance than the other signs that surround it."[28] It is precisely this mode of constructing meaning, one that relies on adjacent forms and patterns, that Eisenman tested with his *Dom-ino* diagrams.

In 1972 (translated into English in 1977), Derrida addresses the question of context specifically in "Signature Event Context," a critique of J.L. Austin's speech act theory, which explores the possibility of a "rigorous and scientific concept of context."[29] In order to be read, Derrida explains, the sign must be repeatable. Yet, each reading and writing or rereading and rewriting is slightly different because of its changed context. Derrida considers: "One can perhaps come to recognize other possibilities in it by inscribing it or grafting it onto other chains. No context can entirely enclose it."[30] Because of its ability to be cited, to be enclosed and protected by quotation marks, the sign "can break with every given context, engendering an infinity of new contexts in a manner which is absolutely illimitable."[31] Correspondingly, there can be no pure context because the context is already tainted by the past iterations of the sign.[32]

Imagine, then, an additional series of Eisenmanian diagrams in which all possible contexts in which *Maison Dom-ino* as a sign in itself (in which the whole is equal to the column or stair) would be drawn. Would these relations then construct new and different meanings? According to Eisenman's method of inquiry, they would: *Dom-ino* on a cliff-edge, *Dom-ino* in the city, and *Dom-ino* in a the savannah might generate different meanings. And probably, in certain contexts, for example in the case where the raising up of the house has become a necessity due to rising sea-levels, the juxtaposition might, in fact, be funny.

FIGURE 9.13 House, Suwanne, Florida. Photo from the series *(Post)line*, a research project on architecture's response to rising sea-levels, by Suzanne Lettieri and Michael Jefferson, 2013. Sponsored by the Eidlitz Travel Fellowship, Cornell University, Department of Architecture.

At the time when Eisenman was diagramming *Dom-ino*, he may have never allowed the consideration of context in the conception of the whole. It would have created a logical impasse, or at the very least a distraction in his analysis of strictly the relationship between formal elements. Derrida might well scoff, as he did at J.L. Austin's speech act theory, which was an attempt to consider broader physical and empirical scenarios as contributors to textual meanings.[33] Here, though, we must be careful as the meaning of *context* itself is beginning to split. There is, on the one hand, the context given by the text, in which the new context embraces and gives new meaning to a citation, or on the other hand there is the context outside of the text itself, the *actual* context in which the text is written or read. When Austin originally notes the inevitability of context (precipitating the chain of texts including Derrida's critique and counter-critique), it is this second context to which he is referring—not the written or spoken words that surround any given word, but a much more basic phenomenon: that the utterer himself is already in a context that is (probably) appropriate to the utterance.[34]

Derrida's essay derides Austin's insistence on the inevitability of actual context at the expense of linguistic context. He derides Austin's consideration of the physical surroundings instead of the speech/text surroundings. Yet as we have seen in the study of humor and contextual incongruity resolution, the relationship between object and its site is crucial to the formulation of its meaning.

While these two understandings of context seem fundamentally at odds, Gregory Bateson offers a bridge in the form of steps between the nested elements of language. Bateson reminds us that context, in fact, acts at a range of scales and that text acquires meaning from a process of continual rescaling from that of a letter, to a phoneme, to a word, to a sentence, to a paragraph and so on.[35] In English, twenty-six symbols are combined to make words. Each symbol, albeit independent, implies the presence or statistical likelihood of other letters adjacent to it. The letter T, for example, suggests that the next letter is likely to be an H, an R, or a vowel. The letters B, D, G, V, W, and Q are unlikely to be preceded by it, and X never will. The simple T provides information about its surroundings. Through a measured process of zooming out from the range of the phoneme to that of the word and then the sentence, Gregory Bateson identifies a sustained relationship that exists between context and content:

> A phoneme exists as such only in combination with other phonemes which make up a word. The word is the *context* of the phoneme. But the word only exists as such—only has "meaning"—in the larger context of the utterance, which again has meaning only in a relationship.[36]

While the contexts studied by Eisenman in the *Dom-ino* diagram are highly localized and, by his own proclamation, self-referential, that is, exclusive of site and other external factors, Eisenman did begin to consider context in its broader sense in his 1978 *Cannaregio Town Square* design. This project, which began with an analysis of both the real and fictional conditions of the site, had a radically transformative effect on Eisenman's trajectory. Subsequently, the acknowledgment of context can be found in a few of his later projects. Proposals ranging

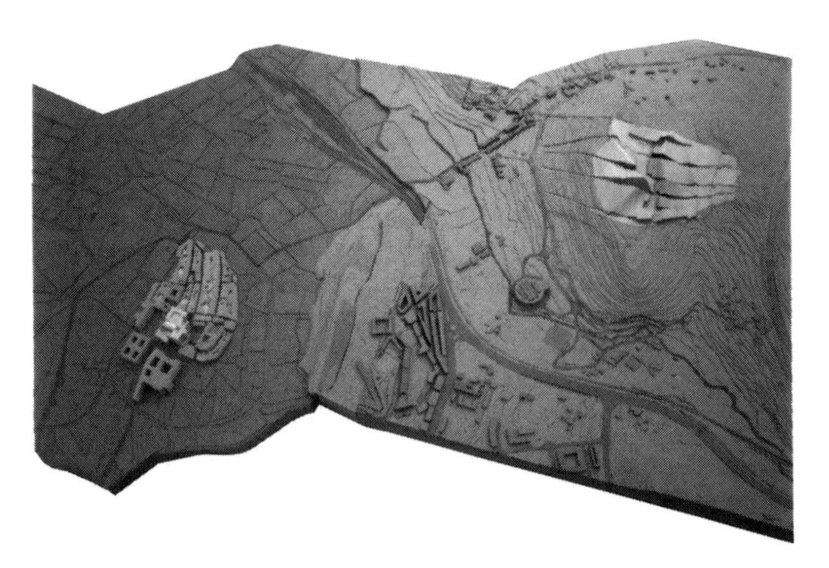

FIGURE 9.14 Model: Eisenman Architects, Santiago de Compostela *City of Culture*, site plan, 1999.

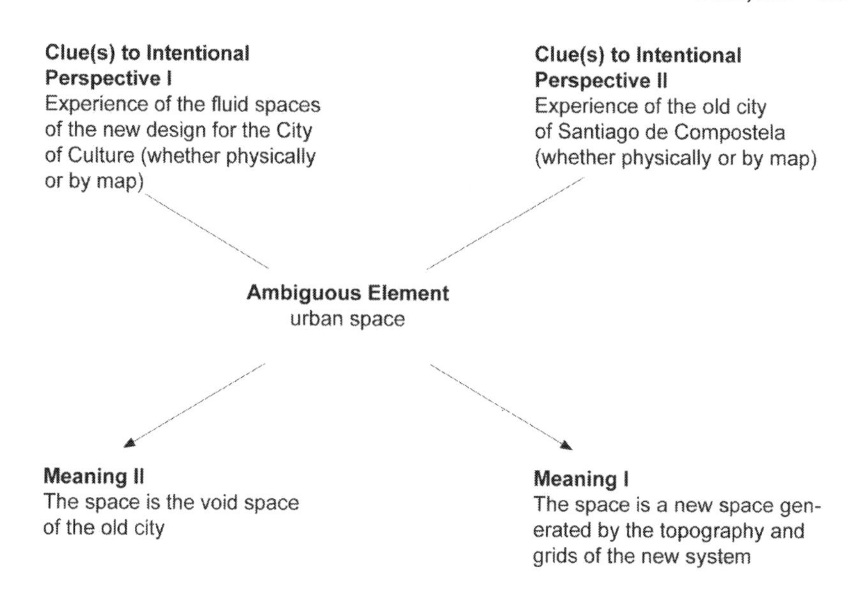

FIGURE 9.15 *City of Culture* joke diagram in the style of Edmond L. Wright. CODA, 2014.

from his *City of Culture* of Galicia in Santiago de Compostela (in the 1990s) to *Pompei Stazione Santuario* (in the 2000s) have engaged deeply with site as a generator of form.[37]

These are site-specific works, and as such they dually derive meaning from and contribute meaning to the experience of the greater environment. And, they may indeed generate a flash of laughter in the attentive student or particularly visceral visitor when he realizes that he is standing in the space of neither the newly built nor the old city of Santiago, but rather that the space of each is the same. In *incongruity resolution* terms, the original context of the *City of Culture* is replaced by the context of the old city of Santiago.

A similar, albeit more abstracted, version of the joke is played in *Pompei Stazione Santuario*, in which the characteristics (both formal and operational) of the ancient city of Pompei are overlaid in the station area, to create a field of familiar grains and grids, but now superimposed. This joke requires more work to decipher, and demonstrates Eisenman's ongoing interest in the issue of legibility.

Despite many proclamations to the contrary,[38] Eisenman admitted in a 2007 interview that "context matters," and that "it is not possible to transform anything without beginning *somewhere*."[39] And, as his later work demonstrates, that material need not be limited to the local contexts of columnar relations as in *Dom-ino*, or even the *Wexner Center*. If the relationship between column and slab generates

FIGURE 9.16 Model: Eisenman Architects, *Pompei Santuario Station*, 2007.

meaning, then, following the same logic, meaning must similarly be generated by the relationship between a built object and its environment.

In a recent response to Eisenman's "Duck Soup," a critique of Charles Jencks's book, *The Iconic Building*, Jencks, in his usual tongue-in-cheek manner, calls Eisenman a "duck-in-denial" and his buildings "non-duck ducks."[40] While these alleged Eisenmanian ducks do not refer to their function in the way that the Long Island Duck did, they are signifiers of other signifieds: Jencks calls out the "Terragni Duck" (Eisenman's *Cardboard Houses*) and other "Volumetric Ducks" (the *Max Reinhardthaus* as an icon of folding and of the arch; and the *Memorial to the Murdered Jews of Europe* as an icon of the graveyard). Jencks is clearly stretching the original meaning of the duck here, using it to mean 'referent' or 'image' rather than the original connotation of 'program,' but the inescapable element of the iconic sign in the image of the whole work is also not untrue.

Yet in light of his rarely admitted contextual tendencies, Eisenman may instead be a different kind of duck. These later works—in which the physical context is 'drawn in' and becomes central to the project—are perhaps more ducks-in-the-duckpond, in the Wrightian sense. The duck (rabbit) gains its identity from the pond, as the duckpond gains its identity from the duck. While Jencks and Eisenman's duck texts remain focused on the building, its formal qualities, and its function, they distract from the heart of a discussion about the ambiguity that lies with both the architectural object and its site, a quality in each that is capable of producing form, meaning, and even jokes, in architecture.[41]

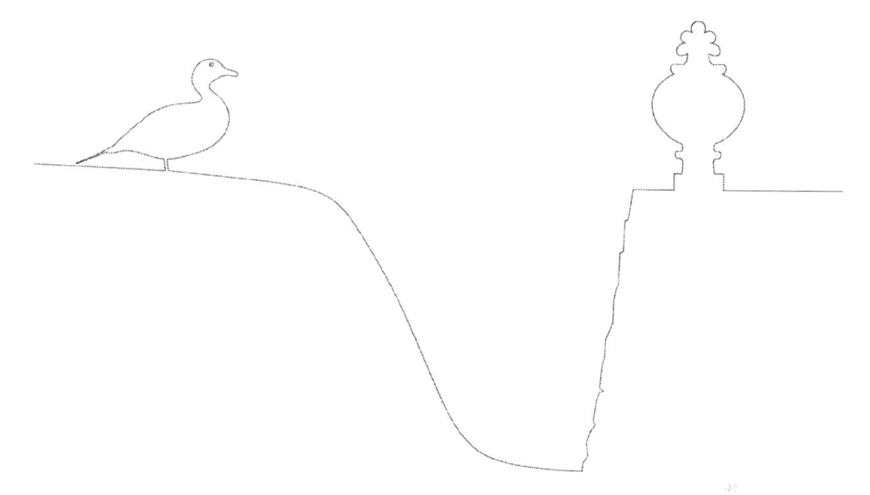

FIGURE 9.17 Ha-Ha Ha-Ha Wall. CODA, 2014.

Notes

1 *Arrested Development*, season 3, episode 11, "Family Ties." Originally aired on *Fox*, 2006.
2 *Arrested Development*, season 2, episode 1, "The One Where Michael Leaves." Originally aired on *Fox*, 2004.
3 Perhaps the mental process that occurs in Incongruity Resolution is comparable to the flickering between states that occurs in the perception of collage or the gestalt created by montage. Thanks to Mark Morris for this observation.
4 Immanuel Kant, *Critique of Judgment* (New York: Cosimo, 2007), 133.
5 Matthew Hurley, Daniel Dennett, and Reginald Adams, *Inside Jokes* (Cambridge, MA: MIT Press, 2013), 47.
6 Edmond L. Wright, "Derrida, Searle, Contexts, Games, Riddles," *New Literary History*, 13, 3 (*Theory: Parodies, Puzzles, Paradigms*) (Spring, 1982), 471. Many other joke diagrams are developed in Edmond Wright, *Narrative, Perception, Language, and Faith* (Basingstoke: Palgrave Macmillan, 2005).
7 Jane Nissen (ed.), *The Oxfam Crack-a-Joke Book* (Harmondsworth: Puffin Books, 1978), 96.
8 Ibid., 80.
9 R.C. Schank and R.P. Abelson, "Scripts," in *Scripts, Plans, Goals, and Understanding: An Inquiry into Human Knowledge Structures* (Hillsdale, NJ: Lawrence Erlbaum, 1977) and M. Minsky, "Frames," in "Music, Mind and Meaning," in *Music Mind and the Brain: The Neuropsychology of Music*, ed. Manfred Clynes (New York: Plenum, 1981).
10 Hurley et al., *Inside Jokes*, 42.
11 Unattributed drawing in *Fliegende Blätter* (October 23, 1892), 147. The caption reads "Which animals are most like each other?"; the answer: "Rabbit and Duck." The image was borrowed by psychologist Joseph Jastrow in several publications, including "The Mind's Eye" (1899), and later by Ludwig Wittgenstein, in *Philosophical Investigations* (1953), and by Ernst Gombrich, in *Art and Illusion* (1960).
12 Joseph Jastrow, "The Mind's Eye," *Popular Science Monthly*, 54 (1899), 299–312.
13 E.H. Gombrich, "Illusion and Art," in *Illusion in Nature and Art*, ed. Richard. L. Gregory and Ernst H. Gombrich (London: Duckworth, 1973), 193–243.
14 Edmond L. Wright, "Arbitrariness and Motivation: A New Theory," *Foundations of Language*, 14, 4 (July, 1976), 505–523. Wright suggests that others are finding similar

evidence, notably R.L. Gregory, in *Concepts and Mechanisms of Perception* (London: Gerald Duckworth, 1974), 536.

15 In Henri Bergson, *Laughter: An Essay on the Meaning of the Comic*, trans. Cloudesley Brereton and Fred Rothwell (New York: Dover, 2005; orig. New York: Macmillan, 1911), 2; Bergson notes that laughter is a strictly human and not animal behavior, implying that those specifically human traits of language, speech, and intelligence are necessary foundations of comedy.

16 Critique written for *Magasin Pittoresque* in 1852, and entitled "Etudes d'architecture en France."

17 Germain Boffrand, *Livre d'architecture* (Paris: Guillaume Cavelier père, 1745), 11.

18 Emil Kaufmann, "Three Revolutionary Architects, Boullée, Ledoux, and Lequeu," *Transactions of the American Philosophical Society*, New Series, 42, 3 (1952), 447.

19 Marcus Pollione Vitruvius, *De architeturra*, trans. F. Granger (London: Loeb Library, 1930), 1, iii, 3.

20 From Peter Blake's "The Long Island Duckling," illustrated in *God's Own Junkyard: The Planned Deterioration of America's Landscape* (New York: Holt, Rinehart and Winston, 1979).

21 Comparable to *Arrested Development*'s conflation of the job-title *analyst* with that of *therapist*, which together become "analrapist." *Arrested Development*, Season 3, episode 3, "Forget-me-now," 2005. Originally aired on *Fox*.

22 Robert Venturi, Denise Scott Brown, and Steven Izenour, *Learning From Las Vegas* (Cambridge, MA: MIT Press, 1972), 12.

23 Colin Rowe and Robert Slutzky, in "Transparency: Literal and Phenomenal," *Perspecta*, 8 (1963), 51.

24 Peter Eisenman, "Aspects of Modernism: Maison Dom-ino and the Self-Referential Sign," *Oppositions*, 15/16 (Winter/Spring, 1979), 119–128.

25 Ibid. Also, "Thus, in cases where a simple geometry exists as a basic diagram, the 'architecture' seems to be reduced to the decorative grafting of some aesthetic skin or the insertion of a particular use into the given geometry. Likewise, if we . . . begin with some program of use of a site context which logically suggests a simple order, the question of whether the diagram is any more or any less architecture would remain exactly the same" (p. 193).

26 Rosalind Krauss, "Death of a Hermeneutic Phantom: Materialization of the Sign in the Work of Peter Eisenman," in *Peter Eisenman, House of Cards* (New York: Oxford University Press, 1987), 174–175.

27 Peter Eisenman, "The End of the Classical: The End of the Beginning, the End of the End," *Perpspecta*, 21 (1984), 154–173.

28 Ferdinand de Saussure, *Course in General Linguistics* (New York: New York Philosophical Library, 1916 [trans. 1959]), 121–122.

29 Jacques Derrida, "Signature Event Context," in *Limited Inc.* (Evanston, IL: Northwestern University Press, 1988), 3.

30 Ibid.

31 Ibid., 12.

32 "To speak or write the word is by necessity a contamination: iterability means impurity." There can be no pure context because the context is "already broached by past uses." Diane Davis reminds us that even 'I love you' is a citation, "a citation ripped from a prior context remixed and repurposed. The most intimate communication between you and someone else . . . is and can only be a citation, in a new context and with a new audience." Every sign inevitably carries with it traces of its former contexts. In many cases the context can radically change the meaning of a word or expression. Davis presents '911' as an example

of such polysemia: in the United States '911' can mean, depending on the context, an emergency phone number, the date of the world trade center disaster, 1973 in Chile, a date in September, a number, a year in the tenth century, and so on. Similarly, '999' may mean an emergency telephone number in England, but in the United States, it may mean the 2012 Republican presidential hopeful Herman Cain's dubious tax plan. Polysemia is the reason one must sometimes ask "Wait, what's the context?" "Where were you at the time, with whom were you speaking, what else was said?" (Diane Davis Lecture: Iterability, Dissemination, and Context, November 15, 2011, at the European Graduate School (EGS), Media and Communication Studies Department, Saas-Fee, Switzerland.)

33 Derrida, "Signature Event Context," 15.

34 For example, an 'I do,' means something different from any other 'I do,' if the utterer is with his almost-bride at the altar.

35 Perhaps another joke here, this time from *Father Ted*: "These are small; but the ones out there are far away." *Father Ted*, Season 2, episode 1, "Hell," Channel 4 Productions. Thanks again to Mark Morris.

36 Gregory Bateson, *Steps to an Ecology of Mind* (Chicago: University of Chicago Press, 1972), 408.

37 The author being less than an innocent by-stander in the latter case.

38 Most recently in "Wobble: The Cat Has Nine Lives," the ninth in a series of conversations between Peter Eisenman and Mark Wigley, with Enrique Walker, at Wood Auditorium, Columbia University GSAPP, September 12, 2012, www.youtube.com/watch?v=Gu4-ErX6hDA.

39 Emphasis added. Interview with Peter Eisenman by Ling Fan and Caroline O'Donnell, *Pidgin*, 4, 95. The quote continues: "In other words, if design is the move from A to B, you have to understand what A is. And A is the context, program, etc. The places with the most context are for me the most interesting because it gives the chance to take a very rich A and transform that rich A into a rich B."

40 Peter Eisenman, "Duck Soup" in *Log*, 7 (Winter/Spring 2006), edited by Cynthia Davidson, co-edited by Denise Bratton; and Charles Jencks, "Eisenman Ducks," *Log*, 9 (Winter/Spring 2007).

41 There are two kinds of people in the world: those who require closure . . .

10

FUGLY

In the fifteenth century, as voyagers explored the world's uncharted territories, they discovered new species that deviated radically from the known types. At first, these novelties were explained as extreme variations within established species—Marco Polo infamously mistook a rhinoceros for an "ugly unicorn."[1] The notion that new species existed, or that species themselves were in flux, was inconceivable.

It was in such an intellectual climate of platonic fixity, as Charles Darwin was nervously preparing his revolutionary *On the Origin of Species*, which would explain evolution as unmotivated rather than aspiring to any platonic ideal, that Karl Rosenkranz published *Aesthetic of Ugliness* (Die Ästhetik des Hässlichen) in 1853. Despite a thorough record of the development of theories of beauty throughout history, there was little documentation of ugliness itself, except in its definition as the opposite of beauty. *Aesthetic of Ugliness* represented a rigorous investigation into the ugly in nature, art, and religion, and at last considered the ugly as a subject in itself, rather than as an erroneous manifestation of the beautiful. The work is founded on, but eventually surpasses, an understanding of the ugly as an opposition to traditional definitions of beauty that rely on harmony, totality, and unity.

Notions of change versus stasis originating with Darwin forced a rethinking of the platonic model of the ecological world, and slowly the evolutionary model has percolated into many fields. Nevertheless, until very recently, the platonic model has dominated the discipline of architecture, from Palladio to Le Corbusier to Colin Rowe.[2] Even today, while a belief in ordering systems may manifest itself differently—the mathematical-geometrical bases may have shifted scale, focusing more on the part now as opposed to the whole—it is arguable whether or not the model of order and proportion has lost its grip on architecture.

In the contemporary climate of anything goes, however, value judgments of what is beautiful or ugly in architecture have begun to lose their power. With beauty no longer the ultimate goal today, Rosenkranz's pre-Darwinian theory of ugliness opens new and unexpected objectives for the production of architecture today.

Formal Ugliness

Beginning with the assumption that unity is the principle condition of all that is beautiful, Rosenkranz lays out the qualities of ugliness in three categories:

1. Formlessness/Amorphousness
2. Deformation/Asymmetry
3. Non-unity/Disharmony differentiated and incompletion.

Formlessness/Amorphousness

> The primary requirements of the beautiful are boundaries; it must acquire unity and relate its differences as organic moments of that unity. This notion of abstract formulation is the logic of the beautiful, because it abstracts itself from the content and imposes the same formal necessity on all beauty, no matter how it is materialized or conceptualized.[3]

According to Rosenkranz, amorphousness is the absence of boundary to the outside and is ugly *only* when a boundary is required and not present (otherwise space, time, reasoning, and desire would be ugly because they are unbounded). Further, monotony or lack of differentiation within the form is also ugly. Unity can itself become ugly with repetition and so difference or dissolution within the unity is necessary to avoid the ugly. This dissolution can become ugly if it occurs where it is not expected or supposed to occur.

Deformation/Asymmetry

> Unrestricted diversity is beautiful, as long as it contains certain logics of grouping.

Symmetry, in the abstract sense, is simply regularity. However, too much regularity is tedious. At the same time, diversity becomes ugly if it lacks organization. Rosenkranz clarifies: "Symmetry is not plain unity, not plain otherness nor simple non-differentiation; not plain regularity, but unity which contains difference within its sameness."[4] Extremes are ugly—only a balance between repetition and differentiation is beautiful.

If symmetry is negated, disproportion, which is ugly, results. If no symmetry was or is potentially present, that is, if a form is complete, it is not ugly. It is the sense of incompleteness or unfinishedness that is ugly. A cripple with shrunken or withered feet demonstrates this ugliness, as does a church with one tower shorter than the other. Again, expectation comes into play: the *absence* of symmetry, where it is expected, is ugly, especially if it has been removed, or if the potential was there but has not been executed.

Non-Unity/Disharmony

> The beautiful can increase difference up to the rupture of the contradiction, as long as it lets the contradiction re-dissolve into unity, for through the *dissolution of rupture* harmony is produced.[5]

With a certain force, nature and art can overcome the rigidity of symmetry. In order to achieve overall harmony, the regularity and symmetry of minor relations is sacrificed, as evident in comprehensive architectonic concepts, such as the much-praised Castle Marienburg.

Harmony is the generation of differences as vivid elements of the integral whole and their unrestricted correlation. It is not unity that dissolves in unrelated differences, it is difference that is reincorporated into the whole. If unity dissolves into difference but those differences cannot re-merge, non-harmony occurs. Disharmony—a step further—occurs if the unity of differences is destroyed by becoming a contradiction without returning to unity.

As a stage in the transition from beauty to ugliness, Rosenkranz repeatedly refers to the comical, which results from "the continuous recurrence of ever the same difference instead of the expected distinct difference, partially from overturning a design from its initial movement into an entirely different, opposite end."[6]

Ugliness as Reaction

> Beautiful is, as Kant rightly states, what pleases apart from all interest; thus ugly is what displeases apart from all interest. The disharmonic can in fact arouse our interest without being beautiful; this we call *interesting*. Something devoid of internal contradiction we will not call interesting. The simple, light, transparent is not interesting; the great, sublime, sacred, are above such expression; they are more than merely interesting. But the complicated, contradictory, amphibolic and therefore the unnatural, the criminal, the strange, even the lunatic are interesting. The seething restlessness in the boiling pot of contradiction has a magical attraction.[7]

In *On Ugliness*, Umberto Eco lists Rosenkranz's use of the terms of negation in his definition of ugliness: incorrectness, absence of form, asymmetry, disharmony, disfigurement, deformation (the wretched, the vile, the banal, the fortuitous, the arbitrary, and the gross), and the repugnant (the ungainly, death and the void, the horrendous, the vacuous, the sickening, the felonious, the spectral, the demoniac, the witchlike, and the satanic), and notes that the richness of these terms is "too much to allow us to carry on saying that ugliness is merely the opposite of beauty understood as harmony, proportion, or integrity."[8] Eco explains that, "whereas all the synonyms for beautiful could be conceived as a reaction of disinterested appreciation, almost all the synonyms for ugly contain a reaction of disgust, if not of violent repulsion, horror or fear."[9] This notion, originating in Kant's idea of "disinterested pleasure" in *Critique of Judgment*, wherein the object of beauty can be appreciated without reaction or engagement, considers the ugly as not merely the opposite of beauty, but something that uniquely provokes a response or action on the part of the subject.

Mark Cousins, whose collection of essays on the subject of the ugly has been the most comprehensive entry of ugliness into architecture, notes similarly that: "Ugliness in its positive dimension, in its force, provokes within the subject a turning away, a retreat."[10] On setting eyes upon the ugly, one scurries into the realm of the defenses, with the impulse of "turning away, closing my eyes, shutting my ears, being bored, killing time, being nowhere, waiting, all investment withdrawn from the object."[11]

Whereas beauty can be looked upon without emotion or real engagement, ugliness, in short, produces a visceral reaction.[12]

Ugliness as Failed Expectation

> When bread is baked some parts split here and there, but the parts that this opens, while contrary to the baker's art, are in a certain sense very fine and above all, they whet the appetite wonderfully. In the same way, ripe figs also split open. Consider olives, when they are fully ripe: it is precisely that almost rotten look that lends a particular beauty to the fruit. Things like ears of corn bent toward the ground, the proud looks of the lion, the slobber running from the jaws of wild boars, and countless other examples, considered separately, are far from beauty. But because they follow nature's order, they help to adorn that order and give pleasure.

This description from Marcus Aurelius (second century, *The Meditations*) may be considered to be in direct contradiction to Rosenkranz's idea of completeness, according to which the bread, in its deviation from the platonic ideal, should be ugly. However, the bread is not *expected* to be perfect—it is meant to have cracks and therefore the cracks appear as a fulfillment and elaboration of the beautiful.

Overriding the categorization of ugliness as formlessness/amorphousness, deformation/asymmetry, and non-unity/disharmony, is a definition of ugliness as something fundamentally unplanned, unexpected, not *supposed* to be. Rosenkranz's amorphousness, for example, has conditions: the amorphous is ugly only when it is *intended* to have a form, yet does not. The asymmetrical is ugly when it has been symmetrical and the symmetry has been destroyed, or if the realization of its potential symmetry has been stilted.

The issue is one of *expectation*. If decay occurs as it is supposed to, as a mountain range disappears behind clouds, it can be beautiful. It is *unexpected* decay that is ugly: the withered arm of a cripple, the gothic cathedral with one unbuilt tower, an amputation. Similarly, Umberto Eco, in his book *On Ugliness*, describes the reaction to a toothless stranger as a deviation from the expected:

> What disturbs us is not the form of the lips or the few remaining teeth, but the fact that the few survivors are not accompanied by the others that *should be* in that mouth . . . Faced with the inconsistency or incompleteness of that whole—we feel compelled to say dispassionately that this face is ugly.[13]

Equally ugly is the asymmetrical growth of a third limb, or the addition of a misplaced window. In his essay "The Renewed Novelty of Symmetry," Greg Lynn studies William Bateson's mutation of the human hand. Here, however, the mutated hand is *more* symmetrical than the normal hand, the thumb having mirrored itself. Bateson proposes that this resultant condition is due to a *loss* of information, arguing that where information is lost, the organism reverts to copying known information and therefore symmetry occurs as a default. "What is both disturbing and beautiful about this example," Lynn writes, "is that the mutation replaces the asymmetry of the opposed thumb with a higher level of symmetry."[14] Yet the increase in symmetry does not have the effect of rendering the hand more beautiful. Instead, the hand is uglier due to its inability to meet expected hand conditions. In other words, the *projection* of an expected image on to any given object is part of one's perception of the ugly.

Ugliness in Art and Architecture

Rosenkranz acknowledges the duality in his conception of beauty, recognizing the inevitable discrepancy between reality and the ideal: "To appreciate beauty as such, the mind has to extract it from nature and to complete it to perfection."[15] This process of abstraction is, for Rosenkranz, how art evolves. However, he assumes that in art we aspire to achieve the beautiful. Extending this assumption, it would follow that in producing art we aspire to produce the harmonious, the unified, and, therefore, the expected, or that which produces no reaction.

Mark Cousins, however, argues for a positive understanding of the ugly in the artistic investigation of possible relations between a subject and an object. Fundamentally, the ugly is interesting (as opposed to the disinterested aesthetic attitude that comes from the beautiful) and, according to Cousins, only "an art which is interesting, which mobilizes libidinal energy without its being side-tracked into the defenses, is one which is able to stage the dramas in which the subject will find itself caught, but in a zone of representation."[16]

Throughout history, ugliness in art has been seen as a necessary contrast with beauty and a reminder of the ceaseless presence of evil. Inevitably, examples of ugliness appear in the form of the human or animal body—distorted, sick, decaying, mutating. The communication of the ugly, as a deviation from the ideal model, inevitably relies on the understanding of the expected human or animal form. Deviations from the expected are allowed and enjoyed, but when extremes are reached, the unexpected form's ugliness is confirmed by a visceral repulsion.

FIGURE 10.1 Odilon Redon, "The misshapen polyp floated on the shores, a sort of smiling and hideous Cyclops," 1840–1916. Plate No. 3 from the set "The Origins," 1883 Lithograph on chine-collé; Image: 21.3 × 19.9 cm (8 3/8 × 7 13/16 in.); Sheet: 32.2 × 26.5 cm (12 11/16 × 10 7/16 in.). Museum of Fine Arts, Boston, Lee M. Friedman Fund, 67.276. Photograph © 2014, Museum of Fine Arts, Boston.

In the twentieth century, the mutilation-beyond-recognition of bodily form, by artists such as Picasso and Boccioni, Dali and Magritte, allowed the ugly to move away from a transformation of the organism toward surrealism and abstraction.

Méret Oppenheim's *Object* (Le Déjeuner en Fourrure, 1936)—a teacup, saucer, and spoon covered with fur—is perhaps the finest example of the non-bodily ugly

FIGURE 10.2 Méret Oppenheim, *Object*, Paris, 1936. Fur-covered cup, saucer, and spoon. Cup 4 3/8 in. (10.9 cm) in diameter; saucer 9 3/8 in. (23.7 cm) in diameter; spoon 8 in. (20.2 cm) long; overall height 2 7/8 in. (7.3 cm). © The Museum of Modern Art/Licensed by SCALA/Art Resource, NY. © 2014 Artists Rights Society (ARS), New York/ ProLitteris, Zurich.

as a deviation from the anticipated. Described in 1988 by conceptual artist Jenny Holzer as "repulsive," *Object* "reverses all sorts of expectations."[17] The disconcerting combination of the everyday tea-set with the fur of a Chinese gazelle plays on the cup's inevitably repelling interaction with the lips and tongue. The fur is what is there but what should not be.

In a sense, the New Brutalist work of the 1960s and 1970s is architecture's first translation of the ugliness seen in Oppenheim's *Object* and other surrealist works. The displacement and replacement of expected meaning through shifts in material, the lack of expected patterns, the lack of expected functions, the lack of expected inhabitation, and so on, caused the *reactive force* of the ugly.

Alison and Peter Smithson, the alleged torchbearers of New Brutalism in England in the 1960s, were criticized for work that was "anti-human, repulsive and 'brutal' in the sense of subhuman."[18] The Smithsons, however, were not radical amorphosists or aformalists, as a superficial understanding of ugliness would suggest. In fact, they were faithful students of Wittkower and believed in the rules of proportion and harmony that had been handed down to them. The ugliness of their work may have had its roots in a second influence cited by the Smithsons: Japanese architecture, which they appreciated for its honest and sensuous use of materials. Their aggressive translation of this material expression, which had been absent in the whiteness of Modernism, produced unforgiving expanses of glass, brick, and concrete in projects such as *Hunstanton School* and *Robin Hood Gardens*. Although the Smithsons connected this material attitude with a truly British sensibility harking back to the warehouses and factories of the industrial revolution, it was shocking to the architectural world and, even more so, to the British public.

Today, 'Brutalist' works (no longer 'New') repeatedly appear on top-ten-ugliest-buildings lists. But, if examined, these works are formally unified in a way that would seem to undermine Rosenkranz's three criteria. Van den Broek and Bakema's *Aula* in Delft, Mathers & Haldenby's *Robarts Library* in Toronto,

FIGURE 10.3 John Carl Warnecke, *AT&T Long Lines Building*, New York, 1974. Photo by CODA, 2014.

John Carl Warnecke's *AT&T Long Lines Building*, and others have all been called ugly, yet they all obey rules of symmetry, order, and harmony. If these works are not ugly due to their failure to meet Rosenkranz's triad, perhaps the ugly can be found through an investigation of the *unexpected* or *incongruous* in these works.

The *AT&T Long Lines Building* (1974), for instance, stands in lower Manhattan, mute among a chorus of glossy skyscrapers. The windowless tower has six protruding bays on each façade, which are extruded along the elevation and project beyond the main envelope as 'visors,' at one third of the height of the building, and at the top. The building has no base, an interstitial condition between ground and tower that is common among its neighbors, both neoclassical and contemporary.

Primarily, it is its closed elevations, in stark contrast with its transparent neighbors, which arouse interest. The monotony of the Swedish granite façade, broken only by the visors (openings that cannot logically be windows) instills a sense of foreboding. The building is all wrong: whereas it should be transparent, it is solid; whereas it is expected to be occupied, it is uninhabitable; whereas it is supposed to touch the ground with a base that is differentiated, it does not acknowledge any adjacent ground.

Van den Broek and Bakema's *Aula* in Delft, albeit similarly accused, also obeys the rules of symmetry, order, and harmony. It is symmetrical around its axial oculus, a single eye that protrudes from the main body of the form, with only minor variations on the side façades. The belly of the building lifts up strenuously, as if allowing us to see something that should remain hidden. Most notably, what appear to be windows on the rear are closed in a way that windows should not be.

Although the 'ugly' works named above are symmetrically intact, they do not meet expectations of punctuation, porosity, and transparency.

This kind of work continues today in projects such as Peter Cook's *Kunsthaus Graz*, which has been called alien or like a sore thumb,[19] and Future Systems' *Selfridges Department Store*, Birmingham, called oppressive, monolithic, and inflexible.[20]

Like New Brutalism before it, 'blob' architecture has been criticized as being insensitive to context—unexpected, one might say, in its particular site. Moving beyond New Brutalism, these forms seem to have lost all regard for an architecture based on proportion. The blobs bulge into a site without apparent order, symmetry, or part-to-whole relationships, which would allow for the harmony required to deem the work 'beautiful.'

Architecture, however, rarely incites feelings of revulsion as strong as ugliness in nature or realistic representations of it. Of the very few examples of real revulsion produced by architecture, our best candidate must be Peter Eisenman's *Greater Columbus Convention Center*, which apparently induced nausea in one early visitor because the multiple diagonal grids confused him and caused vertigo. Cousins defines the act of vomiting as the final and most extreme reaction to ugliness:

FIGURE 10.4 Van den Broek and Bakema, *Aula*, TU Delft, Delft, Netherlands, 1958–1966. Photo courtesy of Luc Hegeman with CODA.

> To vomit is a last ditch attempt to expel aspects of the impending object, but at the same time it is already identified with the ugly object in precisely that action of spreading itself about. The final collapse of the subject and its defenses comes about in precisely the action of the ugly object revealing to the subject that they are the same.[21]

Ugliness Today

Umberto Eco suggests that beauty and ugliness have today become two possible options to be experienced neutrally, and that the opposition no longer has any aesthetic value. While the media reproduce classical ideals of beauty almost unchanged from antiquity (witness Brad Pitt as Achilles in Wolfgang Petersen's *Troy*), audiences are equally enthralled by, and mimic, repugnant rock-stars, so that in the end they look "more like Marilyn Manson than Marilyn Monroe."[22]

As ugliness becomes the norm, becomes no longer shocking, our expectations change. By provoking this constant readjustment of expectations, ugliness is a motor for change. As Asger Jorn writes, "An era without ugliness would be an era without progress."[23]

In beginning to understand ugliness not as an opposite of beauty but a condition in itself, ugliness becomes a valid architectural aspiration. As a condition that interests, engages, and affects the subject, the ugly, like the joke, makes the experience of the world more conscious by manipulating our expectations. This marks the beginning of a movement for which Cousins has appealed, a movement that strives for the creation of the positive ugly.

FIGURE 10.5 Future Systems, *Selfridges Department Store*, Birmingham, England. Photo © Richard Davies.

Notes

This text was originally printed in *Log*, 22 (*The Absurd*), guest edited by Michael Meredith (MOS), and accompanied by excerpts from Karl Rosenkranz's *Aesthetics of Ugliness*, translated by Sarah Haubner.

1 Later Gasper Schott, in his *Physica Curiosa* (Würzburg, 1697), an encyclopedia of curious creatures, depicting all known natural monstrosities including giraffes, elephants, and dugongs, identified the novel creatures in terms of timid variations on known types: an octopus was a fish with legs, an ostrich a winged camel, and so on.

2 Rowe later retracts his ideas on analytic formalism in favor of "collage formalism," precisely because of its reductivist character; he has already propelled a movement against which architects like Venturi, Eisenman, Tschumi began their careers.

3 Karl Rosenkranz, *Die Ästhetik des Häßlichen* (Stuttgart: Reclam Taschenbuchen, 1990), 57. Translated for the author by Sarah Haubner.

4 Karl Rosenkranz, *Aesthetics of Ugliness*, trans. Sarah Haubner, *Log*, 22 (Spring/Summer, 2011) (*The Absurd*), ed. Cynthia Davidson and Michael Meredith (MOS), 105, section B. Asymmetry.

5 Rosenkranz, *Die Ästhetik des Häßlichen*, 99. Translated for the author by Sarah Haubner.

6 In his *Poetics*, Aristotle defines the laughable as the mild ugly: an ugliness that does not hurt: " . . . the laughable is a species of the base or ugly. It consists in some blunder or ugliness that does not cause pain or disaster, an obvious example being the comic mask which is ugly and distorted but not painful." Aristotle, *Aristotle in 23 Volumes*, vol. 23, trans. William Hamilton Fyfe (Cambridge, MA: Harvard University Press; London: William Heinemann, 1932), 1449a.

7 Rosenkranz, *Aesthetics of Ugliness*, 109, section C. Disharmony.

8 Umberto Eco, *On Ugliness*, trans. Alastair McEwen (New York: Rizzoli, 2007), 16.

9 What is considered beautiful is: "Pretty, cute, pleasing, attractive, agreeable, lovely, delightful, fascinating, harmonious, marvelous, delicate, graceful, enchanting, magnificent, stupendous, sublime, exceptional, fabulous, wonderful, fantastic, magical, admirable, exquisite, spectacular, splendid and superb. The ugly is: repellent, horrible, horrendous, disgusting, disagreeable, grotesque, abominable, repulsive, odious, indecent, foul, dirty, obscene, repugnant, frightening, abject, monstrous, horrid, horrifying, unpleasant, terrible, terrifying, frightful, nightmarish, revolting, sickening, foetid, fearsome, ignoble, ungainly, displeasing, tiresome, offensive, deformed and disfigured." Eco, *On Ugliness*, 16.

10 Mark Cousins, "The Ugly Part III," *AA Files*, 30 (Autumn 1995), 65–68.

11 Cousins further illustrates a departure into the subject's defenses, a kind of playing dead which seeks to obliterate the experience of ugliness, describing it as a cowardice that shows itself "in the sudden lack of interest in the object, in the lulling of sensation, in the blurring of perception, in the indifference to space" (ibid.). Although the initial recoil is evident in both texts, Eco cites only reaction, whereas Cousins' reaction is followed by withdrawal.

12 In the eighteenth century, the debate shifted from the definition of beauty to a consideration of the effects of beauty, about our reaction to those natural phenomena the formless, painful, terrifying. Kant's *Critique of Judgement* (1790) talks of a mathematical sublime, the sight of the starry sky, where we have the impression that what we see goes beyond our sensibilities and leads us to postulate the ungraspable. Schiller saw it as something that makes us aware of our limitations. While a discussion of the sublime is beyond our scope, it can be noted that the ugly and the sublime have some overlap but that, whereas the sublime is incomprehensible and awesome, the ugly is reviling. The opposite of beauty's legibility and comprehensibility is not necessarily ugly but neither is it necessarily sublime.

13 Eco, *On Ugliness*, 19. Emphasis added.

14 Greg Lynn, "The Renewed Novelty of Symmetry," in *Folds, Bodies and Blobs* (Brussels: La Lettre Volée, 1998), 64 (caption 1).

15 Rosenkranz, *Die Ästhetik des Häßlichen*, 40. Translated for the author by Sarah Haubner.

16 Cousins, "The Ugly Part III."

17 Artist Jenny Holzer and Curator Anne Umland discuss *Object* in "Listen Up!," www.moma.org/learn/moma_learning/meret-oppenheim-object-paris-1936 (accessed December 10, 2014).

18 Peter Reyner Banham, *The New Brutalism* (New York: Reinhold, 1966), 41. Quote refers to Hunstanton School.

19 Galinsky. "Kunsthaus Graz by Peter Cook," www.galinsky.com/buildings/kunsthausgraz/index.htm (accessed March 3, 2014).

20 Ben Flatman, "History Repeating," *Area: Journal of the Royal Institute of British Architects*, 7 (Autumn, 2003), http://archive.is/Pb54d (accessed April 5, 2014).

21 Cousins, "The Ugly Part III," 4.

22 Eco, *On Ugliness*, 426.

23 Asger Jorn, quoted in Simon Sadler, *The Situationist City* (Cambridge, MA: MIT Press, 1998), 73.

11

HOPEFUL MONSTERS

In his "Aphorisms on the Composition of the Primary History" (1620), Francis Bacon separates nature into three parts: Species, Monsters, and Artificial; or by another set of names: liberty, errors, and bonds. The first and last are described plainly enough: as free and developing ordinarily; and as constrained and molded by human intervention, respectively. The monsters' description, however, is more arresting: the monster is "forced out of her proper state by the perverseness and insubordination of matter and the violence of impediments."[1] That is to say, monsters are so erroneous as to exist separately, outside the "proper" category of the species. They are no longer a bad copy of a platonic model, but, beyond simply a variation, monsters have crossed into another realm.

FIGURE 11.1 German broadside illustrating a monstrous birth in Spalt, 1511. Courtesy of the Bayerische Staatsbibliothek, Munich.

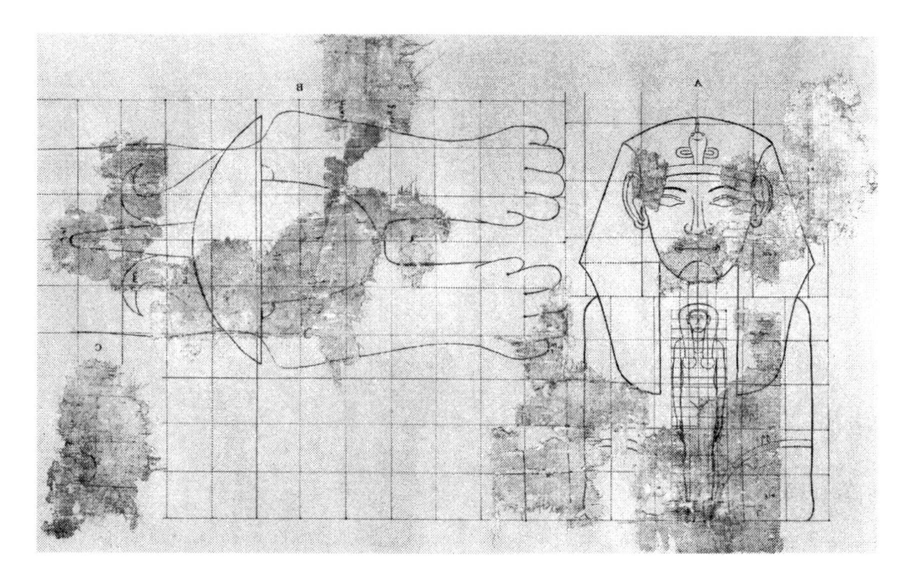

FIGURE 11.2 Papyrus with Sphinx sketch, 304–282 BCE. Papyrus, 33.7 × 57.2 cm. From the Ägyptisches Museum und Papyrussammlung, Staatliche Museen, Berlin, Germany. Photo courtesy of bpk, Berlin/Sandra Steiss/Art Resource, NY.

This transgression is, until the twentieth century, not an internal and genotypic transgression, but one that is external and primarily visual, formal, and geometrical. Pierre Boaistuau's sixteenth-century conception of the monster is one of a nature "inverted, mutilated, and truncated."[2] In this conception, the monster is the natural transformed through an array of geometric operations (think cad-commands) including multiplication, division, rotation, cutting, and trimming. The Monster of Spalt, for example, shows a boy whose legs and face are doubled, and one arm is copied and pasted at a distance below the original.

These geometrical operations do not act exclusively on the organism's own parts, but can (and often do) incorporate parts of other species that do not typically pair with the original form. As such, the parts of a monstrous whole co-exist as fragments of platonic ideals, stitched together. An example of this heterogeneous model is shown in the *Berlin Sphinx Papyrus*. This image uses three regulating systems to represent three species—lion, human, and goddess—combined into one whole. Erwin Panofsky calls the result "monstrous" due to its heterogeneousness as opposed to the homogeneity that would be expected of a single animal.[3]

Such monsters and mythical figures, many of them guardians of gates and cities, were often seen as cautionary signs. In fact, the root of the word *monstrare* means "divine omen portent or sign"[4] and derives from *monere* 'to warn.' In the sixteenth century, for example, word spread across Europe of the Monster of Ravenna, a winged and single-footed child, born as an omen days before the great siege of Ravenna began. This monster was both self-sourced (in the

FIGURE 11.3 The Monster of Ravenna, from *De monstrorum caussis*. Courtesy of the Division of Rare and Manuscript Collections, Cornell University Library.

consolidation of the feet into one and the shrinking of the arms) and heterogeneous (in the addition of components from other species). Beyond its existence as a curiosity, it was the subject of much attention due to the belief in its inherent meaning: a missive, or a warning, from God.[5]

As species began to be catalogued in the seventeenth century, however, the world of mythology and hearsay that surrounded teratology gave way to measured scientific study. By the time Charles Darwin published *On the Origin of Species*, monsters had become accepted, if only as an erroneous and short-lived part of the story of evolution. Darwin accepted that monstrosities occurred, but believed that organisms with such extreme mutations either did not survive to propagate, or were eradicated through breeding with the normal un-mutated forms. Otherwise, according to Darwin, and as D'Arcy Thompson's powerful images of transition between animal and geometry would later depict, variation occurs smoothly and gradually. In Darwinian theory, there is no possibility of the sudden appearance of perfect organs, but rather that improvements are honed as "the consequence of a long struggle between opposing actions, the result of contending forces, the outcome of a conflict between the organism and its environment."[6]

It falls to William Bateson, more than thirty years after *On the Origin of Species*, in 1894, to readdress this subject in *Materials for the Study of Variation*.[7] Although rooted in Darwinism, Bateson's studies develop ideas that contrast with the idea of gradual modification. Bateson notices a contradiction in the widely accepted theories of the time: while environments are continuous, species are discontinuous. Through his research, he observes "total" or "perfect" variations in examples from the tulip—which, although it normally has three petals, has variations with four *complete* petals, to the cockroach tarsus—which, although normally it has five segments, has variations with four *complete* segments, and many other cases, in which the pieces and joints are "properly proportioned and serviceable, showing no sign of unfitness."[8] He argues, then, that changes in the morphology in an organism occur in sharp jumps amid periods of continuity, and that these jumps correlate to external forces.

Bateson asks, in a lengthy but convincing and provocative quote that is worth repeating in its totality: "how does change occur?" His slightly sarcastic tone underscores his frustration toward the great number of questions left unanswered by Darwin:

> Did the variation come first in one member of the series and then in another? Did it occur, for example, simultaneously on the two sides of the body? Did the right and left fore-legs of the Horse cease to develop more than the present number of digits simultaneously or separately? Was the similar form of the hind-legs assumed before, after, or simultaneously with that of the fore-legs? Were the orange markings which are present on both fore- and hind-wings of the Brimstone, or the ocellar markings of the Peacock *(V. Io)* and of the Emperor (*Saturnia carpini*), assumed by both wings at once? Were the four wings of the Plume Moths split simultaneously into the characteristic "plumes"? Did the brown spots on the three leaflets of Medicago, the fimbriation of the petals of Ragged Robin (*Lychnis flos-cuculi*), the series of stripes on the Zebra, the pink slashes on the segments of *Sphinx* larvae, the eyes on the scutes of Chitons, and the thousand other color-marks, sense-organs, appendages and structural features, which throughout organized Nature occurs in Series, vary to their present state of similarity by similar and simultaneous steps, or did each member of such series take these characters by steps which were separate and occurring independently?[9]

Bateson concludes, of course, that symmetrical parts have a special bond, which makes it likely that they *do* change together. Variations offered to nature are

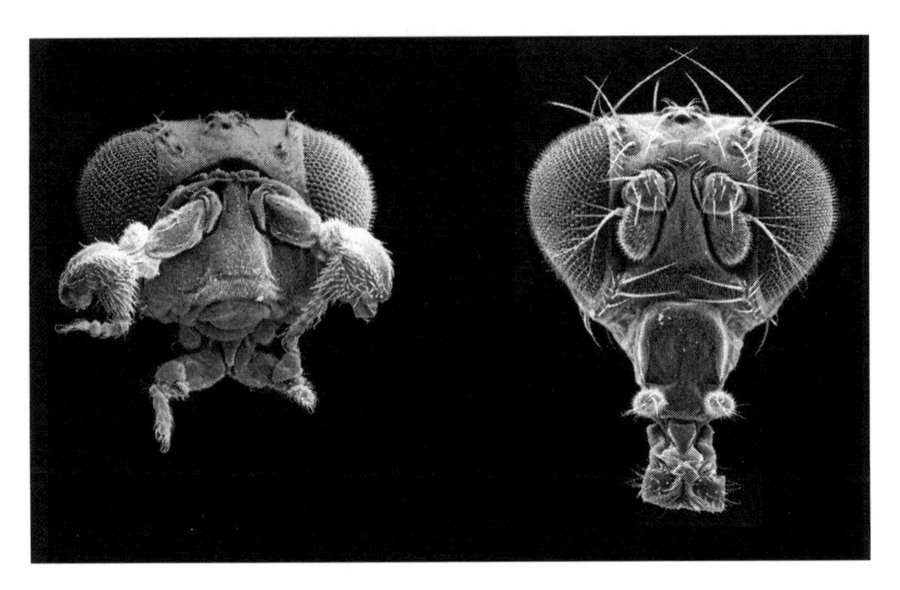

FIGURE 11.4 Scanning electron microscopy of *Drosophila melanogaster* (fruit fly) with/without the *Antennapedia* gene. Image courtesy of F. Rudolf Turner, Indiana University.

complete in and of themselves. Nature chooses between complete variations, not a smooth range (i.e. between red and purple, not a spectrum of color in between).[10] Thus, Bateson's proposal of "essential diversity" through discontinuous variation argues that even monstrosities adhere to rules; to recognizable forms of the so-called normal. Monsters are also complete and perfect in their own way.[11]

A contemporary example[12] might be found in antennapedic *Drosophila:* fruit flies with a genetic malfunction that confuses antenna and leg/foot (pedia) production.[13] This can occur such that the antennae are replaced by an additional pair of legs.[14] With legs sticking out of their heads, according to our definitions, these flies are of the self-sourced operational type (versus the heterogeneous type, since the parts are mathematical operations on their own anatomies and not borrowed from another species). Like the Spalt Monster, although they remain symmetrical, another level of disorder is at work in the location-switching of the extremities.

If the mutation proves beneficial; if it is well suited to survive and propagate in its environment—if it *fits*—such a creature has been named a "hopeful monster." The term was coined in 1933 by Richard Goldschmidt as part of his argument that "mutants producing monstrosities may have played a considerable role in macro-evolution."[15] Rather than Darwin's smooth and gradual evolution, Goldschmidt, like Bateson, believes that monstrosities could allow for the inhabitation of a new niche and produce, in one leap, a new species. While the antennapedic fly may not necessarily benefit from having additional legs on his head, Goldschmidt proposes several examples in which variations may have proven so beneficial as to cause a sharp split in the evolutionary trajectory: a Manx cat with a concrescence of tail

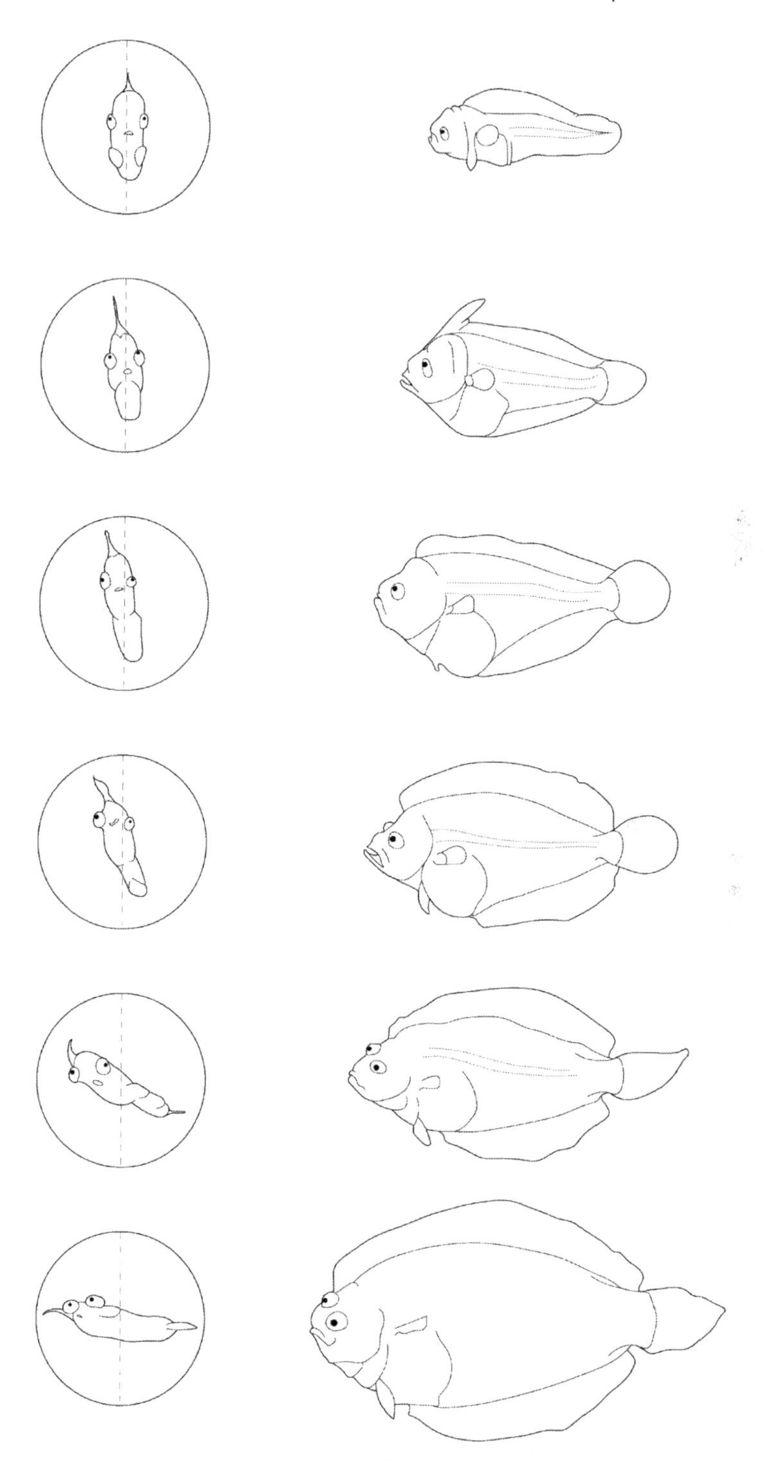

FIGURE 11.5 Flounder fish transformation. Drawn by CODA, 2014.

vertebrae may be considered to be just a monster, but an early mutation of the archaeopteryx producing the same monstrosity might have resulted in a fanlike array of tail feathers that was an improvement in the mechanics of flying, and thus the first flying bird; a fish with a distorted skull carrying both eyes to one side is a monster, but the same monstrosity in a bottom-feeding horizontally swimming fish becomes advantageous in the flatfish; and, in controlled breeding, the dog with achondroplastic bow-legs is monstrous, but once it is used to chase badgers (*dachs*) into their dens, it is a transformation beneficial to a dachshund.[16]

For Goldschmidt, such leaps were the fundaments of evolution.[17] Gradual variation existed, he believed, but accounted only for variation *within* a species. Monsters represented great evolutionary leaps and the origins of *new* species. While they may have begun as erroneous—whether heterogeneous, geometrically operative, or both—and as deviations from the norm, those that happened to fit into a niche were the hopeful monsters that would later become species and enter a newly created normal territory under that heading.[18] They would, conceptually, have a new platonic form created for them, as they moved from the realm of the monster to that of the species.

Writing at the end of the 1930s, however, Goldschmidt was rocking the boat on what was an established and comfortable theory of evolutionary continuity. His theories were much maligned and only recently have they begun to arouse some renewed interest. Even so, the role of the hopeful monster remains questionable to many evolutionary biologists.

One contemporary proponent, biologist Stephen Jay Gould, however, believes that hidden beneath the distraction of Goldschmidt's more radical ideas were important concepts that reintroduced the notion of hierarchical models into evolutionary theory. Goldschmidt's vision, Gould writes in his introduction to the 1982 re-publication of *The Material Basis of Evolution*, "supplied (or rather re-supplied) an essential ingredient that strict Darwinism had expunged from evolutionary theory: the idea that evolution works through a hierarchy of distinct levels with important independent properties."[19] Today, neither Darwinian microevolution nor Goldschmidtian macroevolution is considered solely responsible as an overarching theory of evolution. Instead, evolution occurs more complexly through a hierarchical range of procedures.

What is significant to note in this brief overview of the transition of the monster from the mythical to the genetic, and from being outside of the species to being an integral part of it, is that, in the Goldschmidtian interpretation at least, the monster can be positive and indeed generative. Significantly, for our purposes, this positivity is judged on the relationship of the monster with its environment.

Monsters and Architecture

Vitruvius's analogy of the human body with architecture[20] became animalistic via Leon Battista Alberti who, in *De re aedificatoria*, saw the animal as analogous to architecture, as an embodiment of natural principles of organization and order in its part-to-whole relationships as well as its consideration of climatic and site-related givens.[21] He wrote, for example, that, "the supports of ancient buildings were generally even in number, as animals support themselves on an even number of feet; but the apertures were generally odd in number, in the same way that the mouth is a single opening in the face."[22]

The slip from architecture-as-animal to architecture-as-monster is nearly as effortless. Alberti warns the architect of all possible "errors of excess," which would push architecture to the limits of its species and produce a "monster with limbs disproportionate."[23] Even Bacon, who had originally so clearly distinguished species from monster and from artifice, did not remain strict in the separation of his categories. He granted that, despite their distinctions, the rules for each may apply equally to the others: "For why should not the history of the monsters in the several species be joined with the history of the species themselves?"[24] And, to further extrapolate, why should not the history of monsters and species be joined with the history of the artificial?

Camillo Boito, in the seventeenth century, does just this. Distinguishing between a variation-within-a-species and a monster, Boito writes that "marriages between analogous architectures give birth to hybrids," and "between diverse architectures generate aborts or monsters."[25] That is to say, combinations can be made, but whether the combination results in an animal or a monster is a factor of the similarity or difference of the parts. The antennapedic fly and the Spalt Monster may delight in this definition, as their parts certainly do belong together (just in different locations or in smaller or greater numbers), and thus Boito would classify them as variations rather than full-blown monsters. Such combination of parts in architecture is certainly well practiced enough to waive examples, but how far can such practices go before passing the boundaries of the architectural species and into architectural monstrosity?

In his *Monsters of Architecture*, Marco Frascari describes, among other buildings, James Stirling's addition to the Alte Staatsgalerie in Stuttgart as an architectural monster. The *Neue Staatsgalerie*, he tells us, has been referred to as such by other writers—notably John Summerson, who refers to Stirling's "monstrously ingenious 'Queen Anne' play,"[26] and Susan Doubilet, who calls it a "'faceless' monster, a grotesque exotic animal."[27] Frascari investigates the motivations for such monstrous language and concludes that, at Stuttgart, "impossible things have been unified in a whole . . . classical stone stereonomy has been combined with Pop elements, and with brutalistic concrete mushroom columns . . . a summa of typological and iconographical references."[28] Frascari calls to our attention references to Egyptian temples, a Roman temple of Praeneste, Russian Constructivism, Gilly's detailing, Boullée's megalomaniacism, Shinkel's Altesmuseum, Asplund's City Library, Aalto's finishing, Wright's museum spiral, Mies's steel profiles, Kahn's stone stereonomy, and Corb's guardrails (scaled-up), as well as traces of Stirling's own designs from unrealized competitions.[29]

Considered by Frascari a child of many illicit fathers, the *Neue Staatsgalerie* is monstrous because it is (for the most part) heterogeneous, an organism created out of parts of diverse and unrelated species. Had it come from more analogous origins, it may have been a novel and interesting variation within a species, but its sources were too wildly divergent. As with Panofsky's Sphinx, it is ejected from the world of species and thrust into the world of monsters.

A monster, indeed, by all accounts. But, following Goldschmidt, the story does not end here. Goldschmidt would require a thorough examination of the creature's surroundings in order to understand if this radical mutant might be considered a *hopeful* monster, and, we will recall, its very hopefulness depends on the positivity of this relationship. Frascari's lengthy analysis of the *Neue Staatsgalerie*, however, barely mentions the context of the museum. While considering it as

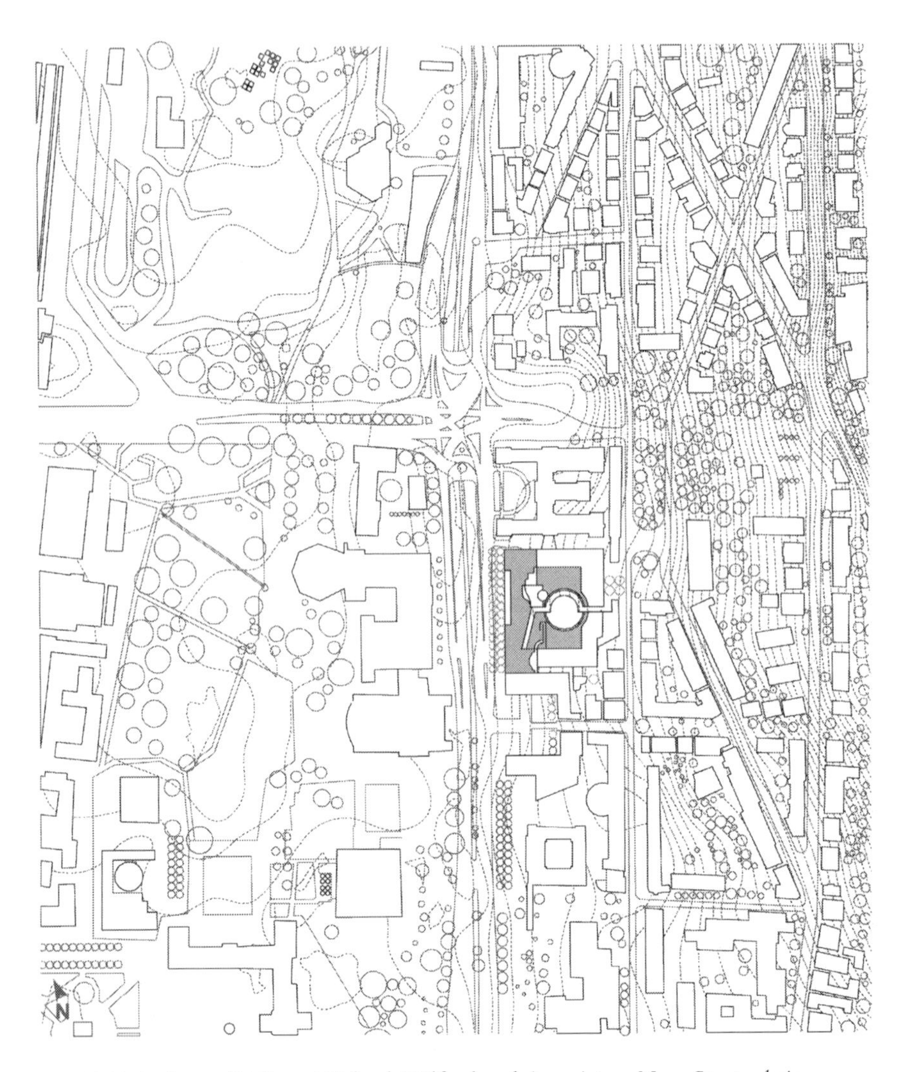

FIGURE 11.6 James Stirling, Michael Wilford and Associates, *Neue Staatsgalerie*, Stuttgart, 1977–1984. Redrawn with site by CODA.

an isolated object of multiple parentages leads inevitably to a monstrous conclusion, zooming out allows its fitness to its context, and thus its hopefulness, to be considered.

The site is compressed between a busy multi-lane road and a steep topographical shift, and between the city and an adjacent but sectionally separated neighborhood. The museum's circular drum and public circulation that run through the building operate at an urban level to connect the two sides of the city. The heterogeneous nature of the fragments allows the building to act as a series of smaller urban parts, a neighborhood in itself that can be conceptually passed through, or alternatively as a piece of infrastructure that can be passed along and on. Seen as a system, rather than a collection of style-samplings into one discreet object, the *Neue Staatsgalerie* appears, like Goldschmidt's archaeopteryx-monstrosity become flying-bird, hopeful indeed. It *affords* something, in the Gibsonian sense: it offers something new in relation to its site. It has advantages over its neighboring like-types (who instead form a barrier between the districts), precisely because this particular mutation is beneficial in relation to the specifics of the context in which it exists.

Type

As the growing numbers of species became unmanageable in the eighteenth century, many natural scientists set to work organizing the world's flora and fauna taxonomically. In Georges-Louis Leclerc Comte de Buffon's *Histoire naturelle* in 1749 and Carl Linnaeus's *Species plantarum* in 1753, plants and animals appeared classified, categorized, and tabulated (Buffon by historical evolution, Linnaeus by reproductive organs).[30] Whatever their system, the tendency was to identify and describe formal characteristics normal to each type.[31]

The graphic techniques and the classification procedures were soon borrowed from the natural scientists by architects. Francois Leroy and then Jean-Nicolas-Louis Durand published treatises in which architecture was taxonomically organized and like-forms were presented as types or species. And, as in the natural science treatise, differences and variations were eliminated in order to deduce the basic model of the type. Architectural types were stripped down to their bare essentials in order that the designer could build up more complex forms from a solid conceptual base.

Although type is presented textually by Durand as programmatic, his diagrams reveal the inevitable truth: that type, and therefore the fundamentals of architecture, are based on geometry. Or, as Giulio Carlo Argan suggests in *On the Typology of Architecture*, "the initial geometric move is the type."[32]

Thinking of type formally in this way allows for like-types to cut across generations of architects and styles, to reveal evolving families of form. Such typologies are well known in the discipline, for example the species of the nine-square from Palladio to Rowe, the species of the sphere from Ledoux and Boullée to Quaroni, or the species of the circle-within-square, demonstrating a long chain of evolutionary variations from Schinkel to Koolhaas (and including Stirling's *Neue Staatsgalerie*).

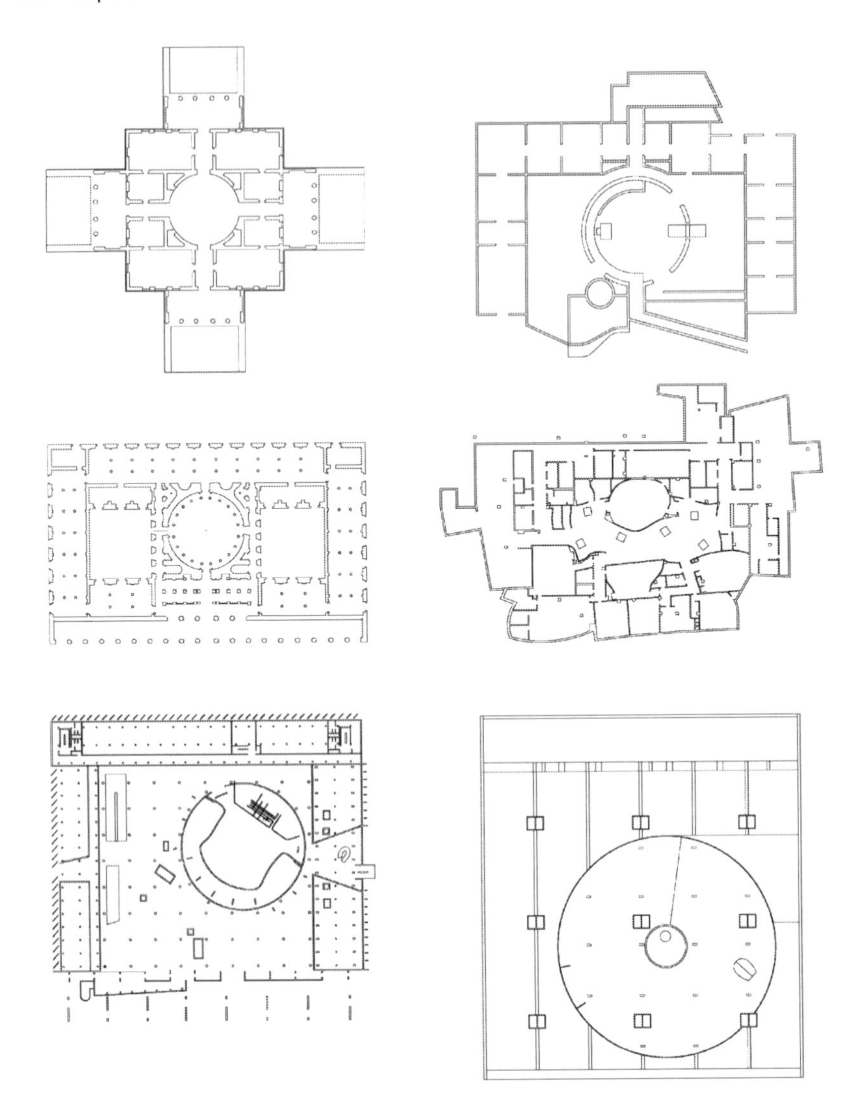

FIGURE 11.7 Schematized versions of Andrea Palladio, *Villa Rotonda*; Karl Friedrich Schinkel, *Altes Museum*; Le Corbusier, *Palace of Assembly*; James Stirling, *Neue Staatsgalerie*; Frank Gehry, *Peter B. Lewis Building*; OMA, *Très Grande Bibliothèque*. CODA 2010.

A second version of typological thinking emerges from the need to engage with machine logics and mass-production of the industrial revolution. Anthony Vidler considers this artificial machine world a mirror of nature in which architecture was "equivalent to the range of mass-production objects, subject themselves to a quasi-Darwinian law of the selection of the fittest."[33] While both of these typologies strive to relate architecture to natural development, and to give value through this relationship, what Vidler defines as a third typology, emerging in the 1970s, breaks this connection and looks inward at architecture itself, where the only nature is the nature of the city: the typology of the artifice. This new internalized typological thinking, in fact, understood in the terms of monstrosity as we have set them out, *enables* architecture to become monstrous. "This typology," Vidler writes, is "ready to be decomposed into fragments." These fragments do not reiterate known forms but are:

> selected and reassembled according to criteria derived from three levels of meaning—the first, inherited from the ascribed means of the past existence of the forms; the second, derived from the specific fragment and its boundaries, and often crossing between previous types; the third, proposed by a recomposition of these fragments in a new context.[34]

Vidler's third typology, which clearly refers to collage techniques in composition and foreshadows deconstructivism, is one that, like its predecessors, considers form platonically, or, more precisely in this case, poly-platonically. And so these new types, which would soon include Stirling's *Neue Staatsgalerie* (the competition for which was held in 1977, the same year that Vidler's essay was published), tend toward the monstrous because of their (collage) heterogeneity.

While typological scholars looked to like-forms for typologies in the nineteenth and twentieth centuries, questions of interplay or points of productive contact between systems and surroundings did not arise. This is not surprising, of course, since the very process of typologizing eliminates context. The notion of the hopeful monster, however, introduces an alternative approach to typological thinking, one which involves taking the geometry and appearance of the organism as a strong indicator of the organism's environmental setting. For example, when the eye of the flatfish migrates to meet the other eye on one side of its skull, it *provokes* the question of what in nature, below or above the fish, has conferred an advantage on the fish that it survived and reproduced better than those without the mutation. The successful mutation *points* to something outside itself in order to make sense of itself. In this sense, Le Corbusier's *Chapel of Nôtre Dame du Haut* at Ronchamp (1950–1954) might be considered a hopeful monster of its time. Unlike the *Neue Staatsgalerie*, it is geometrically operative rather than heterogeneous, and certainly exists far enough outside the bounds of its type—whether type is considered functional (the church as circular temple or basilica form) or formal (the modern style)—to be considered monstrous. Ironically, James Stirling, himself acknowledged this ex-speciality when he reviewed *Ronchamp* shortly after its completion, in the *Architectural Review*, writing that, since the building is so outside its type, one should not "criticize by the rationale of the modern movement."[35] The young architect appears, however, to be able to do little else, writing derisively that the chapel holds "little to appeal to the intellect, and nothing to analyze or stimulate curiosity."[36] Stirling muses that Le Corbusier had stockpiled a plastic and picturesque vocabulary from his global travels that allowed him to transform his initial modern ideas into what he calls a "conscious imperfectionism."

Indeed, the consciously imperfect may be just what the monster seeks to be. Imperfections—we imagine the fresh-faced Stirling confronting the building's asymmetries, bulges, and roughnesses—are arrows that point to disorder and dynamics in the world. The thick southern wall of the *Chapel*, for example, faces the approach and the midday sun, and acts as a great scoop to direct the congregation clockwise, away from the altar(s) and toward the main entrance. Upon entry, the congregation again views this massive, detached, and punctured surface, now from the interior as an illuminated composition of colored voids captive in the wall. This wall, then, begins to reveal its own code only when one looks beyond the object itself and to its environment.

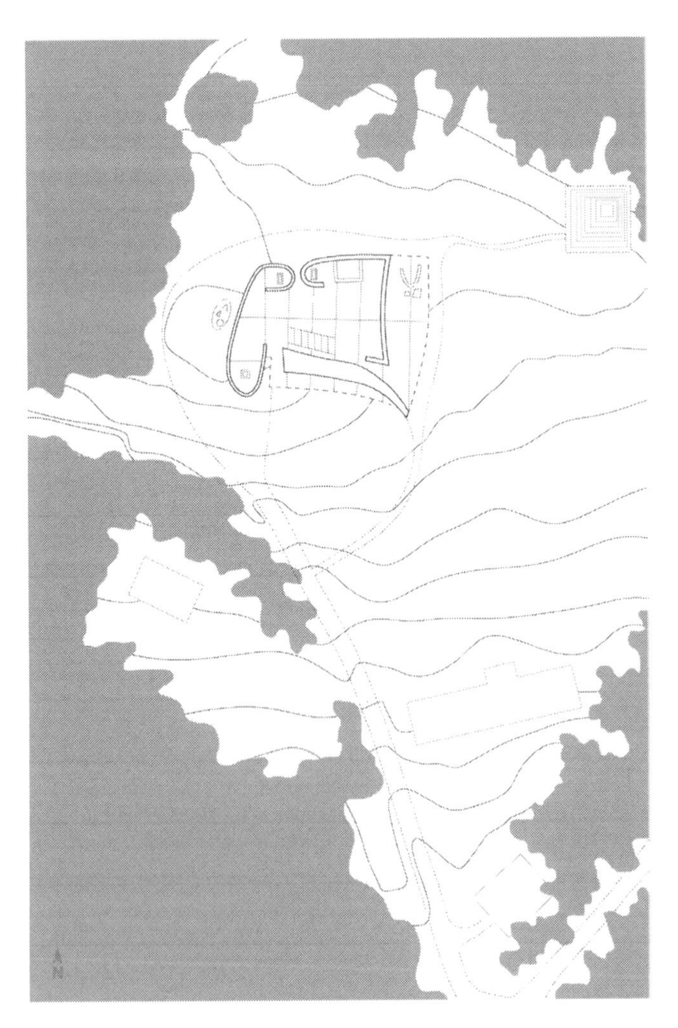

FIGURE 11.8 Le Corbusier, *Chapel of Nôtre Dame du Haut* at Ronchamp, 1950–1954. Site plan by CODA, 2014.

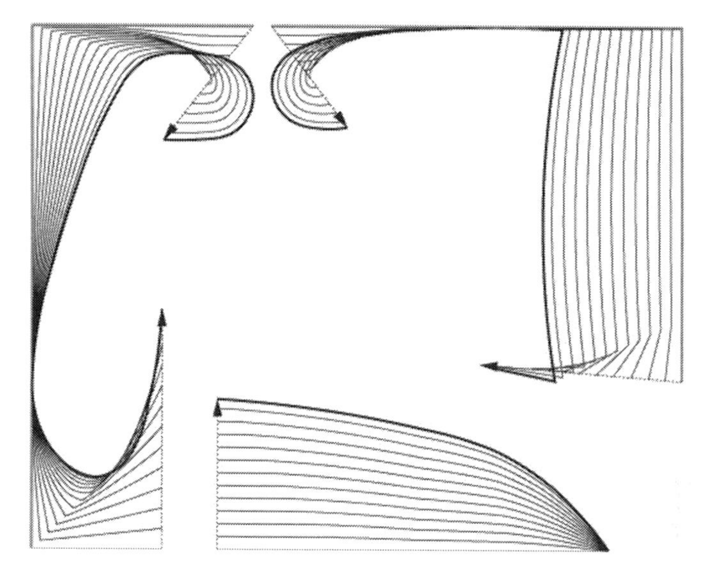

FIGURE 11.9 Diagram of transformations in Le Corbusier, *Chapel of Nôtre Dame du Haut* at Ronchamp, 1950–1954. CODA, 2014.

The south wall stands out as something that is mutated from any typical form, certainly from the early Corbusian pentad and its progeny. As the flounder rotates its eye to engage with the bottom of the ocean surface where it feeds, this heavy 'flipper' detaches from the body of the church, addresses the congregation's approach, the mid-day sun, and the view down (or up) the hill. It has, like *Santa Maria Deformata*, broken free of its expected ideal form and begun to bulge, slit, curl, and in various ways and, in doing so, to point at its own particular extraction of the world.

While this heavy wall is pressed inward, the thinner walls on the north and west bulge outward and furl their edges to produce openings or breaks in the plan. The east façade is read as an extension of the north wall, but acts differently, producing the only corner condition in the plan, and finishing in a straight angle instead of a curve. This façade, behind both the interior and exterior altars respectively, pushes inward slightly.

What is monstrous here, in comparison to early Corbusier projects, is that the curves that were previously contained inside a pristine box have escaped the confines of their enclosure. Although rare in Le Corbusier's oeuvre, the externalized bulging forms can be found in earlier works such as the *Swiss Pavilion*, Paris (1930), and in particular in some of the various iterations of the *Obus* project, Algiers (1931–1942). In the 1933 version of this project, the walls seem to be in the process of becoming Ronchampized, but with important differences: first, the bulging is always inwards and, second, the ends are beginning to furl but never pass 90 degrees.

The section, too, has close relatives at the Palace of Assembly, Chandigarh (1953), and perhaps in the opposite sense (of pushing down rather than lifting up)

FIGURE 11.10 Le Corbusier, *Obus* project, Algiers, 1931–1942. Redrawn by CODA, 2014.

in the *Maison du Brésil*, Paris (1957–1959). What keeps these related projects (with the exception of Algiers, which, had it been built, may too have been monstrous) within the realm of species is that their erroneous bulges are one instance within an otherwise regular plan. At Ronchamp, they have consumed the project so that traces of regularity are left only as imprints in the floor. This consumption is what leads to Stirling's proclaimed inability to criticize this according to accepted norms.

In architecture, monsters—works far outside the bounds of the normal—abound. What makes Ronchamp a potential candidate for consideration as a *hopeful* monster is that its anomalies, its bulbs, its bulges, seem to say something that makes sense only in relation to its site.

But it is a later project, the *Carpenter Center for the Visual Arts*, Cambridge, Massachusetts (1962), that truly ties Le Corbusier's monstrosity to James Stirling's. A critique of the *Carpenter Center* by Stan Allen asks, like Stirling's earlier critique of Ronchamp, if this work can be judged in the terms of the modern movement or if it is itself "a new kind of movement." Allen goes on to explain the building in monstrous terms, through the subversion of expectations, and, as one of a series of late-Corbusian projects that are "hopeful" and "complex paradoxes," which, "rather than looking backward, making incremental adjustments to know solutions . . . look forward . . . propose new projects, and . . . hold out the possibility of as yet unrealized solutions."[37]

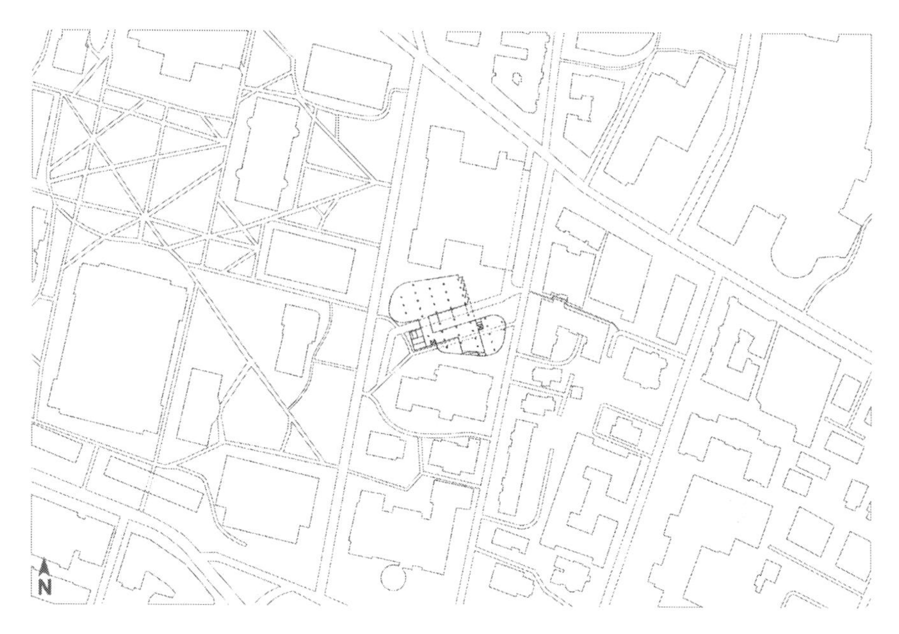

FIGURE 11.11 Le Corbusier, *Carpenter Center*, Cambridge, MA. Site plan by CODA, 2014.

Described by Fred Koetter as a "contextual grotesque,"[38] the *Carpenter Center*'s main volume is rotated and penetrated by an S-shaped ramp, pulling lobes from the cube along its trajectory. This slicing of the public trajectory through rectilinear mass, and the resultant fragmentation, are descendants of Le Corbusier's early paintings and his *promenade architecturale* (as in *Villa Savoye*, Poissy (1928–1931)), but now they have escaped the confines of the box and the frame and have become dominant and exterior (in the genetic sense, perhaps, a genotypic mutation has become phenotypic). In any case, this gesture of the public path pulled through the building, recomposed in Stirling's museum, is one of the moves that allows both buildings to function hopefully, that is, to be a monster in successful interaction with its site.

In both projects, the trajectory is not forced but knitted into the fabric of the city. Further, and again in both cases, the cut is not simply that, but has the effect of shaking the other parts, so that each side, and each corner, is different. They point to their adjacencies but also to the cut itself.

Other versions of this monstrous type exist, perhaps as evidence of the monster's evolutionary success. A third in this lineage, OMA's *Kunsthal*, Rotterdam (1992), is yet another volume penetrated by public pathway, here connecting park and main urban artery (tram, car, bicycle, and pedestrian route as well as dike). Here, too, sides and corners differ and, further, interior spaces are spatialized and materialized to create a series of heterogeneous and unrepeated worlds.

FIGURE 11.12 OMA, *Kunsthal*, Rotterdam, 1992. Photo, CODA 1999.

In Eisenman Architects' *Domplatz Library*, Hamburg (2005) this penetrating trajectory becomes cyclonic, shaking and twisting the entire built volume. Beyond a reference to the building's relation to the ground network, the building's structure points to two adjacent churches, one remaining and one demolished, and ties the visible and invisible together in its multitude of signs.

In all the above cases, it is difficult to capture a whole image of the building from one point of view, as each loses its definition against the backdrop of the world, becomes less object and more system, becomes more monstrous. This lack of definition reinforces Bakhtin's statement that, "the image of the grotesque body is unfinished and open and it is not separated from its surroundings by clearly defined boundaries."[39] This idea recalls Pevsner's picturesque terms *weak form* and *unideal figurality* (see Chapter 4, "An Ecological Approach to the Picturesque"), both of which bind the monstrous form more closely with its context. The monster becomes less a definable object and more an unnameable, unintelligible, and unfinished non-thing.

Hopeful architectural monsters can, of course, exist in a multitude of forms (we have seen many examples of monstrosities in this collection already without necessarily naming them as such), but this particular lineage, like the antennapedic fly, is an example of one normal part of architecture (the path/street) being relocated to a more dominant position, creating new possibilities of how this 'part' might be used and how it might affect newly adjacent parts. The architecture then, points to its other, a partially consumed and endlessly extending network, and to its relationship with it.

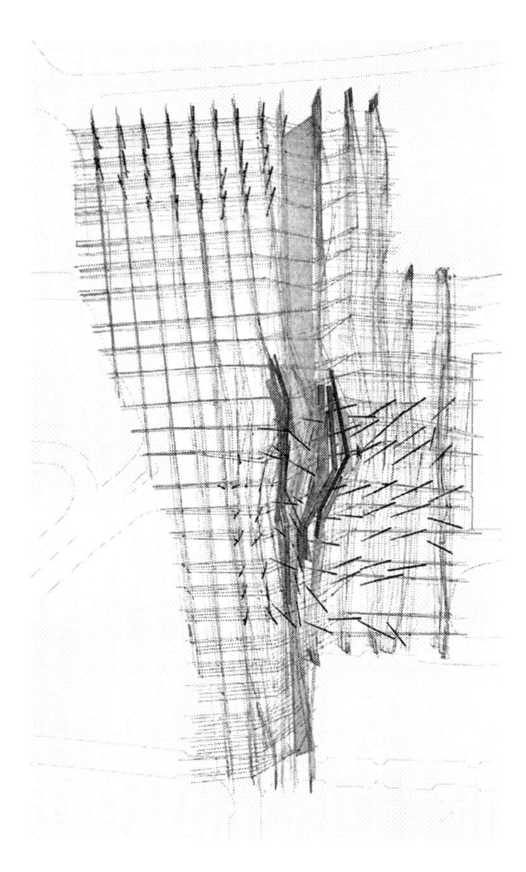

FIGURE 11.13 Eisenman Architects, *Domplatz Library*, Hamburg, 2005. Concept Model.

Desire for Monster

The medieval tales of mixed-species monsters are today attributed to hyperbole usually originating from geometrically operative mutant births. In the case of the Monster of Ravenna, a common birth defect called the sirenomelia sequence is thought to have caused a fusion of legs, upper limb malformation, bulging skull, and wing-shaped fleshy growths, leading to erroneous interpretations of these operations as heterogeneous.[40] Even heterogeneous features, like the presence of an animal tail on a human body, are understood as the activation of a gene already present in the human genome, which connects all creatures together, to varying degrees.

Likewise, architecture's heterogeneous monsters may today be considered an expression of latent genes embedded, but usually dormant, in all architectures. Monstrous architectures, thought in this way, are less collage, and more activation.

Most importantly, perhaps, architectural monsters continue to be understood as a sign. Massimo Scolari, in the 1980s, advocated such an interpretation, arguing that, "an architect must subject the reality proposed by nature to a host of legitimate deformations and 'unnatural relationships' between the facts of construction to produce monsters that are 'enigmas which express precisions.'"[41]

Monsters cannot help but communicate. And their expressed codes contain information describing the generative relationships between the entity and its world. Marco Frascari goes so far as to say that monstrous signs—fantasies—are essential to architectural creativity; that "the phantasmal and compound nature of monsters is at the beginning of the architectural practice of signification, which translates interpretations of construction events into architectural events."[42] Frascari believes that the monster's power is in making the invisible visible, in showing (demonstrating) or revealing that which we cannot see.[43] The monster shows us, perhaps more by way of what it is not, what our norms are and, subsequently, what our world is and what the things in it mean.

Breaking free of the animal's conformism, the hopeful monster is free to express not only displacements and asymmetries, but positive relationships, and to express them forcefully. It is able to be continuous with its environment, not visually, but operatively and systematically. Above all, the hopeful monster can express, finally and demonstratively, the tactical relation between its body and its world.

Notes

1 Francis Bacon, "Aphorisms on the Composition of the Primary History, Aphorism 1," in *The Works of Francis Bacon: Volume 4*, ed. William Rawley (London: Longmans, 1858), 253.
2 Georges Bataille, "The Deviations of Nature," in *Visions of Excess*, trans. Allan Stoekl (Minneapolis, MN: University of Minnesota Press, 1985), 53. (Orig. Pierre Boaistuau, *Histoires prodigieuses*, Paris, 1561.)
3 Erwin Panofsky, "The History of the Theory of the Proportions as a Reflection of the History of Styles," quoted from Greg Lynn, "Body Matters," in *Folds, Bodies and Blobs* (Brussels: La Lettre Volée, 2004), 141.
4 Etymology Online, www.etymonline.com/index.php?term=monster (accessed March 14, 2014).
5 Examples of heterogeneous, geometrically operative, and geometrically operative-heterogeneous monsters abound in mythological history: the Centaur, the Cyclops, the Sphinx, the Sciapod, the Capricorn, Hydra, Pegasus, Cerberus, and so on, and many more unnamed monsters. Named monsters exist in many forms; for example, some named heterogenes include: fish and goat (Capricorn), horse and human (centaur), human and snake (gorgon), tiger and wolf (Succarath), horse with wings (Pegasus), lion and human (sphinx); and some named operational monsters include the three-headed dog (Cerberus), one-legged humans (sciapods), many-headed reptiles (Hydra), and so on, but many more remain nameless as scalar deformations of one of the correct number and species of parts.
6 Francois Jacob, *The Logic of Life: A History of Heredity* (New York: Princeton Architectural Press, 1993), 166–167. Jacob quoting Darwin.
7 Bateson (and his contemporaries) were influenced by the fact that they worked on mutations in lab organisms and particularly on mutations of large effect.
8 William Bateson, *Materials for the Study of Variation Treated with Especial Regard to Discontinuity In the Origin of Species* (London: Macmillan, 1894), 61.
9 Ibid., 26.
10 Ibid., 80.
11 Bateson showed that monstrosities have higher degrees of symmetry than normal (in the example of the thumb). From Greg Lynn, "The Renewed Novelty of Symmetry," in *Folds, Bodies and Blobs*, 68.

12 Michael Weinstock, "Monsters, Mutations and Morphology," *Perspecta*, 40 (2008), 170–175.
13 Such homeotic mutations are more common in insects since they carry only one copy of the homeotic gene, rather than two (in mammals). From http://learn.genetics.utah.edu/archive/bodypatterns/mutation.html (accessed June 4, 2014).
14 In addition to *Antennapedia*, other common mutations include: reducing the extremities (in mammals and birds), hairlessness and taillessness (in mammals), bulldog head (in vertebrates, fish, and mammals), wing rudimentation (in insects and birds), reduced eyes (in insects, crustaceans, and mammals), and telescope eyes (in fish). From Richard Goldschmidt, *The Material Basis of Evolution: Silliman Milestones in Science* (New Haven, CT: Yale University Press, 1982; orig. 1940), 392.
15 Ibid., 390.
16 Ibid., 391.
17 Goldschmidt was not alone in this belief. While many natural scientists cited a lack of mutants in populations as an argument, a number of Goldschmidt's contemporaries believed that "constructive mutations are numerous but have ordinarily remained unnoticed simply because destructive mutations are more easily described, catalogued, and scored, and have therefore been more convenient in genetic research" (Edward Murray East (1936), quoted in Goldschmidt, *The Material Basis of Evolution*, 10). This idea is also put forth by Emanuel Bonavia, in 1895—monsters may have played a large role in evolution by providing specific adaptations in one step—and might have been able to occupy new habitats and continue their special evolution.
18 Such ideas, Goldschmidt points out, were nothing new. Darwin originally believed that mutations (then known innocuously as 'sports') played a major evolutionary role, but later changed his mind. In support of his argument, Goldschmidt provides examples of new traits that cannot possibly have arisen through gradual micro-evolutionary stages: "hair in mammals, feathers in birds, segmentation of arthropods and vertebrates . . . teeth, shells of mollusks, ectoskeletons, compound eyes, blood circulation . . . poison apparatus of snake . . . etc." (ibid., 7). Like Bateson, he believed that these phenomena cannot have appeared gradually.
19 Stephen Jay Gould, in his introduction to Goldschmidt, *The Material Basis of Evolution*, xl.
20 "Without symmetry and proportion, there can be no principles in the design of any temple; that is, if there is no precise relation between its members, as in the case of a well-shaped man." Vitruvius, *The Ten Books of Architecture*, trans. Morris Hickey Morgan (Cambridge, MA: Harvard University Press, 1960).
21 Manfredo Tafuri, *Interpreting the Renaissance: Princes, Cities, Architects* (New Haven, CT: Yale University Press, 2006). From Catherine Ingraham, *Architecture, Animal, Human: The Asymmetrical Condition* (New York: Routledge, 2006), 19.
22 Ingraham, *Architecture, Animal, Human*, 183.
23 Leon Battista Alberti, *The Ten Books of Architecture*, trans. James. Leoni (New York: Dover Publications, 1986), 13–14.
24 Bacon, "Aphorisms on the Composition of the Primary History, Aphorism 1," 253.
25 Camillo Boito, "Sullo stile future dell'architettura Italiana," in *In nuova e l'antico in architettura*, ed. Maria A. Crippa (Milan: Jaca Books, 1988; orig. *c.*1640), 17.
26 John Summerson, "Vitruvius Ludens," *Architectural Review*, 173 (March, 1983), 19.
27 Susan Doubilet, "The Talk of the Town," *Progressive Architecture*, 10 (1984), 74.
28 Marco Frascari, *Monsters of Architecture: Anthropocentrism in Architectural Theory* (Savage, MD: Rowman & Littlefield, 1991), 78.
29 Ibid., 82.
30 Leandro Madrazo, "Durand and the Science of Architecture," *Journal of Architectural Education*, 48, 1 (1994), 12.

31 Ingraham, *Architecture, Animal, Human*, 41.
32 Giulio Carlo Argan, "On the Typology of Architecture," in *Theorizing a New Agenda for Architecture: An Anthology of Architectural Theory 1965–1995*, ed. Kate Nesbitt (New York: Princeton Architectural Press, 1996), 242–246.
33 Anthony Vidler, "The Third Typology," *Oppositions*, 7 (Winter, 1977), quoted from *Oppositions Reader*, 291.
34 Ibid., 292.
35 James Stirling, "Ronchamp: Le Corbusier's Chapel and the Crisis of Rationalism," *Architectural Review* (March, 1956), 155–159.
36 Ibid.
37 Stan Allen, "Le Corbusier and Modernist Movement: The Carpenter Center for the Visual Arts," in *Practice: Architecture, Technique and Representation* (New York: Routledge, 2000), 121.
38 Fred Koetter, quoted in Allen, "Le Corbusier and Modernist Movement," 121.
39 Mikhail Bakhtin, *Rabelais and His World* (Bloomington: Indiana University Press, 1984), 26.
40 Michael T. Walton, Robert M. Fineman, and Phyllis J. Walton, "Of Monsters and Prodigies: The Interpretation of Birth Defects in the Sixteenth Century," *American Journal of Medical Genetics*, xlvii (1993), 12.
41 Franco Rella, "The Gaze of the Argonaut," in *Hypnos* (New York: Rizzoli, 1987), 14. Rella quoting Massimo Scolari.
42 Frascari, *Monsters of Architecture*, 90.
43 Ibid., 15.

12
CODA

Theories and alignments, like those presented in this collection, are most engaging when applied: when they become tactics in practice. Alongside many of the interwoven strands in these texts runs a series of investigations—not answers, but a parallel set of questions, this time in the language of architecture and urban design.

The practice, within the framework of design studio *CODA*, sets as its goal the production of architecture that behaves in a manner advocated in these texts: a niche-tactical architecture that develops through projection, extraction, and response. Such a practice inevitably engages with and results in imbalanced and abnormal conditions: ugliness, roughness, monstrosity, and so on. Most importantly, work of this type points at something beyond itself and draws the salient elements of its environment that make up its niche, whether visible or invisible, into its bubble of interactions and negotiations. The role of the architectural joke becomes crucial here in establishing expectations and transforming them, with the goal of bringing these connections into consciousness.

Bloodline (2010), for example, analyses the parent–child relationship of a pair of umbilically connected baroque palaces outside Stuttgart, Germany, and proposes a third in the lineage. The third 'descendant' then exposes not only the barely concealed monstrosity of the second, but also foregrounds the idea of evolution through the new form itself. The intervention, a *self-consuming grill pavilion*, begins, as its 'grandparent' does, as a perfect form: in its contemporary situation, a cube, clad with local barbecue wood whose color is a perfect match for the existing palaces. As the grill is used, the cladding is removed and consumed, revealing an interior volume, grotesque and programmatically derived (as is the case in the poché spaces of its parent, in which the poché had provided access to stoke the fires from behind).

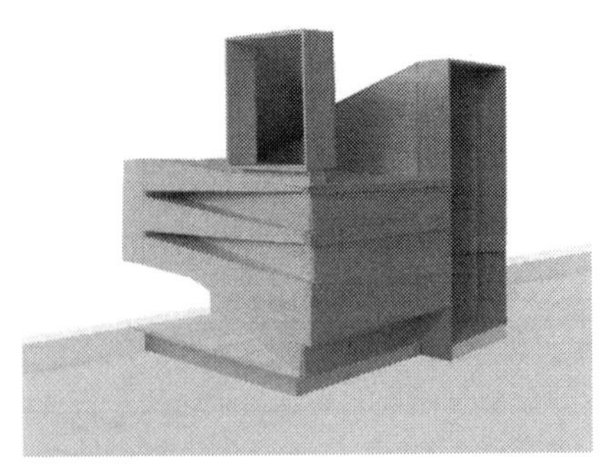

FIGURE 12.1 *Bloodline*, CODA, 2010. Before and after (models).

The shedding and consumption of skin in *Bloodline*, which continues to evolve during its lifetime, is an exploration of architecture's potential transformation from animal to monster. As a perfect cube it represents the ideal form, in a material seemingly connected to the comparably pure (if baroque) form of the adjacent palace. As it transforms, the de-purification of the form and material corresponds to the potential reinterpretation of cladding as fuel (wood affords appropriate enclosure from one perspective, but it affords burning—and grilling—from another), which in itself activates the cube's program to shift from pavilion to barbecue. The articulation of the form—the grill window's alignment with the forest axis (which is missing its 'castle'), or the chimney's alignment with the prevailing wind—points to factors outside itself, while the folds of the exterior point to internal functional needs (fire safety equipment, grilling tools, food storage, ash storage.) The project points too to change itself, as use, interaction, and consumption cause the form to evolve and become a tool to provoke a reading of the object in dynamic dialogue with its niche.

This approach is situated in a territory somewhere between indexical formal theory—in which dynamic diagrams result in a static but legible form— and a material practice, in which change over time is fundamental. As James Lowder has described it: "the processes behind the formal erosion of the skin are not conceptual in nature and occurring in a virtual space, but rather are the actual physical and material processes based on the forces of program in a *literal* temporal field."[1] As an ecdysic spider periodically sheds its skin, or a chameleon adapts to unpredictability of changing backgrounds while preserving its integrity as an organism, CODA engages this active, open, and tactical—if indeterminate—model both in principle and in practice.

The concept of the ecdysis was again key to *Party Wall*, a temporary pavilion constructed as the winner of PS1/MoMA's 2013 Young Architects' Program. Originally, two contradictory briefs were presented to shortlisted competitors, requesting both the maximization of floor area and, at the same time, large areas of seating for various events. The proposal to use the pavilion's façade as a great storage device for seating, shedding, and re-skinning as conditions require, becomes

FIGURE 12.2 *Bloodline*, CODA, 2010. A 1:10 model and 1:1 mock-up presented in "Self-Consuming," an exhibition at Tjaden Experimental Gallery, Cornell, supported by the CCA and the College of Architecture, Art, and Planning, as well as by Akademie Schloss Solitude and Elise Jaffe + Jeffrey Brown.

FIGURE 12.3 *Party Wall*, MoMA/PS1 Young Architects' Program, CODA, 2013. View from dance floor. Photograph by Brent Solomon.

the first experiment in real-time behavior: façade as removable, usable, and returnable, architecture as animal/monster whose skin is, for a time, consumable.

Party Wall considers its fourteen predecessors as co-existing species (like the lions, the buffalo, and the crocodiles at Kruger[2]). The form itself, in an Uexküllian sense, extracts the elements of the environment necessary to create its niche by projecting needs—movement of the sun (because we need shade), minimal

FIGURE 12.4 *Party Wall*, MoMA/PS1 Young Architects' Program, CODA, 2013. View of shadow from above. Photograph by Zachary Tyler Newton.

footing possibilities (because we need space to dance), maximum sitting possibilities (because we need to be an audience), etc., and by observing local opportunities—the proliferation of steel signage, graphic text, and graffiti with which it may enter into dialogue, a walled-in irregular site with multiple sub-sites. In the end, *Party Wall*'s monstrous achievement is not its size, but its engagement with its extracted environment and, in true monster-form, its literal understanding of itself as a sign. Crucially, though, the pavilion as both an architectural and literal sign does not communicate by itself but *relies directly on its context to produce a hint of its true meaning*: under certain lighting conditions (sunny) at certain times of day (1–2pm), at certain times of year (late summer), the clue to understanding most fully the concept at work appeared as a shadow in text on the ground. Read: WALL.

A continuous linear element, *Party Wall* is all-wall at the top, but at the bottom it stands only on four splayed feet, and allows passage through the space it encloses. The object as itself and the object as named are, whether at these particular moments or conceptually at other times, productively conflated. Or, there stands a non-wall as it spells the name of its ambition on the pavement. A wall, or not a wall? In fact, the very form of the letters that make up the sign disrupt the object's ability to be what it says it is, only to provoke endlessly this question of what, in fact, it really is.

When coupled with the slightly larger context of billboards and signs that proliferate like grazing beasts around the site, the object becomes more sign than wall; a sign that by its own definition points to something other than itself. The play between thing itself, sign and signified, is tossed back and forth. The joke may be too subtle or too superficially easy (as in the news headlines: "'Party Wall' at MoMA PS1 Is More Than Just a Pun (It's Two Puns)"[3] and "This Is Not a Wall"[4]). In this sense, *Party Wall* evades categorization as a duck-type, because it does not say what it does. Beyond that, it is syntactical with its environment, and thus represents a progression that extends beyond both Semantic Duck and Syntactic Dom-ino. Like the joke, it plays with the manipulation of expectation and transformation on a number of levels.

At the finer scale, the weaving together of Comet Skateboard's longboard off-cuts into a pattern reminiscent of the recent wave of digital architecture sets up a

FIGURE 12.5 *Party Wall*, MoMA/PS1 Young Architects' Program, CODA, 2013. Detail. Photograph by Zachary Tyler Newton.

similar tension at the level of the façade. The original expectation, one of a digitally designed surface, is overthrown as the voided longboard shape becomes apparent. Mounted on the façade under the woven boards, the solid boards afford enclosure and architectural base-line. When removed, they afford sitting (with legs, we call them benches) or play (with soft-trucks they revert to a strange kind of skateboard). Working backward, in fact, the bench reveals its other affordances by its underside print, which in turn hints at the façade pattern as a functional series of longboard-shaped voids, and a chain of events that potentially conjures up the origins of the material and its many transformations and affordances throughout its own diverse life-cycle.

These projects build on previous investigations that are at times literally dynamic—*Zoom House* in Brisbane, Australia (2012), for example, is an addition that slides away from the main house in summer, revealing a pool and creating a patio space, and then slides back to the house in winter to provide an additional contiguous room; or at other times offer static but complex systems that engage with known constants—*Noatún*, Klaksvik, Faroe Islands (2013), for example, redefines the city fabric as a response to complex but known or predictable solar, topographic, wind, and built conditions.

Other projects exploit the left-over at the urban scale: *Urban Punc.*, Leisnig, Germany (2009), for example, proposes the insertion of a series of three-pronged infrastructural supports into existing gaps in the urban fabric to rehabilitate vacant housing stock. Others still seek to transform affordances in familiar architectural elements: *Counterspace*, Dublin, Ireland (2011), for example, extracts the elements of stair, chimney, garden, street, and row and reconfigures them with new functions (the chimney in particular transforms to becomes a solar device, a periscope, and a vent).These latter works negotiate with familiar site elements but recompose them in ways that aim to force the relationship between the new and the pre-existing context, whether visible, climatic, or otherwise, into our perception of the architecture.

Zooming in and out of scales from the material detail to the scale of the city or territory, we look for networks of connections that exist, or that need to be made, between a series of elements and zones at these differing scales. This zooming,

FIGURE 12.6 *Noatún*, Klaksvik, Faroe Islands, CODA, 2012.

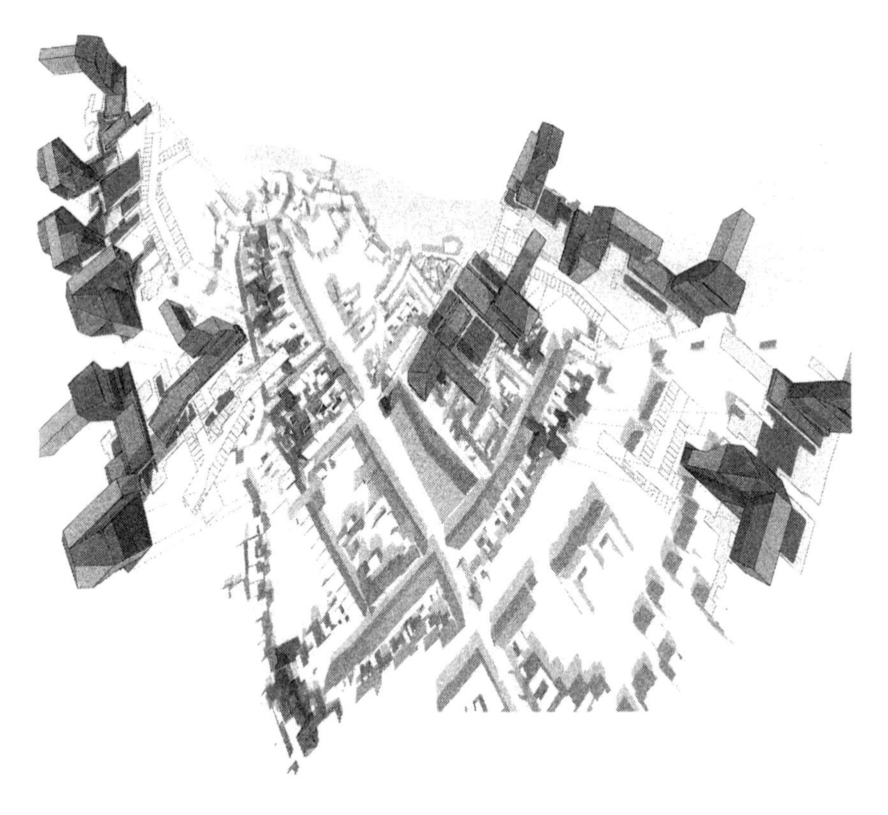

FIGURE 12.7 *Urban Punc.*, Leisnig, Germany, CODA, 2009. Runner-up, Europan 10.

FIGURE 12.8 *Counterspace*, Dublin, Ireland, CODA, 2011. First Prize Europan 11.

envisioned in time as well as in space, draws in, both conceptually and literally—by the mind, the eye, and the hand—connections between select opportunities, needs, desires, and affordances. Such selective 'drawing in' is fundamental to the generation of the responsive architecture proposed in these pages. At what appears to be the end of the book, the above examples, in addition to CODA's past and current experiments, should be considered just the beginnings of a practice of experimentation in niche-tactics.

Notes

1 James Lowder, "Skin Problems," in *103rd ACSA Conference Proceedings: The Expanding Periphery and the Migrating Center*, ed. Lola Sheppard and David Ruy, ACSA, March 19–21, 2015.

2 www.youtube.com/watch?v=u2wOhlWeYpY (accessed March 3, 2014).

3 Kelly Chan, "CODA's 'Party Wall' at MoMA PS1 Is More Than Just a Pun (It's Two Puns)," *Blouin Artinfo*, March 15, 2013, http://blogs.artinfo.com/objectlessons/2013/03/15/codas-party-wall-at-moma-ps1-is-more-than-just-a-pun-its-two-puns/ (accessed February 1, 2014).

4 Justin Allen, "This Is Not a Wall," in *Domus*, July 2, 2013. www.domusweb.it/en/architecture/2013/07/2/coda_architects_ps1yap2013.html (accessed February 1, 2014).

BIBLIOGRAPHY

Ackerman, James S., *Palladio*, ed. John Fleming and Hugh Honour (Harmondsworth: Penguin Books, 1966).

Alberti, Leon Battista, *The Ten Books of Architecture*, trans. James Leoni (New York: Dover Publications, 1986).

———, *On the Art of Building in Ten Books*, trans. Joseph Rykwert, Neil Leach, and Robert Tavernor (Cambridge, MA: MIT Press, 1988).

Allen, Justin, "This Is Not a Wall," in *Domus*, July 2, 2013. www.domusweb.it/en/architecture/2013/07/2/coda_architects_ps1yap2013.html (accessed February 1, 2014).

Allen, Stan, *Practice: Architecture, Technique and Representation* (New York: Routledge, 2000).

———, *Points + Lines: Diagrams and Projects for the City* (New York: Princeton Architectural Press, 1999).

Andersen, Paul and Salomon, David, *The Architecture of Patterns* (New York: W.W.Norton, 2010).

Anonymous, "Etudes d'architecture en France," *Magasin Pittoresque* (1852).

Argan, Giulio Carlo, "On the Typology of Architecture," in *Theorizing a New Agenda for Architecture: An Anthology of Architectural Theory 1965–1995*, ed. Kate Nesbitt (New York: Princeton Architectural Press, 1996), 242–246.

Aristotle, *Aristotle in 23 Volumes*, vol. 23, trans. William Hamilton Fyfe (Cambridge, MA: Harvard University Press; London: William Heinemann, 1932).

Augustyn, Prisca, "Uexküll, Peirce, and Other Affinities Between Biosemiotics and Biolinguistics," *Biosemiotics*, 9 (2009), 1–17.

Aureli, Pier Vittorio, *The Possibility of an Absolute Architecture* (Cambridge, MA: MIT Press, 2011).

Bacon, Francis, *The Essays; or, Councels, Civil and Moral, and the Wisdom of the Ancients* (Boston, MA: Little, Brown, 1856).

———, "Aphorisms on the Composition of the Primary History, Aphorism 1," in *The Works of Francis Bacon: Volume 4*, ed. William Rawley (London: Longmans, 1858).

Bakhtin, Mikhail, *Rabelais and His World* (Bloomington: Indiana University Press, 1984).

Banham, Peter Reyner, "The New Brutalism," *Architecture Review*, 118 (1955).

———, *The New Brutalism* (New York: Reinhold, 1966).

———, "De Wolfe the Author?," letter to the editor, *Architectural Review*, 158 (1975).
———, *Theory and Design in the First Machine Age* (Cambridge, MA: MIT Press, 1980).
———, *Architecture of the Well-Tempered Environment* (Chicago: University of Chicago Press, 1984).

Bataille, Georges, *Visions of Excess*, trans. Allan Stoekl (Minneapolis, MN: University of Minnesota Press, 1985).

Bateson, Gregory, *Steps to an Ecology of Mind* (Chicago: University of Chicago Press, 1972).

Bateson, William, *Materials for the Study of Variation Treated with Especial Regard to Discontinuity In the Origin of Species* (London: Macmillan, 1894).

Beesley, Philip and Bonnemaison, Sarah, *On Growth and Form: Organic Architecture and Beyond* (Toronto: Riverside Architectural Press, 2008).

Belot, Robert and Bermond, Daniel, *Bartholdi* (Paris: Perrin, 2004).

Berenson, Edward, *The Statue of Liberty: A Transatlantic Story* (New Haven, CT: Yale University Press, 2012).

Bergson, Henri, *Laughter: An Essay on the Meaning of the Comic*, trans. Cloudesley Brereton and Fred Rothwell (New York: Dover, 2005; orig. New York: Macmillan, 1911).

Biological Sciences Curriculum Study, *Biological Science: Molecules to Man* (Boston, MA: Houghton Mifflin, 1963).

Blake, Peter, *God's Own Junkyard: The Planned Deterioration of America's Landscape* (New York: Holt, Rinehart and Winston, 1979).

Boffrand, Germain, *Livre d'architecture* (Paris: Guillaume Cavelier père, 1745).

Bois, Yve-Alain, "A Picturesque Stroll around Clara-Clara," *October Files: Richard Serra*, ed. Hal Foster with Gordon Hughes (Cambridge, MA: MIT Press, 2000).

Boito, Camillo, "Sullo stile future dell'architettura Italiana," in *In nuova e l'antico in architettura*, ed. Maria A. Crippa (Milan: Jaca Books, 1988; orig. *c.*1640)

Bosker, Bianca, *Original Copies: Architectural Mimicry in Contemporary China* (Honolulu, HI: University of Hawai'i Press; Hong Kong: Hong Kong University Press, 2013).

Britton, John, *Devonshire Illustrated, in a Series of Views of Cities, Towns, Public Buildings, Streets, Docks, Churches, Antiques, Abbeys, Picturesque Scenery, Castles, Seats of the Nobility, &c. &c.* (London: Fisher, Son & Co., 1829).

Brownlee, "Evolution of the Giraffe," *Nature*, 200 (1983).

Burns, Carol J. and Kahn, Andrea (eds), *Site Matters: Design Concepts, Histories, and Strategies* (New York: Routledge, 2005).

Burrows, Edwin G. and Wallace, Mike, *Gotham: A History of New York City to 1898* (New York: Oxford University Press, 1999).

Canguilhem, Georges, *The Normal and the Pathological* (New York: Zone Books, 1991).

Carpo, Mario, *The Alphabet and the Algorithm* (Cambridge, MA: MIT Press, 2011).

Celan, Paul, *Sites of the Uncanny: Specularity and the Visual Arts* (Berlin: Walter De Gruyter, 2007).

Chan, Kelly, "CODA's 'Party Wall' at MoMA PS1 Is More Than Just a Pun (It's Two Puns)," *Blouin Artinfo*, March 15, 2013, http://blogs.artinfo.com/objectlessons/2013/03/15/codas-party-wall-at-moma-ps1-is-more-than-just-a-pun-its-two-puns/ (accessed February 1, 2014)

Choisy, Auguste, *Histoire de l'architecture* (Paris: Gauthier-Villars, 1889).

Cohen, Stuart E., "Contextualism: From Urbanism to a Theory of Appropriate Form," *Inland Architect* (May/June 1987).
———, "Physical Context/Cultural Context: Including It All," in *Oppositions Reader*, ed. K. Michael Hays (New York: Princeton Architectural Press, 1998).

Colquhoun, Alan, *Collected Essays in Architectural Criticism* (London: Black Dog Publishing, 2009).

Cosgrove, Denis, *The Palladian Landscape: Geographical Change and Its Cultural Representations In Sixteenth-Century Italy* (University Park: Pennsylvania State University Press, 1993).

Cousins, Mark, "The Ugly Part III," *AA Files*, 30 (Autumn, 1995), 65–68.

Craine, Joseph M., *Resource Strategies of Wild Plants* (New York: Princeton University Press, 2009).

Darwin, Charles, *On the Origin of Species*, 6th ed. (New York: Digireads Publishing, 2010).

Davis, Diane, "Diane Davis Lecture: Iterability, Dissemination, and Context," November 15, 2011, at the European Graduate School (EGS), Media and Communication Studies Department, Saas-Fee, Switzerland.

de Certeau, Michel, *The Practice of Everyday Life* (Berkeley: University of California Press, 1984).

Deetz, James, *Invitation to Archaeology* (New York: Doubleday, 1940).

de la Croix, Horst, "Military Architecture and the Radial City Plan in Sixteenth Century Italy," *Art Bulletin*, XLII, 4 (1960).

Deleuze, Gilles, *Cinema 1: The Movement-Image* (Minneapolis, MN: University of Minnesota Press, 1986).

de Marchi, Francesco, *Della architettura militare* (Gaspare dall'Oglio, 1599).

Derrida, Jacques, *Limited Inc.* (Evanston, IL: Northwestern University Press, 1988).

———, *Of Grammatology*, trans. Gayatri Chakravorty Spivak (Baltimore, MD: Johns Hopkins University Press, 1998).

de Saussure, Ferdinand, *Course in General Linguistics* (New York: New York Philosophical Library, 1916).

de Wolfe, Ivor (Hubert de Cronin Hastings), writing as The Editor, "Exterior Furnishing or Sharawaggi: The Art of Making Urban Landscape," *Architectural Review*, 95 (1944), 5.

———, "Townscape: A Plea for an English Visual Philosophy Founded on the True Rock of Sir Uvedale Price," *Architectural Review*, 106 (1949), 354–362.

Disson, Sian, "Wangjing SOHO/Meiquan 22nd Century: The Sincerest Form of Flattery?," *WorldArchitectureNews.com*, January 7, 2013, www.worldarchitecturenews.com/index.php?fuseaction=wanappln.projectview&upload_id=21660&q=wangjing (accessed March 3, 2014).

Doubilet, Susan, "The Talk of the Town," *Progressive Architecture*, 10 (1984).

Eastlake, Charles, L., *A History of the Gothic Revival* (London: Longmans, Green, 1872).

Eco, Umberto, *On Ugliness*, trans. Alastair McEwen (New York: Rizzoli, 2007).

Eidlitz, Leopold, *The Nature and Function of Art, More Especially of Architecture* (London: Sampson Low, 1881).

Eisenman, Peter, "Aspects of Modernism: The Maison Dom-ino and the Self-Referential Sign," *Oppositions*, 15–16 (Winter/Spring, 1979), 119–128.

———, "The End of the Classical: The End of the Beginning, the End of the End," *Perspecta*, 21 (1984), 154–173.

———, "Strong Form, Weak Form," in *Re:Working Eisenman* (London: Academy Editions, 1993).

———, *Architecture in Transition: Between Deconstruction and New Modernism*, ed. Peter Noever (Munich: Prestel, 1997).

———, *Eisenman Inside Out: Selected Writings, 1963–1988* (New Haven, CT: Yale University Press, 2004).

———, "Duck Soup," *Log*, 7 (Winter/Spring, 2006). Edited by Cynthia Davidson, co-edited by Denise Bratton.

———, *The Formal Basis of Modern Architecture* (Zürich: Lars Müller, 2006).

———, *Written into the Void: Selected Writings, 1990–2004* (New Haven, CT: Yale University Press, 2007).

———, *Ten Canonical Buildings* (New York: Rizzoli, 2008).

———, *Palladio Virtuel Exhibition Catalog*, Yale School of Architecture Gallery, August 20–October 27, 2012.

———, Interview by Ling Fan and Caroline O'Donnell, *Pidgin*, 4, 95.

Eisenstein, Sergei M., "Montage and Architecture," *Assemblage*, 10 (December 1989), 111–131.

Elton, Charles Sutherland, *Animal Ecology* (Chicago: University of Chicago Press, 2001), 64.

Etymology Online, www.etymonline.com/index.php?term=monster (accessed March 14, 2014).

Evans, Robin, *Translations from Drawing to Building and Other Essays* (Cambridge, MA: MIT Press, 1997).

Filarete (Antonio di Pietro Averlino), *Trattato di architettura di Antonio Filareto* (Florence, 1465). Reprinted as *Filarete's Treatise on Architecture, Volume 2: The Facsimile* (New Haven, CT: Yale University Press, 1965).

Flatman, Ben, "History Repeating," *Area: Journal of the Royal Institute of British Architects*, 7 (Autumn, 2003).

Fletcher, Banister, *A History of Architecture*, ed. John Musgrove (London; Boston, MA: Butterworths, 1987).

Forty, Adrian, *Words and Buildings: A Vocabulary of Modern Architecture* (New York: Thames & Hudson, 2000).

Fournier, Colin, "Kunsthaus Graz, Research Outputs 1 and 2," http://discovery.ucl.ac.uk/13132/1/13132.pdf (accessed January 5, 2013).

———, "Kunsthaus Graz," http://eprints.ucl.ac.uk/13132/ (accessed January 5, 2014).

Frampton, Kenneth, "Towards a Critical Regionalism: Six Points for an Architecture of Resistance," in *Anti-Aesthetic: Essays on Postmodern Culture* (Seattle, WA: Bay Press, 1983).

Frascari, Marco, *Monsters of Architecture: Anthropocentrism in Architectural Theory* (Savage, MD: Rowman & Littlefield, 1991).

Frazer, John, *An Evolutionary Architecture* (London: AA Publications, 1995).

Galinsky, "Kunsthaus Graz by Peter Cook," www.galinsky.com/buildings/kunsthausgraz/index.htm (accessed March 3, 2014).

Gibson, James J., *The Ecological Approach to Visual Perception* (Hillsdale, NJ: Lawrence Erlbaum Assoc., 1986).

Gilchrist, George W., "Specialists and Generalists in Changing Environments. I. Fitness Landscapes of Thermal Sensitivity," *The American Naturalist*, 146, 2 (August, 1995), 252–270.

Gilpin, William, *Three Essays: On Picturesque Beauty: On Picturesque Travel: And On Sketching Landscape: To Which is Added a Poem on Landscape Painting* (London: R. Blamire, 1792).

Gissen, David, *Subnature: Architecture's Other Environments* (New York: Princeton Architectural Press, 2009).

Glassberg, David, "Rethinking the Statue of Liberty: Old Meanings, New Contexts," paper prepared for the National Park Service, December 2003, https://archives.iupui.edu/bitstream/handle/2450/678/RethinkingTheStatue-Glassberg.pdf (accessed March 9, 2014).

Goldschmidt, Richard, *The Material Basis of Evolution: Silliman Milestones in Science* (New Haven, CT: Yale University Press, 1982; orig. 1940).

Gould, Stephen Jay, *The Structure of Evolutionary Theory* (Cambridge, MA: The Belknap Press of Harvard University, 2002).

Graafland, Arie (ed.), *The Critical Landscape* (Rotterdam: 010 Publishers, 1996).

Gregory, Richard L., *Concepts and Mechanisms of Perception* (London: Gerald Duckworth, 1974).

——— and Gombrich, Ernst H. (eds), *Illusion in Nature and Art* (London: Duckworth, 1973).

Gregotti, Vittorio, Introduction to the French edition, *Le territoire de l'architecture* (1966), French trans. from Italian by Vittorio Hugo (Paris: L'Equerre, 1982).

Grinnell, Joseph, "The Niche-Relationships of the California Thrasher," *The Auk*, 34, 4 (1917), 427–433.

Hadley, Elizabeth A., "Evolutionary and Ecological Response of Pocket Gophers (*Thomomys talpoides*) to Late-Holocene Climatic Change," *Biological Journal of the Linnean Society*, 60 (1997), 277–296.

Hale, John R., *Renaissance Fortification: Art or Engineering* (London: Thames and Hudson, 1977).

Hall, Edward T., *Beyond Culture* (New York: Random House, 1978).

Hargens, Alan R., Millard, Ronald W., Petterson, Knut, and Johansen, Kjell, "Gravitational Haemodynamics and Oedema Prevention in the Giraffe," *Nature*, 329 (1987), 59–60.

Heller, Steven, "Duplitectural Marvels: Exploring China's Replica Western Cities," *The Atlantic*, February 21, 2013, www.theatlantic.com/entertainment/archive/2013/02/duplitectural-marvels-exploring-chinas-replica-western-cities/273366/ (accessed March 3, 2014).

Hersey, George L. and Freedman, Richard, *Possible Palladian Villas: (Plus a Few Instructively Impossible Ones)* (Cambridge, MA: MIT Press, 1992).

Hitchcock, Henry-Russell and Johnson, Philip, *The International Style* (New York: W.W. Norton, 1995).

Holden Platt, Kevin, "Zaha Hadid vs. the Pirates: Copycat Architects in China Take Aim at the Stars," *Spiegel Online International*, December 28, 2012, www.spiegel.de/international/zeitgeist/pirated-copy-of-design-by-star-architect-hadid-being-built-in-china-a-874390.html (accessed March 3, 2014).

Holzer, Jenny and Umland, Anne, "Listen Up!," www.moma.org/learn/moma_learning/meret-oppenheim-object-paris-1936 (accessed December 10, 2014).

Hurley, Matthew, Dennett, Daniel, and Adams, Reginald, *Inside Jokes* (Cambridge, MA: MIT Press, 2013).

Ingold, Tim, *Being Alive, Essays on Movement, Knowledge and Description* (New York: Routledge, 2011).

Ingraham, Catherine, *Architecture and the Burdens of Linearity* (New Haven, CT: Yale University Press, 1998).

———, Architecture, *Animal, Human: The Asymmetrical Condition* (New York: Routledge, 2006).

Jacob, Francois, *The Logic of Life: A History of Heredity* (New York: Princeton Architectural Press, 1993).

Jastrow, Joseph, "The Mind's Eye," *Popular Science Monthly*, 54 (1899), 299–312.

Jencks, Charles, *The Iconic Building* (New York: Rizzoli, 2005).

———, "Eisenman Ducks," *Log*, 9 (Winter/Spring, 2007). Edited by Cynthia Davidson.

Kant, Immanuel, *Critique of Judgment* (New York: Cosimo, 2007).

Kaufmann, Emil, "Three Revolutionary Architects, Boullée, Ledoux, and Lequeu," *Transactions of the American Philosophical Society*, New Series, 42, 3 (1952).

Kemp, Martin, "Doing What Comes Naturally: Morphogenesis and the Limits of the Genetic Code," *Art Journal*, 55, 1 (*Contemporary Art and the Genetic Code*) (Spring, 1996), 27–32.

Kipnis, Jeffrey, "Toward a New Architecture," in *AD: Folding and Pliancy* (London: Academy Editions, 1993).

Knight, Richard Payne, *The Landscape: A Didactic Poem* (London: Bulmer, 1795).

Koetter, Fred and Rowe, Colin, "The Crisis of the Object: The Predicament of Texture," *Perspecta*, 16 (1980).

Koffka, Kurt, *The Growth of the Mind* (New York; London: Routledge & Kegan Paul, 1928).
Köhler, Wolfgang, *Gestalt Psychology: An Introduction to New Concepts in Modern Psychology* (New York: Liveright Publishing, 1947).
Koolhaas, Rem, *S,M,L,XL* (New York: The Monacelli Press, 1995).
———, *Delirious New York: A Retroactive Manifesto for Manhattan* (New York: The Monacelli Press, 1997).
———, "Rem Koolhaas Revisits Fundamentals for the 2014 Venice Architecture Biennale," *Design Boom*, January 25, 2013, www.designboom.com/architecture/rem-koolhaas-revisits-fundamentals-for-the-2014-venice-architecture-biennale/ (accessed April 17, 2013).
Krauss, Rosalind, "Death of a Hermeneutic Phantom: Materialization of the Sign in the Work of Peter Eisenman," in *Peter Eisenman, House of Cards* (New York: Oxford University Press, 1987).
———, "The Scantology of Anywhere: Modernism against the Grain," in *Anywhere*, ed. Cynthia Davidson (New York: Rizzoli, 1992).
———, *The Picasso Papers* (Cambridge, MA: MIT Press, 1999).
Kuleshov, Lev, *Kuleshov on Film: Writings of Lev Kuleshov*, trans. Ronald Levaco (Berkeley: University of California Press, 1974).
Kwinter, Sanford, *Architectures of Time: Toward a Theory of the Event in Modernist Culture* (Cambridge, MA: MIT Press, 1999).
Lamarck, Jean Baptiste, *Zoological Philosophy: An Exposition With Regard to the Natural History of Animals* (London: Forgotten Books, 2012).
Lang, Susan, "The Ideal City from Plato to Howard," *Architectural Review*, 112, 668 (August, 1952).
———, "Sforzinda, Filarete, and Filelfo," *Journal of the Warburg and Courtauld Institutes*, 35 (1972).
Laugier, Marc-Antoine (Abbé), *An Essay on Architecture* (London, 1755).
Le Corbusier, *Quand les cathédrales étaient blanches* (Paris: La Librairie Plon, 1937; reprint 1965)
———, *La ville radieuse Paris: Editions de l'architecture d'aujord'hui*, trans. Pamela Knight, Eleanor Levieux, and Derek Coltman (New York: The Orion Press, 1967).
———, *Toward a New Architecture* (1927), trans. Frederick Etchells (New York: Holt, Rinehart and Winston, 1986)
———, *The City of To-morrow and its Planning*, trans. Frederick Etchells (New York: Dover Publications, 1987).
———, *Toward a New Architecture* (1927), trans. John Goodman (Los Angeles: Getty Publications, 2007).
——— and Pierre Jeanneret, *Oeuvre complète 1929–1934* (Zurich: Les Editions Architecture, 1946)
——— and ———, *Oeuvre complète 1910–1929* (Zurich: Girsberger, 1964).
Lefaivre, Liane and Tzonis, Alexander, *Critical Regionalism: Architecture and Identity in a Globalized World* (Munich: Prestel, 2003).
Levaco, Ronald, "Introduction," in *Kuleshov on Film: Writings of Lev Kuleshov*, trans. Ronald Levaco (Berkeley: University of California Press, 1974).
Linden, Blanche M.G., *Silent City on a Hill: Picturesque Landscapes of Memory and Boston's Mount Auburn Cemetery* (Minneapolis, MN: University of Minnesota Press, 2007).
Lomolino, Mark V., Riddle, Brett R., and Brown, James H., "Single Species Patterns," in *Biogeography*, 2nd ed. (Sunderland, MA: Sinauer Associates, 2006).
Loos, Adolf, *Adolf Loos, Spoken into the Void: Collected Essays 1897–1900*, trans. Jane O. Newman and John H. Smith (Cambridge, MA: MIT Press, 1982).

Lowder, James, "Skin Problems," in *103rd ACSA Conference Proceedings: The Expanding Periphery and the Migrating Center*, ed. Lola Sheppard and David Ruy, ACSA, March 19–21, 2015.
Lynch, Kevin, *The Image of the City* (Cambridge, MA: MIT Press, 1960).
Lynn, Greg, "Multiplicitous and Inorganic Bodies," *Assemblage*, 19 (1992), 33–49.
———, "Architectural Curvilinearity: The Folded, the Pliant and the Supple," in *Folding in Architecture* (London: Architectural Design, 1992).
———, "The Renewed Novelty of Symmetry," *Assemblage*, 26, April 1995.
———, *Folds, Bodies and Blobs: Collected Essays* (Brussels: La Lettre Volée, 1998).
———, *Animate Form* (New York: Princeton Architectural Press, 1999).
Macarthur, John, *The Picturesque: Architecture, Disgust and Other Irregularities* (New York; London: Routledge, 2007).
——— and Aitchison, Mathew, "Pevsner's Townscape," in Nikolaus Pevsner, *Visual Planning and the Picturesque*, ed. Mathew Aitchison (Los Angeles: Getty Publications, 2010).
Madden, Derek and Young, Truman P., "Symbiotic Ants as an Alternative Defense against Giraffe Herbivory in Spinescent *Acacia drepanolobium*," *Oecologia*, 91 (1992), 235–238.
Madrazo, Leandro, "Durand and the Science of Architecture," *Journal of Architectural Education*, 48, 1 (1994).
Maturana, Humberto R. and Varela, Francisco J., *Autopoiesis and Cognition—The Realization of the Living* (Dordrecht: D. Reidel Publishing, 1980).
McHale, John, *The Ecological Context* (New York: George Braziller, 1970).
Mertins, Detlef, *Research and Design: The Architecture of Variation* (New York: Thames and Hudson, 2009).
Milewski, Antoni V., Young, Truman P., and Madden, Derek, "Thorns as Induced Defenses," *Oecologia*, 86, 1 (1991), 70–75.
Minsky, Marvin, *Music Mind and the Brain: The Neuropsychology of Music*, ed. Manfred Clynes (New York: Plenum, 1981).
Müller, Sabine and Quednau, Andreas, *City Boids—Molecular Urbanism*, Office Pamphlet (SMAQ, Berlin, 2004).
Nissen, Jane (ed.), *The Oxfam Crack-a-Joke Book* (Harmondsworth: Puffin Books, 1978).
Office of Metropolitan Architecture, "Whitney Museum Extension, USA, New York, 2001," http://oma.eu/projects/2001/whitney-museum-extension (accessed January 5, 2014).
Palladio, Andrea, *Quattro Libri*, trans. Isaac Ware (London: Dover, 1965; reprint edition).
———, *The Four Books on Architecture*, trans. Robert Tavernor and Richard Schofield (Cambridge, MA: MIT Press, 1997).
Pedley, Timothy J., Brook, Bindi S., and Seymour, Russell S., "Blood Pressure and Flow Rate in the Giraffe Jugular Vein," *Philosophical Transactions: Biological Sciences*, 351, 1342 (1996).
Pevsner, Nikolaus, "Twentieth Century Picturesque," *Architectural Review*, 115, 688 (1954), 228–229.
———, *Pioneers of Modern Design* (originally published as *Pioneers of the Modern Movement*, 1936, 2nd ed., New York: Museum of Modern Art, 1949; revised and partly rewritten, Penguin Books, 1960).
———, *Visual Planning and the Picturesque*, ed. Mathew Aitchison (Los Angeles: Getty Publications, 2010).
Pincher, Chapman, "Evolution of the Giraffe," *Nature*, 164 (1949), 29–30.
Plato, *Laws*, 360 BC, trans. Benjamin Jowett, http://classics.mit.edu/Plato/laws.6.vi.html (accessed March 3, 2014).
Podos, Jeffrey, "Correlated Evolution of Morphology and Vocal Signal Structure in Darwin's Finches," *Nature*, 409, 11 (2001), 185–188.

Pollak, Martha, *Turin, 1564–1680: Urban Design, Military Culture, and the Creation of the Absolutist Capital* (Chicago: University of Chicago Press, 1991).
Pomorska, Krystyna, *Russian Formalism Theory and its Poetic Ambiance* (The Hague: Mouton, 1968).
Price, Uvedale, *An Essay on the Picturesque, as Compared with the Sublime and the Beautiful: And, on the Use of Studying Pictures, for the Purpose of Improving Real Landscape*, 3 vols (London: printed for J. Mawman, 1810).
Pudovkin, Vsevolod, *Film Technique and Film Acting*, trans. Ivor Montagu (London: Vision, 1954).
Reiser, Jesse (Reiser + Umemoto), *Atlas of Novel Tectonics* (New York: Princeton Architectural Press, 2006).
——— and Payne, Jason, "Chum: Computation in a Super-saturated Milieu," in *Kenchiku Bunka* (Tokyo: Shokokusha Publishing, May 1998).
Reiss, Michael J., *The Allometry of Growth and Reproduction* (Cambridge: Cambridge University Press, 1989).
Rella, Franco, "The Gaze of the Argonaut," *Hypnos* (New York: Rizzoli, 1987).
Repton, Humphry, *Sketches and Hints on Landscape Gardening* (London: Bulmer, 1794).
———, *The Landscape Gardening and Landscape Architecture of the Late Humphry Repton Esq.*, ed. John Cladius Loudon (London, 1840).
Reynolds, Joshua, *The Works of Sir Joshua Reynolds, To Which Is Prefixed an Account of the Life and Writings of the Author*, by Edmond Malone, 4th ed. (London: T. Cadell & W. Davies, 1809).
Ricoeur, Paul, *History and Truth*, trans. Chas. A. Kelbley (Evanston, IL: Northwestern University Press, 1965).
Rimmer, Matthew, "Crystal Palaces: Copyright Law and Public Architecture," *Bond Law Review*, 14, 2, Article 4 (2002), 320–346, http://works.bepress.com/matthew_rimmer/30 (accessed March 3, 2014).
Roberts, Sam, "200th Birthday for the Map That Made New York," *New York Times*, May 20, 2011, www.nytimes.com/2011/03/21/nyregion/21grid.html?pagewanted=all&_r=0 (accessed March 15, 2014).
Rogers, Ernesto, "The Existing Environment and the Practical Content of Contemporary Architecture," *Casabella* (February, 1955).
———, "L'architettura Moderna dopo la generazione dei Maestri," *Casabella-Continuá*, 211 (June–July, 1956).
———, "L'Evolution dell'architettura, " in *Casabella-Continuá*, 228 (June, 1959). Trans. into English by Joan Ockman, *Architecture Culture 1943–1968* (New York: Columbia, 1993), 300–308.
Rosenkranz, Karl, *Die Ästhetik des Häßlichen* (Stuttgart: Reclam Taschenbuchen, 1990). Translated for the author by Sarah Haubner.
———, *Aesthetics of Ugliness*, trans. Sarah Haubner, *Log*, 22 (Spring/Summer, 2011) (*The Absurd*), ed. Cynthia Davidson and Michael Meredith (MOS).
Rossi, Aldo, *The Architecture of the City* (Cambridge, MA: MIT Press, 1984).
Rowe, Colin, *The Mathematics of the Ideal Villa, and Other Essays* (Cambridge, MA: MIT Press, 1976).
———, *As I Was Saying: Recollections and Miscellaneous Essays*, vol. 3, ed. Alexander Carragone (Cambridge, MA: MIT Press, 1996).
——— and Koetter, Fred, *Collage City* (Cambridge, MA: MIT Press, 1978).
——— and Slutzky, Robert, "Transparency: Literal and Phenomenal," *Perspecta*, 8 (1963).
Rudofsky, Bernard, *Architecture Without Architects* (Albuquerque, NM: University of New Mexico Press, 1987).
Sadler, Simon, *The Situationist City* (Cambridge, MA: MIT Press, 1998).
Schank, Roger C. and Abelson, Robert P., *Scripts, Plans, Goals, and Understanding: An Inquiry into Human Knowledge Structures* (Hillsdale, NJ: Lawrence Erlbaum, 1977).

Schluter, Dolph, *The Ecology of Adaptive Radiation* (Oxford: Oxford University Press, 2000).

Schott, Gasper, *Physica Curiosa* (Würzburg, 1697).

Schumacher, Patrik, *The Autopoiesis of Architecture: A New Framework for Architecture, vol. 1.* (London: Wiley and Sons, 2011).

Schumacher, Thomas L., "Contextualism: Urban Ideals + Deformations," *Casabella*, 359–360 (*The City as an Artifact*) (1971), 84.

———, "The Outside Is the Result of an Inside: Some Sources of One of Modernism's Most Persistent Doctrines, "*Journal of Architectural Education*, 56, 1 (2002).

Seebohm, Thomas, "Response to the Review by Terry Knight of *Possible Palladian Villas* (MIT Press, 1992)," *Journal of Architectural Education*, 49, 1 (1995).

Silbergeld, Jerome, "Foreword," in Bianca Bosker, *Original Copies: Architectural Mimicry in Contemporary China* (Honolulu, HI: University of Hawai'i Press; Hong Kong: Hong Kong University Press, 2013), ix.

Simitch, Andrea, "Re-Collage," *The Cornell Journal of Architecture*, 8 (2011).

Simmons, Robert and Scheepers, Lue, "Winning by a Neck: Sexual Selection in the Evolution of the Giraffe," *The American Naturalist*, 148 (1996), 771–786.

Sitte, Camillo, *The Birth of Modern City Planning* (New York: Dover, 1986).

Slobodkin, Lawrence B., "An Appreciation: George Evelyn Hutchinson," *Journal of Animal Ecology*, 62, 2 (1993), 391.

Smith, Margaret F. and Patton, James L., "Subspecies of Pocket Gophers: Causal Bases for Geographic Differentiation in Thomomys bottae," *Sysematic Zoology*, 37 (1988), 163–178.

Somol, Robert E., "Speciating Sites," in *Anywhere*, ed. Cynthia Davidson (New York: Rizzoli, 1992).

———, "Oublier Rowe," *ANY 7/8, Form Work: Colin Rowe* (1994).

Stewart, Janet, *Fashioning Vienna: Adolf Loos' Cultural Criticism* (New York: Routledge, 2003).

Stiny, George N., "Introduction to Shape and Shape Grammars," *Environment and Planning B: Planning and Design*, 7 (1980), 343–351.

———, "Computing with Form and Meaning in Architecture," *Journal of Architectural Education*, 39, 1 (1985).

——— and Gips, James, *Algorithmic Aesthetics: Computer Models for Criticism and Design in the Arts* (Berkeley: University of California Press, 1978).

——— and Mitchell, William J., "The Palladian Grammar," *Environment and Planning B: Planning and Design*, 5, 1 (1978), 5–18.

Stirling, James, "Ronchamp: Le Corbusier's Chapel and the Crisis of Rationalism," *Architectural Review* (March, 1956), 155–159.

Sudjic, Deyan, "Australia Looks Back in Allegory at its Inglorious Past," *The Guardian*, March 4, 2001, www.theguardian.com/theobserver/2001/mar/04/featuresreview.review2 (accessed March 3, 2014).

Summerson, John, "The Case for a Theory of Modern Architecture," *Journal of the Royal Institute of British Architects*, 64, ser. 3 (June 1957), 307–314.

———, "Vitruvius Ludens," *Architectural Review*, 173 (March, 1983).

Tafuri, Manfredo, *Interpreting the Renaissance: Princes, Cities, Architects* (New Haven, CT: Yale University Press, 2006).

Temple, William, *Miscellanea, the Second Part . . . II. Upon the Gardens of Epicurious* (London: printed by T.M. for Ri. and Ra. Simpson, 1690).

Thompson, D'Arcy, *On Growth and Form*, ed. John Tyler (Cambridge: Cambridge University Press, 1961; orig. 1917).

Thornbury, Walter and Walford, Edward, *Old and New London* (London: Cassell, Petter and Galpin, *c.*1897).

Tsui, Eugene, *Evolutionary Architecture: Nature as a Basis for Design* (New York: J. Wiley and Sons, 1999).

Tsukamoto, Yoshiharu and Kaijima, Moyomo (Atelier Bow-Wow) *Behaviorology* (New York: Rizzoli, 2010).
Tzonis, Alex and Lefaivre, Liane, "The Grid and the Pathway: An Introduction to the Work of Dimitris and Suzana Antonakakis," *Architecture in Greece*, 15 (1981), 164–178.
van de Velde, Henry, *Die Künstlerische Hebung der Frauentracht* (Krefeld: Druck und Verlag Kramer & Baum, 1900).
Vellinga, Marcel, "The Inventiveness of Tradition: Vernacular Architecture and the Future," *Perspectives in Vernacular Architecture*, 13, 2 (2006/2007), 115–128.
Venturi, Robert, *Complexity and Contradiction in Architecture* (New York: The Museum of Modern Art, 1966).
———, Scott Brown, Denise, and Izenour, Steven, *Learning From Las Vegas* (Cambridge, MA: MIT Press, 1972).
Vidler, Anthony, "The Third Typology," *Oppositions*, 7 (Winter, 1977).
———, *The Architectural Uncanny: Essays in the Modern Unhomely* (Cambridge, MA: MIT Press, 1994).
———, *Histories of the Immediate Present* (Cambridge, MA: MIT Press, 1994).
———, *Claude-Nicolas Ledoux* (Basel: Birkhäuser, 2006).
———, *Architecture Between Spectacle and Use* (Williamstown, MA: Clark Art Institute, 2008).
Vitruvio, *I dieci libri dell'architettura tradotti e commentate da Daniele Barbaro*, ed. M. Tafuri and M. Morresi (Milan, 1567), 1.2.5–7, 6.5.1–3.
Vitruvius, *De architeturra*, trans. Frank Granger (London: Loeb Library, 1930).
———, *The Ten Books on Architecture*, trans. Morris Hicky Morgan (New York: Dover, 1960).
von Uexküll, Jakob, "A Stroll Through the Worlds of Animals and Men: A Picture Book of Invisible Worlds," in *Instinctive Behavior: The Development of a Modern Concept*, ed. and trans. Claire H. Schiller (New York: International Universities Press, 1957).
———, *The Theory of Meaning*, trans. Barry Stone and Herbert Weiner from *Bedeutungsslehre*, ed. Thure von Uexküll, *Semiotica*, 41, 1 (1982), 25–82.
———, *A Foray into the Worlds of Animals and Humans*, trans. Joseph D. O'Neill (Minneapolis, MN: University of Minnesota Press, 2010).
Walton, Michael T., Fineman, Robert M., and Walton, Phyllis J., "Of Monsters and Prodigies: The Interpretation of Birth Defects in the Sixteenth Century," *American Journal of Medical Genetics*, xlvii (1993).
Warke, Val, "Prolegomena to a Rethinking of Context in Architecture," *Cornell Journal of Architecture*, 5 (1996).
———, guest lecture in the seminar "Contexts: Niche Tactics and the Possibility of Ugliness," Cornell University, Dept of Architecture, March 13, 2014.
Weinstock, Michael, "Monsters, Mutations and Morphology," *Perspecta*, 40 (2008), 170–175.
Wigley, Mark, "White-out: Fashioning the Modern [Part 2],"*Assemblage*, 22 (1993), 6–49.
——— and Johnson, Philip, *Deconstructivist Architecture: The Museum of Modern Art, New York* (Boston, MA: Little, Brown, 1988).
Wittkower, Rudolf, "Principles of Palladio's Architecture," *Journal of the Warburg and Courtauld Institutes*, 7 (1944).
———, *Architectural Principles in the Age of Humanism* (New York; London, W.W. Norton, 1971).
Wright, Edmond L., "Arbitrariness and Motivation: A New Theory," *Foundations of Language*, 14, 4 (July, 1976), 505–523.
———, "Derrida, Searle, Contexts, Games, Riddles," *New Literary History*, 13, 3 (*Theory: Parodies, Puzzles, Paradigms*) (Spring, 1982).
———, *Narrative, Perception, Language, and Faith* (Basingstoke: Palgrave Macmillan, 2005).
Zizek, Slavoj, *The Fragile Absolute* (New York: Verso, 2009).

INDEX